FAMILY SAVE-ALL

EXCELLENT DISHES FOR BREAKFAST, LUNCHEON,

DINNER, AND, SUPPER, FROM COLD AND

OTHER FRAGMENTS

INVALUABLE HINTS

FOR ECONOMY IN THE USE OF EVERY ARTICLE OF
HOUSEHOLD CONSUMPTION

REVISED EDITION.

Published by
Marquis of Fosseway
Edinburgh
EH8 7SW

REVISED EDITION

Copyright © Philip Nicklin Esq. 2009

ISBN 978-0-9561561-0-5

Printed and bound
CPI Anthony Rowe, East Sussex

PREFACE

A LITTLE while ago, Professor Faraday delivered in the theatre of one of our National Institutions a Series of Lectures upon the "Philosophy of a Candle." Interesting as that Philosophy may be, the teachings of the "Save-All" surpass it in importance and utility; for the latter include the former and, in addition thereto, suggest a practical moral lesson. The introduction of gas, and the application of various oils to the purposes of illumination, have almost thrown into oblivion the simple domestic instrument which we have adopted as our emblem, and the name of which we have chosen as our Title - prepared to endure criticism.

In the compilation of the following pages, we have done our utmost to apply the economical teachings of the "Save-All" to every article of Household Consumption. The first division of the work will be found to consist of a carefully prepared system of Secondary Cookery, comprising Recipes for preparing good and tempting Dishes from Cold Meats, Vegetables, and Sweets, which may be re-served, with all the warmth and nicety of appearance of original Cookery. That such information was greatly needed - that no previous work gave satisfactory information upon the subject, or even attempted to supply it — every housekeeper must be aware. Perhaps there are none but the houses of the wealthier classes in which joints and other eatables are not, as a general rule, sent to the table twice or even thrice.
That cold meats are acceptable at times, no one will deny; but that, to the English appetite, a good warm and savoury meal is always preferable to the cheerless repast of "cold mutton," and the like, is proverbially established.

The First Division of the Work contains also numerous Receipts for Cooking what may be termed the Secondary Parts of Animals, such as the heart, liver, tripe, head, feet, etc., and compounding from these usually cheap and slightly esteemed portions, dishes of many kinds that will rival the best joints, and win the suffrages of those who rejoice in what is plainly but appropriately termed "A Good Family Dinner."

The Second Division consists of Invaluable Hints for the performance of Practical Matters in the Household, the Garden, and the Farm; and many excellent suggestions, hitherto unpublished, are given in this portion of the work. These Suggestions are in no respect theoretical, but have been well tried, and their value ascertained.

The Family Save All must not be regarded as a mere Cookery Book with a new Title; nor as a Book of old Receipts put forth with false pretension to novelty. The contents are, for the most part, entirely new; and there is not a page of the work upon which some really useful piece of information may not be found: information calculated to simplify Household Duties, to Increase the Comforts of Home, and Enlarge the Profits of Labour.

We do not hesitate to say, that, if the Hints that will be found in the work are generally acted upon in any Household, the expenditure upon the total consumption of that Household will be reduced One Fourth. That is to say: If Two' Hundred Pounds a Year have hitherto been expended, the general adoption of the Frugal Hints here given will effect a Saving of Fifty Pounds annually, and yet yield a great increase of Comfort.

The Editor avails himself of the present opportunity of thanking the Public for the high estimation in which for several years they have held his Domestic and Educational Works. Of his various productions, such as "Enquire Within," "The Reason Why," etc., etc., more than Half-a-Million Volumes have been sold in Great Britain, and quite as large a number in the American States. Such a mark of public approval constitutes a great reward, of which perhaps there can be no better acknowledgment than to continue industriously and perseveringly in the course of usefulness already so successfully pursued.

London, 1861

THERE'S NOTHING LOST

There's nothing lost. The tiniest flower
That grows within the darkest vale,
Though hid from view, has still the power
The rarest perfume to exhale; —
That perfume, borne on sephyr's wings,
May visit some lone sick one's bed.
And like the balm affection brings,
*Twill scatter gladness round her head.

There's nothing lost. The drop of dew
That trembles in the rosebud's breast
Will' seek its home of ether blue.
And fall again as pore and blest;
Perchance to revel in the spray,
To cool the dry and parching sod,
To mingle in the fountain spray
Or sparkle in the bow of God.

There's nothing lost. The seed that's cast
By careless hand upon the ground
Will yet take root, and may at last
A green and glorious tree be found;
Beneath its shade, some pilgrim may
Seek shelter from the heat of noon.
While in its boughs the breezes play,
And songbirds sing their sweetest tune.

There's nothing lost. The slightest tone
Or whisper from a loved one's voice
Hay melt a heart of hardest stone.
And make a saddened breast rejoice;
And then, perchance, the careless word
Our thoughtless lips too often speak
May touch a heart already stirred.
And cause that troubled heart to break.

There's nothing lost. The faintest strain
Of breathings from some dear one's lute
In memory's dream may come again
Though every mournful string be mute:
The music of some happier hour—
The harp that swirls with love's own word!
May thrill me soul with deepest power,
When still the hands that swept its chords.

Then let s make the plan our own -
For heaven's teachings are the best:
The blessing that is widely used,
Increases, and we're doubly blessed!
And, be our lot with rich or poor,
Be sunshine warmed, or tempest tossed,
So guide our hands that we may say –
"There's nothing wasted, nothing lost."

THE

FAMILY SAVE-ALL

PART I.

SECONDARY COOKERY

An Excellent Pudding from Cold Roast Beef

Hint 1   Mince about a pound of the cold Beef, add to it one tea - spoonful of salt, the same of flour, and half that quantity of pepper; mix well; fill the paste with the prepared meat, and add a gill of water; a little chopped onions and parsley may be added; cover in the ordinary manner, shake well, and tie in a cloth. Boil for half an hour, or longer, if the paste is thick. Chopped gherkins, pickled walnuts, or mushrooms, may be added, or a little of the vinegar of any well-seasoned pickle.

Hint 2   Puddings of cold Veal and Bacon, Mutton, Lamb, Fowls, Rabbits, or Game, may be made in a similar manner.

Cold Beef Hashed in a Plain but Relishable manner,
with or without Bones

Hint 3   Slice the Beef in very thin pieces, and shake a little flour over it. Chop a middle-sized onion, and put it into a stewpan with a tablespoonful of Harvey sauce, an equal quantity of mushroom ketchup; boil these together for two minutes, and then add half a pint of stock or gravy. Boil this down to half its quantity, throw in the beef, set the hash to boil for five minutes longer, and then serve with sippets of bread round it.

Hint 4   The sauce may be served with bones of the beef Broiled and Deviled. The bones may be placed, if broken into small pieces, in the centre of the hash, or on a separate dish.

A very agreeable dish from Cold Beef minced with Bread Sippets, etc

Hint 5   Cut the cold Beef into small dice, and put it into a stewpan with any savings of beef gravy; add a little warm water, some mace, sliced shallot, salt, and black pepper. Let it simmer very gently for an hour, a few minutes before it is to be served, take out the meat and dish it; add to the gravy some walnut ketchup, and a little lemon juice, or walnut pickle. Boil up the gravy once more, and, when hot, pour it over the meat. Garnish with bread sippets.

A capital and ready dish from Fragments of Raw Beef

Hint 6   In trimming, boning, and rolling joints of Beef, there are very often loose bits cut off. These, with other beef, may be made useful in the following way:— Chop the beef very small, and add salt and pepper. Put this, in its raw state, into small jars, and pour on the top some clarified butter. When intended for use, scrape off the clarified butter, and put it into a frying pan; slice some onions into the pan and fry them. Add a little water, and then put in the minced meat. Stew it a few minutes, and it will be ready to serve up. This keeps well, and is always ready at hand to make an extra dish, when a guest accidentally drops in, and provisions are short.

A Snack from Roasted Beef Bones

Hint 7   Divide the Bones, leaving good pickings of meat on each; score them in squares; pour a little melted butter on them, and sprinkle them with pepper and salt; put them on a dish; set them in a Dutch oven for half or three quarters of an hour, according to the thickness of the meat; keep turning until they are quite hot and brown; or broil them on the gridiron. Brown them, but don't burn. Serve with a nice gravy or grill sauce.

Hint 8   A very relishing luncheon or supper, prepared - with Poached or Fried Eggs and Mashed Potatoes as accompaniments.

A Dish from Cold Beef or Mutton, with Potatoes and Bone Gravy

Hint 9   Mince either of the above cold meats. Take all the bones you have saved for some days, and chopping them in pieces, put them in a saucepan, with cold potatoes, or potatoes boiled at the time for the purpose; or peeled and sliced raw. When the potatoes are thoroughly incorporated with the gravy, take out the bones, and put in the meat; stew the whole together for an hour before serving.

A nice dish from Cold Beef with Mashed Potatoes

Hint 10   Mash potatoes, either in a plain way, or with hot milk, and the yolk of an egg, and add some butter and salt. Slice the cold Beef and lay it at the bottom of a pie dish, adding to it some sliced shallots, pepper, salt, and a little beef gravy; cover the whole with a thick paste of the potatoes, and make the crust to rise like a pie crust. Score the potato crust with the point of a knife in squares of equal size. Put the dish before a fire in a Dutch oven, and brown it on all sides. When nicely browned, serve immediately. This, with an apple tart or dumpling to follow, is a capital makeshift dinner for a small family; or a nice supper for a winter's evening.

"Rissoles" of Cold Beef, Mutton or Veal

Hint 11   Mince cold Beef or Mutton, season it to liking, and moisten with a little mushroom or walnut ketchup. Make with beef dripping a very thin paste, and roll it into thin pieces about four inches square; enclose in each piece some of the mince, in the same way as for puffs, cutting each neatly round; fry them in dripping of a very light brown. The paste can scarcely be rolled out too thin. Cold Veal may be dressed in the same way, grating into it some bits of cooked ham, and mixing with white sauce, flavoured with mushrooms. The same mince may be fried in balls without pastry, being first cemented together with egg and breadcrumbs.

To make a very relishable dish from Cold Beef or Mutton, with the addition of Poached Eggs

Hint 12   Take the inside of a sirloin of Beef or of a leg of Mutton, (These parts are recommended, but any other parts may be used.) Cut into slices of equal thickness, and broil them carefully over a clear smart fire, until slightly brown. Lay them upon a dish before the fire to keep hot; then poach some eggs, and lay around the meat, or mashed potatoes, or both. For sauce, add a few drops of shallot wine or vinegar, or any favourite gravy or sauce. This is a savoury zest for luncheon or supper; and it is proper to observe that the under-done parts of meat are best for the purpose.

Nice Patties from Underdone Beef

Hint 13   Cut the meat into small dice, season with pepper, salt, and a little chopped onion. Make a plain paste, and roll it out thin; fill it with the mince, close up, and fry or bake to a light brown.

Hint 14   Or make Rolls or Pasties in a similar manner. Add a little warm beef gravy, when the pasties are served. This may be done by making a hole in the paste, and pouring in the gravy before they are sent to table.

Underdone Beef, served as Steaks, with Cold Cabbage or Potatoes warmed

Hint 15   Cut the meat in slices, an inch and a half thick, securing a good proportion of fat; lay them on a gridiron over a quick fire; turn often, but do not stick a fork into them; as soon as brown, lay them on a very hot dish, which has been rubbed with shallot, and pour over some hot gravy of the joint, and a spoonful of warmed ketchup. Add salt and pepper.

Hint 16   If the seasoning is added while the meat is being broiled, the latter will be hardened, and the pieces wasted. The steaks will be found excellent served upon Warmed Cabbage chopped, with butter, pepper, and salt added; or the cabbage in a separate dish, with sliced Fried Potatoes round it.

A nice Dish from Cold Carrots and Beef

Hint 17   Slice the Beef and the carrots; put an onion to a good gravy, either from the joint, or stewed from the bones; let the carrots and beef simmer in the gravy; add vinegar, pepper, and salt; thicken the gravy, and take out the onion, or not. Serve hot, with bread sippets.

A nice Breakfast, Luncheon, or Supper Relish, from Potted Cold Beef

Hint 18   Having a joint of dressed Beef, which cannot be consumed, proceed in the following manner:— Drain the meat from gravy, pull it to pieces, and beat it in a mortar with mixed spices, and oiled fresh butter, until it resembles a stiff paste. Flavour it with anchovy, shallot, chervil, or tarragon, dried and powdered. Put it into small potting cans, press down, and cover with plenty of clarified butter.

Hint 19   The more it is beaten in the mortar, the better it will be, and keep longer.

A very nice Family Dish from Cold Beef and Mashed Potatoes and Flour

Hint 20   Cut the cold meat into slices, half an inch thick, four inches long, and two inches broad, as nearly as possible. Season the slices, and spread thinly over them a forcemeat of breadcrumbs, and a little shred suet or marrow. Take the gravy left from the joint, or stew a gravy from the bones; thicken with butter, rolled in flour, and season it with an anchovy, or a little ketchup.

Hint 21   Or, the bits of meat, when not large enough to be sliced, as above, may be minced, seasoned, and rolled, in a paste of Mashed Potatoes and Flour, Close the rolls, fry them in dripping, and brown before the fire.

An excellent method of re-dressing Cold Roast Beef Mutton, or Lamb

Hint 22   Cut the meat into small thin slices, season well with pepper and salt, and dip each lightly in breadcrumbs, moistened in gravy or melted butter; lay them on a dish, and cover them with a thin layer of chopped pickles, and moisten with pickle-vinegar, and the gravy from the cold meat; warm in a Dutch oven, and garnish with fried sippets, or potato-balls.

To re-dress Cold Stewed Rump of Beef

Hint 23   Cut into slices a quarter of an inch thick; trim them neatly; soak them till heated in a little broth; or glaze them, after heating through in an oven, and serve with tomato sauce, or sauce piquant.

Another Method of Dressing Cold Sirloin of Beef

Hint 24   Cut the underdone parts of the meat in long narrow slices, about an inch thick, leaving, if possible, a little fat attached to each piece. Season with salt and mixed spices, dredge with flour, and heat them in gravy from the joint; season to liking with anchovy, shallot, or shredded onion, and a little vinegar.

Hint 25   The slices may be Broiled, and served with the hot sauce, with Fried or Mashed Potatoes.

A Fricassee from Fragments of Cold Beef

Hint 26   Cut the meat into thin slices, and free them from gristle and fat. Take some stock, and thicken it with butter rolled in flour; and, for seasoning, use parsley, young onions, pepper, and salt; strain the sauce, and warm the meat in it, standing by the side of the fire.

Hint 27   If something a little better is required, add a glass of Fort Wine, the yolk of an Egg, beaten, and the juice of a Lemon. Stir the Fricassee, and do not allow it to boil.

Cold Beef, Mutton, Veal, Game, or Poultry re-cooked in Egg Croquettes

Hint 28   Take a pound or more of cold meat, and mince it very fine; then put it into a mortar, with a small Spanish onion, about a tablespoonful of parsley chopped fine, add an ounce of good butter, with salt and pepper, and work all well together. Boil six fresh eggs for twelve minutes, dress them in cold water, and take off the shells and skins; take out the meat from the mortar, moisten it with well-beaten white of egg, and cover the eggs with the meat so prepared, about half an inch thick. Roll them in flour, or fine breadcrumbs; fry them in boiling oil; drain them well; make a gravy from the bones of the cold meat, then stew it, and flavour to liking. Cut the croquettes lengthways with a sharp knife; set them in the dish, with the thick sauce in the middle.

Hint 29   This gives a little trouble; but, as an occasional side dish, it will be found very pleasing both to the eye and the taste.

A very nice Dish of Minced Mutton and Mashed Potatoes

Hint 30   Mince the Mutton finely, and stew it in a little gravy, to which add a dessertspoonful of mushroom or walnut ketchup, and a little butter. Stew till hot; thicken with a little flour, and serve on a dish surrounded by mashed potatoes.

Hint 31   An inexpensive Gravy for all Stews, Hashes, Minces, Haricots, etc., may be made of a large onion, some whole pepper, a piece of bread highly toasted, but not burned, and a dessert-spoonful of walnut ketchup, boiled two hours in a pint of water.

A nice Hash of Mutton, with the addition of Herbs

Hint 32   Melt a piece of butter with some finely chopped shallot, parsley, and half a pint or less of mushrooms; boil them gently in the butter; then, by degrees, mix in a large spoonful of flour, half a pint of broth, and stew till the ingredients are well combined. Let it become a little cool, and then put some minced underdone Mutton into it, without boiling.

An Economical Family Dinner of Mutton, warmed with Sauce and Vegetables

Hint 33   Cut the meat into chops, and trim off the fat, etc. Take some well-seasoned stock; if you have none, prepare some by previously by stewing the bones, fat, gristle, etc., not only of the mutton, but also of any other meats.

Simmer the meat in the stock, and add, already boiled, half a dozen or more button onions, some sliced carrot, or carrot cut in squares, and a turnip cut into diamonds.

Hint 34   Lamb may be re-dressed in all the ways recommended for Mutton.

Very Nice Sausages, or Balls, from Cold Mutton

Hint 35   Take, say a pound, of the most underdone part of a boiled leg of Mutton; chop it very fine, and season with pepper, salt, mace, and nutmeg; add six ounces of beef suet, some pounded sweet herbs, a quarter of a pound of grated bread, and the yolks and whites of two eggs well beaten, and a clove of garlic or shallot. Mix well, and press down into a pot. Use as sausages; or roll into balls, and fry a nice brown.

Mutton Hashed in a homely but savoury way

Hint 36   Take three pints of stock gravy, a large onion cut into rings, some pepper and salt; let them boil until the onion is done; then add a little thickening; or, if there should be any cold melted butter left from the day before, it will do as well; put in your meat, and let it simmer for ten minutes. Toast a round of bread, cut it into sippets, and place them round the dish; then pour the hash into the dish, and serve with hot potatoes.

Mutton Hashed in the style of Venison

Hint 37   Take three pints of stock gravy, put it into a saucepan, and let them boil; then add a gill of port wine, some cayenne pepper and salt, some flour to thicken, and a little bit of butter. Cut the Mutton into slices and put it in, and let it simmer for four or five minutes; do not let it boil, or the meat will become hard; make a nice puff paste, roll it out, then cut into diamonds and fry them in boiling fat; then dish the hash, placing the sippets of puff paste as a border round the dish. Serve with currant jelly.

Hint 38   To improve Hashes a well seasoned Gravy may be prepared by stewing Bones, Gristles, and Trimmings, well seasoned with pepper, salt, and onions.

"Bubble and Squeak" or a nice way of serving up Cold Beef, Pork, or Mutton, with seasoned Cabbage

Hint 39   Bubble and Squeak is usually made with slices of old boiled salted beef fried in butter; but any underdone Beef or Mutton will do. Cut the meat into slices; pepper, salt, and fry them lightly.

When done, lay them on a hot dish or drainer, and while the butter or fat is draining from the beef, take a cabbage, already boiled in two waters, or left cold from yesterday; chop it small, put it into the pan, and add the fat that may have drained from the meat, with a little more, if required. Season with pepper and salt, and keep stirring, that it may be equally warmed and seasoned. When taken from the fire, sprinkle over the cabbage a little vinegar, just enough to give it a slightly acid taste. In dishing up, lay the cabbage in the middle of the dish, and the slices of meat around it. For sauce, if desired, anything adapted for steaks, chops, or cutlets.

Cold Breast of Mutton or Veal, Grilled

Hint 40   Pare and trim the joint; egg and crumb it, and broil, or warm it in a Dutch oven. Serve Veal with White Sauce, made thus:— Put equal parts of broth and milk into a stewpan, with an onion and a blade of mace; set it on the fire to boil ten minutes. Rub together on a plate an ounce each of flour and butter; put it into a stewpan, stir well till it boils; then stand it near the fire on the stove, stirring it every now and then till it becomes quite smooth; then strain it through a sieve into a basin; put it back into the stewpan; season it with salt and the juice of a small lemon; beat up the yolks of two eggs, with about three tablespoonfuls of milk; strain it through a sieve into your sauce; stir it well, and keep it near the fire, but do not let it boil. Serve Mutton with Caper Sauce, or with Wow-Wow Sauce, as follows:— Chop some parsley-leaves very fine, quarter two or three pickled cucumbers or walnuts, and divide them into small squares. Put into a saucepan a bit of butter the size of an egg; when melted, stir to it a table-spoonful of vinegar, the same quantity of mushroom ketchup, and a teaspoonful of made mustard; let it simmer together until as thick as you desire, and then put in the parsley and pickles to warm.

Hint 41   If greater piquancy is required in the sauce, add any other pickles or condiments to taste.

A very nice Pie of Cold Boiled Veal and Ham with Liver

Hint 42   Take one pound of cold boiled Liver, chop and pound it in a mortar, and one pound of Sausage Meat. Take also about a pound of cold Veal, chop and pound it; add pepper and salt, a little parsley minced, and a little of the green parts of young onions, chopped fine; mix these in a mortar, and set aside until wanted; take about one pound of cooked Ham, fat and lean, which also chop and pound in a mortar, and set aside. Prepare a pie dish by putting a crust all round the bottom.

Place in the dish a thin layer of the sausage meat, with slices of truffles stuck here and there; now a layer of the pounded ham; then truffles again; then veal and more truffles; then liver; and proceed in this way until the dish is full. Cover with a light flaky crust, and bake; add a little gravy.

Hint 43   Good either hot or cold; it may be made as a Raised Pie; and will be found a great improvement upon the ordinary Veal and Ham pie.

A nice Ragout of Cold Veal

Hint 44   Cut the cold meat into small found cutlets, trimming off the rough parts, bones, etc. With the bones and trimmings, an onion, a turnip, and carrot, make a little good gravy. Melt some fresh butter in a frying pan, and flour and brown the slices of Veal of a light brown; take them up, strain the gravy into the pan, and thicken the sauce to a proper consistence with butter rolled in flour. When smooth and well mixed, put in the cutlets, and let them simmer very slowly. Season to liking with pepper, mace, ketchup, and anchovy, or mushroom powder. Skim the sauce, and pour it hot over the cutlets.

A nice Haricot from Cold Neck of Veal

Hint 45   Saw or break the bones off short. Have ready a pint of green peas, boiled, a cucumber pared and cut into thin slices, and two cabbage/lettuces cut into quarters; stew these in a pint of gravy until they are tender. Then put them to the peas and the Veal, and stew gently for a few minutes. Add a little more gravy if necessary. Serve hot, with forcemeat balls round the dish.

Hint 46   The proportion of vegetables must, of course, always be determined by the quantity of meat. For instance: a large cucumber may be too large; two large cabbage/lettuces may be too great a quantity.

Cold Veal and Fowl Minced, and served on Sippets

Hint 47   Mince the white part of a cold Fowl, either roasted or boiled; put it, together with some thin slices of Veal, into a saucepan, also some white stock, a squeeze of lemon, a few drops of shallot vinegar, and a little sugar; simmer for a short time, and serve upon bread sippets, laying the slices of veal upon the mince.

Another very nice way of Dressing Cold Veal

Hint 48   Mince the fat and lean of cold roast Veal together; season it well with grated nutmeg, lemon peel, white pepper, and salt.

Moisten with a little rich white stock, and a beaten egg; butter a pudding shape; put in the mince, and press it firmly; cover it closely, and set it into a pan of boiling water; let it boil an hour. Serve it with a white gravy thickened; or, when turned out of the shape, rub it over the top with the beaten yolk of an egg; sift bread crumbs thickly over, and brown it in a Dutch oven; baste it with a little melted butter. Garnish with fried parsley, or sliced lemon.

Minced Veal with Gravy from the Bone

Hint 49 Take the bones and trimmings of the Veal, and stew them down to a nice gravy. If you have no bones or trimmings, a few spoonfuls of veal or mutton broth, or pot liquor, will do; add a little mace, white pepper, salt, lemon peel grated, and a tablespoon of mushroom ketchup. Take out some of the gravy when nearly done, and letting it get cool, thicken it with flour and a little butter, and boil it up with the rest of the gravy. Cut the meat into small dice, and put it into the stewpan with the gravy. Serve it up quickly after the meat has been put in. Garnish with bread sippets. A little lemon juice added to the gravy improves its flavour.

Hint 50 This makes a very nice dish, put into scallop shells, covered with Bread Crumbs, sprinkled with bits of butter, and browned in a Dutch oven, or a cheese toaster.

Hint 51 Another nice dish may be made by mincing stewed Mushrooms with the veal, thickening the liquor, putting a little cream to it, and serving garnished with toasted sippets.

A nice Hash of Cold Veal

Hint 52 Having cut the meat into thin slices, and trimmed them, warm it in gravy drawn from the bones and trimmings, to which add any left from the joint. Thicken with a little butter rolled in flour, and season with mace. minced lemon peel, a spoonful of lemon pickle, or the juice of a lemon. Serve with bread sippets and slices of lemon.

A capital Hash of Cold Calf's Head, or other parts of Veal

Hint 53 Gather all the pieces of flesh from the bones, cutting the palate, etc., into smaller pieces than the other parts of the meat. Take about three pints of the liquor in which the head was boiled; break the bones, and stew them with a small bunch of savoury herbs. Also add a carrot, an onion carefully fried in slices, a dozen corns of pepper, and either a slice or two of lean ham or smoked beef. Simmer until the liquid is reduced nearly one half strain, and skim off the fat.

Thicken with a little butter rolled in flour, and add a little spice, mushroom ketchup or Harvey's sauce, and a small quantity of chilli vinegar. Heat the meat slowly in the sauce.

Hint 54 Other parts of Veal, especially the Neck, Breast, Knuckle, and Feet, may be dressed or warmed in the same way.

A Fricassee of Cold Veal

Hint 55 Take some slices of cooked Veal, and put them into a stew-pan with water, a bundle of sweet herbs, and a blade of mace, and let it stew until tender; then take out the herbs, add a little flour and butter boiled together, to thicken it a little, then add half a pint of milk, and the yolk of an egg beat very fine; add some pickled mushrooms, but some fresh mushrooms should be put in first, if they are to be had; keep stirring until it boils, and then add the juice of a lemon; stir well to keep it from curdling; then serve it in a dish, garnished with lemon.

Cold Veal dressed with White Sauce

Hint 56 Boil milk with a thickening of flour and butter; put into it thin slices of cold Veal, and simmer in the gravy until it is made hot, without boiling. When nearly done, beat up the yolk of an egg, with a little anchovy and White Sauce; pour it gently with the rest, stirring it all the time; simmer the whole together, and serve it with sippets of bread, and curled slices of bacon, laid alternately.

To re-cook Roasted Veal

Hint 57 Take a piece of Veal that has been roasted (but not overdone), cut it into thin slices; take from it the skin and gristle; melt some butter, in which put some chopped onions; fry the onions a little, then shake some flour over them; shake the pan round, and put in some veal stock gravy, a bunch of sweet herbs, and some spice; then put in the veal, with the yolk of two eggs, beat up with milk, some grated nutmeg, parsley shred small, lemon peel grated, and a little juice; stir it one way until thick and smooth, and put it into the dish. This converts an insipid cold meat into a very relishable entree.

Hint 58 Remember that meats when re-dressed, having lost some of their original flavour, require more seasoning than at the first.

A very nice dish of Calf's Chitterlings

Hint 59 Clean some of the largest Chitterlings, cut into lengths proper for puddings; tie one of the ends close; take some Bacon, and cut it like dice, a Calf's Udder, and the fat that comes off the chitterlings.

Put them into a stew-pan, with a bay leaf, salt, and pepper, an shallot cut small, some mace, and pepper, with half a pint or more of milk, and let it just simmer; then take off the pan, and thicken with four or five yolks of eggs, and some crumbs of bread; fill the chitterlings with this mixture, which must be kept warm; make the links like hog's puddings. Before they are sent to table, they must be boiled over a moderate fire; let them cool in their own liquor. Very nice and light eating in the summer time.

A nice Luncheon or Supper Cake from Cold Veal

Hint 60   Take as much cold roasted lean Veal as will fill a small cake mould, and pound it in a mortar, together with a slice of Ham or Bacon, a piece of the crumb of bread soaked in cold milk, two eggs well beaten, a small bit of butter, the same of shallot, or onion; season with pepper and salt, and mix all together well; butter the mould; fill it in, and bake in an oven for about an hour; turn it out when cold, and cut into slices.

Hint 61   To be eaten cold. Garnish with pickled eggs and parsley.

A very nice dish of Cold Lamb and Cucumbers, or Spinach

Hint 62   Fry slices or chops of cold Lamb in butter until they are slightly browned. Serve them on a puree of cucumbers. Or on a dish of spinach; or dip the slices in breadcrumbs, chopped parsley, and yolk of egg. Some grated lemon, and a little nutmeg may be added. Fry them, and pour a little good gravy over them when served.

Hint 63   The various methods of re-dressing Mutton are applicable generally to Lamb.

The only "Cold Shoulder" which can be shown to a Friend without Offence

Hint 64   A shoulder of Lamb, or a material part of one, being left cold, proceed in the following manner. Score the shoulder in squares, rub it with the yolk of an egg, pepper and salt it; and rub with breadcrumbs and dried parsley, or sweet herbs. Broil it over a clear fire; or put it in a Dutch oven, until nicely browned. Send it to table with Grill Sauce, made of half a pint of gravy, to which has been added an ounce of fresh butter rubbed into a tablespoonful of flour, the same of mushroom or walnut ketchup, two teaspoonfuls of lemon juice, one of black pepper, a quarter of a rind of lemon, grated very fine, a teaspoonful of essence of anchovies, a little shallot wine and chilli vinegar, or a few grains of cayenne.

Simmer together for a few minutes, pour a little of the sauce over the grill, and send up the rest in a tureen.

Hint 65   The Sauce may be simplified at discretion, if the above ingredients are not all at hand.

Hint 66   A cold shoulder of Mutton, having only a little meat upon the blade bone, may be dressed in the same way. Serve with Caper Sauce poured over it, or Melted Butter in which should be mixed some Mushroom ketchup, Lemon, Pickle and Harvey Sauce, say a tablespoonful each.

A nice Ragout from Cold Lamb

Hint 67   Separate the Lamb from the bones, and cut into convenient pieces; lard with Bacon fried of a light brown; and stew very lightly in mutton gravy, sufficient to cover it; season with sweet herbs, pepper, salt, and spice. Strain off the gravy, keeping the meat hot, and add to it some oysters browned in a frying pan, and freed from the fat in which they were fried; half a glass of port wine; a few mushrooms, and a bit of butter, rolled in flour; the juice of half a lemon; boil together for a few minutes in the gravy, and pour the sauce over the lamb.

Hint 68   Mutton may be served in the same way.

Cutlets of Cold Lamb or Mutton

Hint 69   Take the cutlets from the remains of a roast loin or neck of an underdone stewed or boiled joint; dip them into well-seasoned breadcrumbs, and broil or fry them over a quick fire, that they may be browned and heated through, without being overdone. When the cutlets are broiled, they should be dipped into or sprinkled with butter just dissolved. A few additional crumbs should be made to adhere to them after they are moistened with this.

Hint 70   This is a very good method of serving a half- roasted Loin or Neck.

A capital Dish, with which may he used up Cold or
other Vegetables, of various kinds

Hint 71   Cut some rather fat Ham or Bacon into slices, and fry to a nice brown; lay the slices aside to get warm; then mix equal quantities, or any proportions that you may happen to have, of potatoes and cabbage, cauliflower, or broccoli, and fry the mixture in the fat from the meat. The newly blown broccoli or cauliflower - will answer quite as well as the ripe. Well season with pepper.

To re-dress Cold Roast Pig

Hint 72   Carve the remains into neat pieces, and warm them in a sauce made of stock and sweet milk, the yolk of an egg beaten, and stirred gradually into it. Season with peppercorns, onions, a few sprigs of parsley and lemon thyme, and a bit of lemon peel. Strain the sauce, and warm the meat in it.

Another method of re-dressing Cold Sucking Pig

Hint 73   When the shoulders are left entire, remove from them the skin, turn them, dip them into clarified butter, or best salad oil; then in breadcrumbs, highly seasoned with cayenne and salt. Broil them over a clear fire, and send them to table while hot. Serve with tomato sauce.

Hint 74   Curried Crumbs, and a Curry Sauce, will give an excellent variety; and savoury herbs, with two or three shallots chopped, and mixed with the breadcrumbs, and brown shallot sauce to accompany the broil, will be liked by many.

A very nice Entree from Cold Sucking Pig

Hint 75   Remove the flesh from the bones, and also the skin; cut into convenient pieces. Melt a bit of butter, the size of an egg, and throw in six or eight button mushrooms, cleaned and sliced; shake them over the fire for three or four minutes; then stir to them a dessert spoonful of flour, and continue to shake or toss them gently; but do not allow them to burn. Add a small bunch of parsley, a bay leaf, a middling-sized blade of mace, some salt, a small quantity of cayenne or white pepper, half a pint of white stock, and from two to three glasses of light white wine. Let these boil gently until reduced nearly one-third; take out the parsley and mace, lay in the meat, and bring it slowly to the point of simmering; stir to it the beaten yolks of three fresh eggs, and the strained juice of half a lemon. Serve hot.

Pork Cutlets re-dressed, with Sauce

Hint 76   Pork Cutlets may be re-dressed by broiling; they may be cut from the cold neck or loin; the skin should be left on and scored. Serve them with pepper and salt, and broil over a clear fire, taking care that they do not become scorched.

Hint 77   Serve them with Sage and Onion Sauce, and gravy, shallot, plain onions, or fine herbs; or with gherkin, tomato, or poor man's sauce.

To make a nice Dish of Cold underdone Porky either Roasted or Boiled

Hint 78   Cut the Pork into slices, and fry lightly; make applesauce, and place it in the centre of a dish, laying the slices, of pork around it. Cold boiled pork may be made into Rissoles, being minced very fine, like sausage meat, and seasoned to liking. Either of these forms an excellent side or corner dish. Careful as the cook may be to send Pork to table well done, she is apt to be misled by appearances; and, as underdone pork is absolutely un-eatable, it is very desirable to know how to dispose of it to advantage. One criterion which the cook will do well to observe, is this, if the gravy latest from the meat is of a red colour, the joint is still under-done.

Excellent Sausages from Cold Pork, to be eaten cold

Hint 79   Season fat and lean Pork with salt, black pepper, and allspice, all in fine powder, and rub into the meat. Mince very fine, and fill the skins; tie up the ends, and hang the sausages to smoke, as hams are done, but first wrap them in a fold or two of old muslin.

A nice Hash, or Curry, from Cold Pork or other Cold Meat

Hint 80   Cut the meat into small pieces, having a fair proportion of lean and fat. Put into a stewpan, or a frying pan, two ounces of butter or dripping; when hot, add the meat, stir occasionally, and season with salt, spice, and pepper. When the meat is hot, pat in a teaspoonful of flour, water sufficient to make a good gravy; let it simmer; and add shallot, chives, or onions to liking.

Hint 81   Beef, Mutton, Veal, and Lamb may be done in the same way. For veal, lamb, or pork, the sauce may be kept white, and milk may be used.

Hint 82   A good Curry may be made in this way, by the addition of Curry Powder.

A nice Hash from Cold Venison

Hint 83   Make a gravy by stewing the bones and trimmings; season with a few peppercorns and some salt; strain, and thicken it with a bit of butter rolled in flour; add a glass of port wine, and a tablespoonful of mushroom ketchup, and one of currant jelly. When hot, put in the Venison, cut into thin slices. Heat it by simmering slowly, and serve with toasted sippets.

Hint 84   Should the meat be lean, add a little firm Mutton fat to the gravy, and let it stew before putting in the meat.

A nice Stew from Cold Venison

Hint 85   Make a gravy from the fragments and bones, and add thereto, if convenient, a little strong unseasoned mutton stock, and a bundle of fine herbs. Let this simmer; then skim, and add browned butter, thickened with flour, some ketchup, mixed spices, a little claret, if approved, and a spoonful of currant jelly. Take out the herbs, and squeeze in a little lemon; give a boil, and then while simmering add the pieces of Venison, thinly sliced. Garnish with cut pickles; or with slices of lemon, and fried sippets.

A nice Pasty from cold Venison

Hint 86   Cut the Venison into small squares, and rub them over with a seasoning of sweet herbs, grated nutmeg, pepper, and salt; line the sides and edges of a dish with thin puff paste, lay in the meat, and add half a pint of rich gravy, made with the trimmings of the venison; add a glass of port wine, and the juice of half a lemon, or a teaspoonful of vinegar; cover the dish with a thin paste, and bake.

Hint 87   Pour a little more gravy into the pasty when it comes from the oven. Good, either hot or cold.

Hint 88   Pieces of cold Venison are also suitable for "devilling."

An Economical and Nice Dish, with Apples boiled

Hint 89   Cut thin slices of meat from cold spare rib of Pork, in pieces of about four inches long and two wide; then mix in a plate some pepper, salt, and powdered sage; sprinkle a little of this mixture upon each piece of meat; then make it into a roll about the size of the thumb 5 put the rolls on one side for a moment. Then get a pie dish; lay on the bottom some slices of potatoes about half an inch thick; over these, some slices of onions cut thin; over the onions some slices of Apple, about the same thickness as the potato. If the pie dish is deep, another layer of each will be required; then place over these layers the meat rolled up; cover it with a nice pudding paste; tie it in a cloth, and boil it in a large kettle. A pudding in a twelve-inch dish will require one hour's boiling. This is much more economical than baking or roasting the sparerib; the bones can be put into the stockpot, or be stewed down for gravy.

Hint 90   This may be made into a standing pie, but is not so good in that way. Slices of fat Cold Pork may be used.

Relishable Meat Cakes from Scraps of Cold Meat,
Game, or Poultry

Hint 91   Take any cold Game, Poultry, or Meat, and to give it a little richness, add a little fat bacon or ham, and an anchovy; mince it fine; season with pepper and salt to liking; mix thoroughly, and make into small cakes, with bread crumbs, yolks of boiled eggs, onions, sweet herbs, curry powder, or any of the forcemeats. Fry the cakes a light brown, and serve them with good gravy; or put the mixture into a mould, and boil or bake it. A nice relish for suppers.

Cold Meat of any kind, Game or Poultry, Fish or
Fruits, re-dressed as Fritters

Hint 92   Ascertain the quantity of cold meat you have, and then pot an equal weight of breadcrumbs to soak in cold water; let there be a little fat with the meat, and chop it into small dice.
Squeeze the water from the bread; put in the pan two ounces of butter, lard, or dripping, and two tablespoonfuls of sliced onions; fry for two minutes, then add the bread, stir with a wooden spoon until rather dry; then add the meat. Season with salt and pepper to taste, and a little nutmeg, if approved; stir until quite hot; then add two eggs, one at a time; mix quickly, and pour on a dish to cool. Roll into the shape of small eggs, or as pancakes, egg and breadcrumb them, and fry. Serve plain, or with any appropriate sauce.

Hint 93   The above is the process for Cold Meats; for Fish, or Fruits, the seasoning must be appropriate, as a little anchovy, Reading sauce, cayenne pepper, etc., for the former; and sugar, lemon peel, cloves, etc., for the latter. In the above manner, any kind of scraps may be turned to good account.

"Toad in the Hole" from Cold Meat

Hint 94   Get about two pounds of pieces of underdone Beef, Mutton, Veal, or Lamb, and cut them into bits about the size of an egg; season with salt and pepper; make about two quarts of Batter; grease a baking pan well; put in the meat and batter, and place in a slow oven. Cover the meat with the batter, that it may not be dried.

Hint 95   Cold Boiled Potatoes may be sliced, and placed around the pan.

Hint 96   Cold Boiled Peas and Beans may also be warmed and served in this manner.

*An Excellent and Economical Family Dinner, served
in a homely way*

Hint 97   Take any joint of meat, such as a loin of Veal, or a large shoulder of Mutton, and prepare it as for roasting. Make a suet pudding without eggs, and place it round the side of the dish; fill the remainder of the dish with potatoes, over which place the joint, set upon a trivet, and bake; the gravy of the meat will be absorbed in part by the potatoes and the pudding.

Hint 98   Recommended to the heads of large families. Serve it in the dish in which it was baked.

*Capital Stew made in a Frying-pan, with pieces of
Stale Bread*

Hint 99   Cut in small dice half a pound of solid meat, keeping the bones, if any, for soup; put the frying pan, which should be quite clean, upon the fire; when hot, add an ounce of fat; melt it, and put in the meat; season with half a teaspoonful of salt; fry for ten minutes, stirring now and then; add a teaspoonful of flour; mix all well, put in half a pint of water, and let it simmer for fifteen minutes. Then add some stale bread, the pieces of which have been previously soaked, and when hot serve. The addition of a little pepper, or a little pepper and sugar, will be an improvement; or a pinch of cayenne, curry powder, spice, sauces, pickle vinegar, or chopped pickles.

Hint 100   Salt Meat may be dressed as above, omitting the salt.

Hint 101   Or, for a change, boil the meat plainly, or with Greens, Cabbage, or Dumplings, as for boiled beef; the next day cut what is left into small dice, put in the pan an ounce of fat, and when very hot, add the following: — Mix in a basin a tablespoonful of flour, moisten with water to the consistence of thick melted butter, then pour it into the pan, letting it remain for one or two minutes until set; put in the meat, shake the pan to loosen it, turn it over, let it remain for a few minutes longer, and serve.

*A Frugal, Agreeable, and Nutritive Meal for Eight
Persons, that will neither lighten the Purse, nor Lie
heavy on the Stomach*

Hint 102   Wash three quarters of a pound of Scotch barley in a little cold water; put it in a soup pot with a shin or leg of beef, of about ten pounds weight, severed into four pieces (tell the butcher to do this for you); cover it well with cold water; set it on the fire; when it boils, skim it very cleanly, and put in two onions of about three ounces weight each.

Re-set it by the side of the fire to simmer very gently for about two hours; then skim all the fat cleanly off, and put in two heads of celery, and a large turnip cut into small squares; season it with salt, and let it boil an hour and a half longer, and it is ready. Take out the meat with a slice, cover it up, and set it by the fire to keep warm, and skim the broth well before you put it into the tureen. Put a quart of the soup into a basin, put about an ounce of flour into a stewpan, and pour the broth to it by degrees, stirring it well together; set it on the fire, and stir until it boils then let it boil up, and it is ready. Put the meat in a ragout dish, and strain the sauce through a sieve over the meat; add, if liked, some capers or minced jerkins or walnuts, etc. If the beef has been stewed with proper care in a very gentle manner, and been taken up at the right moment, you will obtain an excellent savoury meal for eight people. Plenty of hot vegetables according to season. Capital for schoolboys when they come in with their noses frost-bitten; or labourers hungry from the field.

A very Economical and Savoury Meal, equal to the most Expensive Dish

Hint 103   Take an Ox Cheek, and prepare it as follows, the day before it is required: clean it and put it in soft water, just warm; let it lie three or four hours, then change it to cold water, and let it soak all night. Next day wipe it clean, put it into a stewpan, and just cover it with water; skim it well just before it comes to a boil; then put in two whole onions, with two or three cloves stuck into each; three turnips quartered, a couple of carrots sliced, two bay leaves, and twenty four corns of allspice, a head of celery, and a bundle of sweet herbs, pepper, and salt. Let it stew gently until perfectly tender, about three hours; then take out the cheek, divide it into convenient pieces suitable for the table; skim and strain the gravy; melt an ounce and a half of butter in the stew-pan; stir into it as much flour as it will take up; mix it by degrees with a pint and a half of the gravy; add to it a tablespoonful of elder vinegar, or mushroom or walnut ketchup, and give it a boil serve in a soup dish; or it may be made into a good Barley Broth.

A capital dish of Rice, with the Extract of Bones

Hint 104   Six pounds or more of bones, of any kind of meat; break them into small pieces, and boil in ten quarts of water for four hours; add three ounces of salt, a small bunch of thyme, bay leaf, and savoury. Put into a stewpan two ounces of dripping, two onions cut thin and half a pound of carrots, turnips, celery, or other vegetables, cut thin; and half an ounce of sugar; set it on the fire for fifteen minutes, stirring occasionally; add half a pound of oatmeal, and mix well; moisten with two gallons of stock from the bones; add one pound and a quarter of rice, previously soaked; boil until tender, and serve.

A method of Cooking Old Fowls, Pheasants, Black Cock, and other Birds, not fit for Roasting

Hint 105   Let the Birds be kept as long as possible, hung up where there is a free circulation of air; and, when picked and prepared for dressing, cover the bottom of a saucepan with slices of good fresh English bacon, upon which lay the bird; then add a pint of good, strong, well seasoned gravy. Place the saucepan upon a slow fire, the cover being on, and let the contents simmer for an hour and a half or two hours, turning the bird occasionally. Supplying more gravy, if necessary; when done, let the contents be put away in a dish to cool. Birds dressed in this manner, are good hot; but they are far better when cold.

Hint 106   Snipes and Woodcocks are also excellent when cooked in this manner; but require much less time. The principal thing to be attended to is the fire, that it be not too quick, as old birds can only be rendered tender by a gradual process.

Hint 107   In roasting Game the principal desideratum is continuous basting, in which case the fire cannot be too ardent.

A nice way of Warming Cold Fowl or Veal

Hint 108   Beat the white of two eggs to a thick froth; add a small bit of butter, or some salad oil, flour, a little lukewarm water, and two tablespoonfuls of beer, beaten together until of the consistency of very thick cream. Cut tip the Fowl or Veal into small pieces; strew over them some chopped parsley and shallot, pepper, salt, and a little vinegar, and let them lie until dinner time; dip the pieces in the butter, and fry, in boiling lard, to a nice brown.

Hint 109   Cold Fowl and Veal, usually dry eating, may thus be converted into a choice and new dish.

A very cheap way of Potting Birds

Hint 110   In seasons when Partridges are very plentiful, and cannot be kept, on account of the hot weather, they may be advantageously potted in the following manner. Clean them thoroughly, and season with mace, allspice, white pepper, and salt, in fine powder. Rub every part well; then lay the breasts downwards in a pan, and pack them as closely as possible. Put a good deal of butter on them; then cover the pan with a coarse flour paste, and a paper cover; tie it close, and bake. When cold, cut them into proper pieces for serving, pack them close in a large potting pot, and cover them again with butter.

Hint 111   The Butter which has been used to cover Potted Meats will afterwards serve for Basting, or for Paste for Meat Pies.

Very nice Scallops from Cold Chicken

Hint 112   Bone the meat, and mince it small; set it over the fire in a little cream, and season with nutmeg, pepper, and salt; then put it into scallop shells, and fill with crumbs of bread, over which put some bits of butter, and brown before the fire.

Hint 113   Cold Veal may be done the same way. Either Veal or Chicken looks and eats well, served thus; or lightly covered with Breadcrumbs, fried; or they may be put on in little heaps.

Fricassee from Cold Chicken or Fowl

Hint 114   Cut up the Chicken, and put it to simmer in a little gravy, made of some of the water in which it was boiled, and the head, neck, feet, liver, and gizzard, stewed well together; an onion, some pepper, and a faggot of sweet herbs. Keep it hot, while you thicken the sauce in this manner:— Strain it off; put it back into the saucepan, with a little salt, nutmeg, and a bit of butter rolled in flour; give it a boil. Know add a little cream, and stir it over the fire; but do not boil again. Pour the sauce upon the chicken, and add some small nicely fried forcemeat balls. Garnish with thin slices of lemon.

Broiled Cold Chicken or Fowl

Hint 115   Split them right down the back, then rub them with egg and breadcrumbs, and sprinkle with clarified butter, over which some more breadcrumbs, and broil over a clear gentle fire.

Hint 116   The Neck, Feet, and Gizzard, may be boiled down, with a small quantity of onion and carrot, previously browned in butter, to make gravy; and the liver, after having been simmered with them for five or six minutes, may be used to thicken it after straining. Season with lemon juice, cayenne, and a little minced parsley; thicken with arrowroot, or flour and butter.

Hint 117   Serve very hot, with Mushroom Sauce, or with a little good plain gravy, thickened and flavoured with a teaspoonful of mushroom powder, mixed with half as much flour, and a little butter. The bird should be pressed as flat as possible, that the fire may take equal effect, and to this end, the legs should be trussed like those of a boiled fowl, and the breastbone may be removed.

Hint 118   Cold Fowls may be Broiled and Deviled.

Sausages from Cold Fowl, Turkey, or Veal

Hint 119   Mince the meat, and add suitable proportions of suet, grated bread, ham, a little parsley, lemon thyme, and chives. Mix these with pepper, salt, pounded mace, egg yolk, and flour. Roll and fry.

Hint 120   These sausages, made in small quantity, form an excellent Garnish to a Fricassee, or to Minced Veal.

An excellent Hash from Cold Roast Fowl

Hint 121   Cut a cold roast Fowl into pieces, and put the trimmings into a saucepan, with two or three shallots, some fine herbs, a bay leaf, pepper, salt, a slice of lean ham, and a little gravy. Simmer this for half an hour, then strain it off. Put a little brown gravy into another stewpan, to which add the above gravy; let it boil a minute, and then put in the fowl. Before serving, squeeze in a little lemon juice.

Cold Roast Fowls Fried, with warmed Vegetables

Hint 122   Beat the yolks of two eggs, with butter, mace, nutmeg, etc. Cut the Fowls into joints, and dip them in this, and roll the egged pieces in crumbs and fried parsley. Fry the cut pieces nicely in butter, or clarified dripping, and pour over the dish any white or green vegetable, chopped, and made hot. Parmesan Cheese grated, may be used to give a piquant flavour.

Hint 123   Slices of Bacon may be fried and sent to table with this.

Hint 124   The pieces of Fowl, instead of being fried, may be warmed in a Dutch oven.

A Delicate Dish from Cold Fowl or Veal

Hint 125   Stew a few small mushrooms in their own liquor, and a bit of butter, for quarter of an hour. Mince them very small and add them, with their liquor, to minced Veal, or parts of Fowl. Add a little pepper and salt, some cream, and a bit of butter rubbed in a little flour. Simmer three or four minutes, and serve on sippets of bread.

Deviled Fowl, Duck, Goose, Turkey, etc., Meat, Bones, etc

Hint 126   The Legs, Bumps, Backs, Gizzards are the parts for "devilling." But, besides these parts of birds.

Pieces of Venison, Veal, Mutton, Kidneys, Beef ribs, etc., are favourite relishes. The devils must be boiled on & strong clear fire, and served upon very hot plates. The meat must be scored, that the hot seasonings may find their way to the inner parts. The seasonings consist principally of cayenne, with salt, curry, mushroom, anchovy, or truffle powder.

Hint 127   When a Moist Devil is desired, the proper sauces are Grill, Anchovy, or anything very piquant, with Indian Gherkins finely chopped, or Chow-Chow pickle.

Hint 128   Take the Rump, Gizzard, and Drumstick of a Turkey, and rub them with seasoning of salt, pepper, and cayenne. Broil them, and while as hot as possible, cut into pieces; pour over a spoonful of mustard, ditto of melted butter, ditto of soy, ditto of lemon juice, and some gravy, mixed, and made very hot.

An Excellent and Economical Dish of Stewed Rabbits, Bacon, and Onions

Hint 129   Take a pipkin, having a tightly fitting cover, and of sufficient size to hold a couple of Rabbits, cut into small pieces, with four middling sized Spanish onions, in thin slices. Put a layer of onion in the bottom of the pipkin; on this a layer of the pieces of Rabbit, previously seasoned with salt, pepper, and any other favourite condiments; cover with a second layer of onions, then rabbit again, and so on until the whole of the rabbit is laid; then a layer of Bacon or Ham, and over the whole a final layer of onion. Put the cover on, and stew gently for two hours, either in a slack oven, or upon a hot plate or hearth.

Hint 130   As no water is added, should the pipkin be placed on the fire, the stew will be liable to burn. When ready, let it be turned out into a dish, and served immediately. It will be found to supply a delicious, tender, succulent, moist dish — far superior to the insipid, dry, fitringy, boiled rabbit and onion sauce of ordinary cookery.

Hint 131   English onions answer very well; and should the gravy, of which a large quantity will be produced, be required to be slightly thickened, a teaspoonful of flour should be added to the seasoning when it is rubbed over the pieces of rabbit.

Hashed Hare, Rabbit, Turkey, Fowl, Pheasant, etc

Hint 132   Cut the remains into pieces of moderate size; put them into a clean. dish, and pour all the cold gravy over them. Break the bones, and put them with the trimmings into a saucepan of broth or water, enough to cover them; add an onion cut in slices, half a teaspoonful each of white pepper and salt, and a blade of mace.

Boil it gently for an hour; then strain off the liquor through a sieve into a basin; and when cold, take off the cake of fat from the top, and mix the gravy in a basin with two teaspoonfuls of flour; then let it boil gently for a minute or two. Lay the meat in a stew-pan, strain over it the gravy, and place it near the fire to simmer, without boiling, for about half an hour. Five minutes before it is done, put in some stuffing. Serve with the slices of stuffing, and sippets of toasted bread, at the sides.

Hint 133   With Hashed Hare, put a little Currant Jelly. If you have no Stuffing left, make a little, and fry or bake it; or boil with the liquor a few sweet herbs, and a little lemon peel.

Pulled Cold Turkey, or Fowl

Hint 134   Divide the meat of the breast by pulling it, instead of cutting; then warm it gradually in a little white gravy, add a little cream, grated nutmeg, salt, and a little flour and butter. While this is being done, broil the drumstick, and put into the dish with the above round it.

Very nice Patties from Cold Turkey, Fowl, Pheasant, etc

Hint 135   Mince the white part of the flesh, and mix it with a little grated ham. Stew this in a little good gravy, or melted butter. Put a spoonful of cream to the mince, and season with white pepper, salt, and mace.

Hint 136   Patties may be made of cold Lamb, Veal, Turkey, Fowl, Fowl and Ham, Pheasant, Guinea Fowl, Hare, Rabbit, etc., and of Lobsters, Oysters, Shrimps, etc.

Hint 137   Patties may be either baked in their paste, without the intervention of a pan, having a piece of paper under each; or they may be baked in tin or earthenware pans of various forms. Those baked in pans will generally be most approved, because the paste will be more delicate; or the paste may be baked separately, and the meat afterwards put upon it. Puff paste should be employed.

Hint 138   Or, Patties may be made with Fried Breads cut the crumb of a loaf into square or round pieces, nearly three inches high, and cut bits the same width for tops; mark them neatly with a knife; fry the bread of a light brown colour in clarified beef dripping, or fine lard. Scoop out the inside crumb, taking care not to go too near the bottom; fill the space with the minced meat; put on the tops, and serve upon a napkin.

Hint 139   Patties of Forcemeats, such as those compounded of Sweetbreads, Herbs, and Panada, or any other light forcemeat, must be united with the yolk and white of egg, and baked in the paste. When baked, the covers must be removed and some rich Sauce poured in; or it may be introduced through a small funnel.

Ducks Stewed with Red Cabbage

Hint 140   Cut the cold Ducks into convenient pieces, and warm them very gradually in a good clear gravy, by the side of the fire. Shred some Red Cabbage very fine, wash it, and drain it on a sieve; put it to stew with a good proportion of butter, and a little pepper and salt, in a stew pan closely covered, shaking it frequently. If it should get too dry, add a spoonful or two of the gravy. When well done and tender, add a small glass of vinegar; lay it on a dish; place the pieces of duck upon it, and serve.

Ducks warmed, with a Puree of Carrots

Hint 141   Scrape and cut in quarters eight or nine Carrots, boil them very tender, put them in a sieve, and when drained, stir them well on the fire, with a good proportion of butter; when well mashed, and the butter begins to fry, put in half a ladle of clear soup or gravy, and add a little salt, and a small bit of sugar; rub the whole through a tammy into a dish; warm it again in a stewpan, and stir it well on the fire with a wooden spoon. Having, during this process, warmed the pieces of Duck in gravy, set the whole upon a dish; lay the duck upon the top.

Cold Duck Stewed with Peas

Hint 142   Put a pint of good gravy and a pint of green peas together in a stewpan, and let them stew until the peas are soft; then add a glass of red wine, or this may be omitted. Add some onion chopped small, or garlic, if liked. A little more gravy, to make up the loss by stewing. Season with lemon peel, sweet herbs, cayenne pepper, and salt. Put in the Duck, and warm gently, under a close cover. Add a little walnut ketchup, and serve hot.

Hint 143   For a nice variation of this dish the peas may be stewed in Cream Sauce, with two yolks of eggs beaten in a little cream, and served in a dish with a border of mashed potatoes.

Excellent Dishes of Hashed Duck, or Goose, etc

Hint 144   Cut the bird into pieces, as in ordinary carving; skin, and soak the pieces in a little hot gravy, set by the side of the fire. Add a small glass of wine, and sufficient mixed spices to give the sauce a high relish.

Or, add a gravy of the trimmings to some onions nicely fried; thicken it, when strained, with butter browned with flour; stew the Duck gently, and serve with the seasoned sauce, upon a deep dish, with fried sippets.

Hint 145   For Goose, a little Sage should be added to the onion sauce.

An excellent Hash from Cold Wild Fowl, Partridges, Pheasants, etc

Hint 146   Carve as for the table, and soak the pieces until hot in boiling gravy, thickened with breadcrumbs, and seasoned with salt, mixed spices, a glass of claret, and a spoonful of lemon pickle or orange juice. Garnish with fried sippets.

Hint 147   Partridges or Pheasants, use white pepper, and white wine.

Hint 148   A good Sauce for warming Wild Fowl may be made as follows: — Simmer a teacupful of port wine, the same quantity of good meat gravy, a little shallot, and a bit of mace, for ten minutes; put in a bit of butter and flour, give it all one boil; then place it on the side of the hob, and steep the pieces of fowl to warm.

Hint 149   For a good common Hash of Wild Duck, or Teal, boil the skin and trimmings in some broth or gravy, with a couple of lightly fried shallots; then strain, heat, and thicken it slightly, with a little brown gravy, or browned flour; add a wine glassful of port wine, some lemon juice, and cayenne; warm the birds thoroughly in it, and serve as soon as they are hot.

Hint 150   Ducks may also be re-dressed as Curry, brown ragout, or Stew soup.

Ragout from Cold Wild Duck or Teal

Hint 151   Score the breasts, and rub into the incisions mixed spices and cayenne pepper; squeeze lemon juice over them. Warm them very gradually in a good brown gravy. Take out the Birds, and keep hot before the fire; then add a glass of wine, and three finely shredded shallots to the gravy; pour it hot over the birds, and serve.

Delicious Stew from Cold Roasted Moorfowl

Hint 152   Cut them into joints, and warm the pieces by stewing very gently. Brown some butter and flour, and put it to some good gravy, seasoned with pepper, salt, mace, and two cloves.

Boil the sauce, and put in the Fowl to warm. Just before taking them from the fire, add a spoonful of mushroom ketchup.

A Delicious Entree from Cold Grouse, Pheasants, or Partridges

Hint 153   Cut the Birds, and take away the skin and fat; put the skin and trimmings into a stewpan, add two or three sliced shallots, a bay leaf, a small blade of mace, and a few peppercorns; then pour in a pint or rather more of good veal gravy, or strong broth, and boil it briskly, until reduced nearly one half; strain the gravy, and skim off the fat; return to the stewpan, and put in the pieces of bird to warm gradually on the hob. When hot, take out the pieces, and lay in the centre of a dish; squeeze into the sauce a little lemon juice, and a sprinkle of cayenne. Give the sauce a momentary boil, and pour it over the bird. Serve with fried sippets.

Hint 154   As the spongy substance in the inside of the Moorfowl is apt to become bitter when the birds have been long kept, it should he removed.

Hint 155   The dish, thus prepared, may be garnished with Liver Sausages, made as follows: — Chop one pound of calf's liver with ten ounces of fat bacon, and six ounces of bread crumbs; season with black pepper, salt, grated nutmeg, and lemon peel, some parsley, thyme, one bay leaf, and some sweet basil, all chopped fine; add the yolks of three eggs, mix the whole thoroughly, and then form into round or oval sausages, wrap in pig's caul, and fry of a brown colour.

Pheasant, Stewed with Artichokes

Hint 156   Take veal broth, enough to cover the bird; make it hot, and put in some parboiled Artichoke Bottoms, a bit of mace, a glass of white wine, and season with pepper and salt, a little lemon juice, butter and flour. Before adding the wine and lemon juice, put in the pieces of Pheasant, and let them stew gently, until warmed. Then lay the bird in the centre of a dish, and pour the hot sauce over it. A few forcemeat balls set round the dish will be an improvement.

A nice Breakfast, Luncheon, or Supper Dish, from Cold Woodcock

Hint 157   Cut up the Woodcock, and warm it in a gravy made as follows: — Beat up the entrails, and mix them in a sauce of red wine and water, a spoonful of vinegar, and a sliced onion; to which add butter and flour; boil this for a minute or two, and then put in tilie bird; when hot, lay the pieces of bird upon a slice of buttered toast, and pour the sauce over the whole.

Hint 158   Snipes may be served in the same way. So may Peewits and Plovers.

Very nice Pasties from Cold Meat and Potatoes

Hint 159   These pasties may be made covered with paste, three-cornered in shape, as in the Cornish fashion; or be made in tin moulds, the meat being laid in the bottom, and potatoes, mashed, upon the top, as in what is commonly called "Sanders." These moulds are sold at the ironmongers' shops. Cut, trim, and season the meat, and lay it in the mould, as if making a pie, or meat pudding. A little fat should be secured for the potatoes. Add water or gravy, cayenne and ketchup, or whatever kind of seasoning is best adapted to the meat used, at discretion; also mushrooms, ketchup, or curry powder, with Veal; and with Fish, a little Harvey's sauce. Put the perforated cover down into the mould, and upon it, to the thickness of three or four inches, rising conically, heap potatoes mashed with milk, and a good bit of butter; season with pepper and salt, and a little shred onion, if liked. Potatoes left from previous days may be thus used. Bake until the potato crust is nicely browned, and have ready a little nice gravy to serve with the meat.

Hint 160   If the pasty is to be baked in a Paste, the tin mould is quite unnecessary. Cut and season the meat; roll out the paste, in the form of a large circle; cover one half of it with a thin layer of cold mashed or sliced potatoes; over this, a thick layer of meat, and a little gravy, if the meat is very lean, or dry; over the meat a final layer of mashed potatoes, stuck with bits of butter, or cold fat meat; pepper and salt; turn one half of the paste over this, and nip the edges with the finger and thumb. Bake until the paste is a nice brown.

Hint 161   Beef, Mutton, Veal, Veal and Oysters, Pork, Hare, Rabbit, all other kinds of Game, Poultry, and Fish, may be re-dressed in this manner.

Hint 162   The same baked in deep dishes, with a savoury Paste Crust, produce excellent Meat and Potato Pies.

A delicious pie of Sheep's Head and Trotters, to be eaten Cold

Hint 163   Scald and clean a Sheep's Head and Trotters; parboil them, and when cold, cut off all the meat in square bits; season with pepper and salt, and a little finely minced onion. Pack the meat closely into a pudding dish or shape, adding some bits of butter; and fill the dish with some rich highly seasoned gravy, or with some of the liquor that the head and feet were boiled in. Cover with a plain paste and bake for an hour. To be serve cold, the pie to be cut into slices, like potted meat, and garnished with curled parsley.

Hint 164   Remnants of Ox Cheek and Tongue, Calf's Head, Tongue, and Brains, etc., may be made into pies in the same manner.

A Medley Pie, of Cold Boast Meat and Apples, Leicestershire Fashion

Hint 165   Cut some Apples into quarters, take out the core (preserving the pips, and sticking them into the pulp); cut thick slices of cold fat Bacon, and any sort of cold roasted meat; season with pounded ginger, pepper, and salt; put into the dish a layer of each, and pour over the top a large cupful of ale; cover the dish with a paste made with dripping or lard; bake until nicely browned.

A nice Pie of Cold Veal, or Chicken, and Ham

Hint 166   Layer a crust into a shallow tart-dish, and fill it with the meat prepared as follows:— Shred cold Veal or Fowl, and half the quantity of ham, mostly lean; put to it a little cream; season with white pepper, salt, a grate or two of nutmeg, and a bit of garlic or shallot, minced as fine as possible. Cover with crust, and turn it out of the dish when baked; or bake the crust with a basin inside to keep it hollow; warm the meat with a little cream, and put it in when the paste is sufficient baked.

Hint 167   Another, and a very nice kind of Veal or Chicken Pie, may be made by scalding some parsley that is picked from the stems, and squeezing it dry; chop, and lay it at the bottom of the dish; then put the meat; then parsley again, and so on, in layers. Pour into the dish new milk, but do not let it touch the crust. When ready, add a little scalded cream; or the latter may be dispensed with.

An Excellent Pie from the Remains of a Calf's Head

Hint 168   Cut all the flesh from the bone, and cut into square bits; put a layer of Ham, either cold boiled, or lightly broiled in slices, at the bottom of the dish; then some pieces of the Head, well seasoned with pepper and salt, and a little of the brain sauce, if any; put here and there forcemeat balls, or veal stuffing, and hard boiled eggs cut into slices; and so on until the dish is full. Make a gravy, by stewing a knuckle of veal till tender, with two onions, a faggot of herbs, a blade of mace, and six peppercorns, in three pints of water; let it simmer, with the bones in it, removing sufficient meat to make balls for the pie. Add the rest of the meat to the flesh of the head. Put a little of the gravy into the dish, cover with a tolerably thick crust, and bake in a slow oven. When done, fill up with gravy, but do not cut the pie until it is cold.

Hint 169   Or, Oysters and Mushrooms may be introduced, and the pie be eaten warm, instead of cold.

Hint 170   Small pies may be made to eat hot, which, with high seasoning. Truffles, Morels, etc., will be found very nice.

Hint 171   The cold pie will keep several days, and slices of it make a pretty side dish, garnished with parsley.

Hint 172   Calf's Foot or Cow Heel may be used instead of knuckle of veal; but these make the pie drier and harder.

Hint 173   Pickled Tongues of calves' heads, or sheep's heads may be cut in to vary the colour and improve the flavour, instead of, or in addition to. Ham.

Sea Pie; a Capital Dish

Hint 174   Make a thick pudding crust; line a dish with it; put a layer of sliced onions at the bottom; then a layer of salt Beef, cut in slices, with a fair proportion of fat; next, a layer of sliced potatoes; then a layer of Pork, and another of onions; strew pepper over all; cover with the crust, and tie down tightly with a cloth, previously dipped in boiling water, and floured. Boil for two hours, and serve in the dish.

Pork Pies of Meat left after trimming Flitches etc

Hint 175   Cut the meat left after trimming flitches that are being prepared for salting into small pieces, together with trimmings from the griskins, and the meat from the sweet bone; keep the fat and lean separate, and season both with pepper and salt. Then raise the crust, and when ready, fill the pies closely with layers of lean and fat, those of the lean being of greater depth than of the fat. Unite the lids firmly to the sides, and bake. Add no water or gravy.

A capital Pie from Goose Giblets

Hint 176   Clean the Giblets of one, two, or three Geese; cut the legs in two, the wing and neck into three, and the gizzard into four pieces; stew them well; preserve the liquor, and set the giblets apart until cold; season them with black pepper and salt, and put them into a deep dish; cover with paste, and bake in a moderate oven. In the mean time, take the liquor the giblets were stewed in, skim it free from fat, put it over a fire in a clean stewpan; thicken with a little flour and butter, and season with pepper and salt, and the juice of half a lemon; add a few drops of browning; strain through a fine sieve; when the pie comes from the oven, pour some of this into it through a funnel.

Hint 177   If you have any cold Game or Poultry, it may be cut into pieces, and included in the pie; the Bones may be stewed with the Giblets.

A "West Country" Squab Pie

Hint 178   This is made with good plain paste. Apples pared and cut into pieces, onions sliced, and pieces of Mutton tolerably fat. Slice the onions and apples, cover the bottom of the dish with them, well intermixed, strew over them some sugar; and then lay upon them some mutton chops, or slices, seasoned with pepper and salt; then more apple, and so on, until the dish is full. Add water in quantity proportionate to the size of the pie.

Very Savoury Puffs from Cold Meat and Potatoes

Hint 179   Cut any kind of Cold Meat into small pieces, and season them well with pepper and salt; add a little shredded onion, if liked. Take the Cold Potatoes, mash them, roll them fine with a rolling pin, and dust with a little flour; break an egg upon the potatoes, mix all well together, and make into a paste of the same thickness as for paste for ordinary pies, stiffening with a little more flour, if necessary; roll it out in portions of convenient size; put the seasoned meat upon these portions, and fold in the usual puff form; pinch the edges together, and fry them slowly on all sides.

Hint 180   For Supper or Luncheon, these Puffs are excellent; or as a bottom or side dish, to help out a spare dinner.

Various ways of Cooking and re-cooking that unmanageable dish, Ox-heart

Hint 181   Trim and clean the Heart, and wipe it dry; fill the cavities with a stuffing made thus:— Crumbs of bread (the quantity must depend upon the size of the heart), chopped suet or butter, say about two ounces, parsley and sweet marjoram, chopped lemon peel grated, pepper, salt, and nutmeg, with the yolk of an egg; mix, and fill the cavities of the heart. Serve it with gravy, melted butter, and currant jelly. Prepared in this way, it may be either baked or roasted, and will require a quarter of an hour for each pound Weight.

Hint 182   Or, clean and cut the Heart in large pieces lengthwise. Put these into a stew pot with cold water and salt, and carefully skim away the blood, which will rise in large quantities; parboil; take up the parboiled pieces, and carve them into mouthful; strain the liquor, and return the cut meat, with plenty of shred onion, a shred head or two of celery, pepper, and allspice, and a dozen or more peeled potatoes, or some sliced carrots. This is a nourishing and economical Stew soup, and half a full-sized bullock's heart will be sufficient etc make it.

Hint 183   Or, cut into pieces lengthwise, the pieces not being thicker than half an inch; Broily with a piece of fat or bacon, for ten minutes; serve with a little currant jelly and butter, under the slices.

Hint 184   Or, wash in several waters, cut it into pieces lengthwise; take a baking dish, and lay some slices of potatoes at the bottom, then a few slices of bacon, then the pieces of heart, another layer of bacon; season each layer to liking, and fill up the spaces with veal stuffing made into balls; add water, and Bake about an hour.

Hint 185   Kidney and Heart may be mixed, or the flesh of Cowheel be mixed with either heart or kidney.

Hint 186   Calf's Heart may be dressed in the same way or be stuffed with veal stuffing, and Baked upon potatoes.

Hint 187   Or, Bullock's Heart, stuffed as for baking, may be Boiled, Small hearts, as of Sheep, Lambs, etc., may be stuffed, enclosed in paste, with a bit of fat bacon wrapped round them, and Baked, like Savoury Dumplings.

Hint 188   Cold Heart may be Hashed the same as Beef or Hare, the stuffing being mixed with the gravy, and accompanied by Currant Jelly.

Various Methods of Cooking Ox, Calf, Sheep, Lamb,
Pigs and other Livers

Hint 189   The claims of Ox Liver, as an article of food, are not sufficiently appreciated. In the following manner it will supply a capital breakfast relish:— Slice, season well with pepper and salt, and Broil over a clear fire; rub cold butter on it, and serve hot, with small slices of fat bacon. Calf's Liver in the same way.

Hint 190   Ox Liver may be made into excellent and savoury skin Puddings: — Boil the liver and grate it; mix, in equal quantities, grated liver, grated bread, and minced suet; season well with black pepper, a little grated nutmeg, salt, and a glass of rum. Half fill the skins, and manage them in the same way as other skin puddings. Some persons use double the quantity of suet, or add some bacon fat, chopped fine.

Hint 191   Or, into excellent Paste Puddings, being cut into slices, with bacon, seasoned with salt and pepper, chopped onion, etc. The liver should be dipped into flour and be laid alternately with slices of bacon in the pudding, which should be made in a dish, a little water or gravy added, and Boiled. Sheep, Lamb, and Pig Livers, may be dressed the same way.

Ox Liver and Kidneys may be combined in Puddings, being browned and seasoned in a frying pan with bacon fat first, but not fully cooked; then put into the pudding, and boiled.

Hint 192 Ox or Calf's Liver Fried with Bacon:— Cut some liver into slices about half an inch thick; melt two ounces of nice clear dripping in a frying pan; dredge the sliced liver with flour, and fry it over a pretty quick fire. Then fry rashers of Bacon; lay the liver in a hot dish, and the bacon upon it; fry, and place round it, if liked, onions shred fine and nicely browned. Or garnish with crisp parsley, and the edges with sliced lemon. Or serve with melted butter. Or pour over the liver and bacon, a sauce made of a little butter and flour, as for rump steaks.

Hint 193 Calf's Liver may be dressed with Herbs in the following manner: — Clean and drain a good quantity of spinach leaves, two large handfuls of parsley, and a handful of green onions. Chop the parsley and onions, and sprinkle them among the spinach. Set them all on to stew, with some salt, and a bit of butter, the size of a walnut; shake the pan when it grows warm, and let it be closely covered over a slow fire, till done enough. Broil the slices of liver, and fry rashers of bacon and eggs; put the latter on the herbs, the other on a separate dish.

Hint 194 Calf's Liver may be Roasted:— Clean and wipe it; then cut a large hole in it, and stuff it with crumbs of bread, chopped anchovy, herbs, a good deal of fat bacon, onions, salt, pepper. Also add a bit of butter, and an egg; sew the liver up; then lard it, or wrap it in veal caul, and roast it. Serve with good brown gravy, and currant jelly. Or it may be larded upon the surface, or have large thin strips of highly seasoned bacon skewered on to it. Or it may be wrapped in well-buttered paper, and be roasted gradually before a clear fire, being constantly basted.

Hint 195 Bits of the Liver may be trimmed off, floured, and lightly Fried, with a sliced onion, and stewed down for gravy in water, with the addition of a few peppercorns, and a small bunch of herbs, salt, and any kind of approved ketchup, or pickle.

Hint 196 Calf's Liver may be Stewed in good broth or gravy, heated very, gradually; when it comes to a simmer, add a sliced carrot, a small onion cut in halves, a little parsley, and mace; stew very gently; thicken the gravy with butter rolled in flour; and add a little white wine, if agreeable; take out the herbs, and season.

Hint 197 Or Calf's Liver may be steeped in vinegar and water for half an hour; then cut into thin slices, rolled in flour, fried very crisp, and served with Fried onions, without any other sauce.

Hint 198   Calf, Pig, Sheep, Lamb, Poultry, or Game Livers, may be made into Stuffing, by being added to ordinary Veal stuffing, in any proportion that is found agreeable. Or may be Curried, to which refer.

Hint 199   The Livers of Poultry, Game, etc., may be made into a Ragout: — Soak them in water, and clean them; put them into a saucepan with gravy, pickled mushrooms, or a little ketchup, and a bit of butter rolled in flour or pure starch; season with pepper and salt; stew for ten or twelve minutes. The Liver of a Turkey may be used, and set in the centre of the dish, with the other livers, or fried sausages, round. Garnish with lemon.

Hint 200   Or Small Livers of any kind may be made into a very useful Liver Sauce:— Boil the liver of a fowl, etc., a few minutes in water, and rub it through a sieve, with a part of the water in which it has been boiled; then make some melted butter, adding a little cream; and when it is hot, put the grated livers into it, seasoning with pepper, salt, grated lemon peel, and nutmeg. This is usually eaten with roasted fowl, being poured over it.

Hint 201   Livers of Fish are variously used in Fish Sauces, and will be economised in various ways in our instructions respecting Fish.

Various Ways of Serving Tripe

Hint 202   The time required for dressing Tripe, depends upon the degree to which it has been prepared by the tripe dealers. In general, an hour's boiling will be sufficient; but tripe that has not been prepared by previous boiling, will take three to five hours to make it tender. Raw tripe should be first boiled in plain water for two hours; then be taken out, and allowed to get cold, and the collection of fat scraped off, before it is stewed in milk and water.

Hint 203   To Boil Tripe cut it in pieces of moderate size and simmer it in milk and water until tender, and the milk thickish. Peel and boil a dozen or more button onions. Dish the tripe in a deep tureen, thicken the milk with flour and put the onions to it; or stew the onions in the milk after taking out the tripe, and then pour hot upon the latter. Some persons prefer Spanish onions, either whole or cut in halves or quarters. Some like the sauce very thick, in which case, a smaller quantity of milk may be employed, and more thickening; others like plenty thin sauce.

Hint 204   Some persons like Tripe boiled plainly in water, and served with Onion Sauce and Mustard. Others boil in Veal Broth; or put a fresh Beef Bone, or Veal Shank to the water.

Hint 205   Tripe may be Fried in Egg and Bread Crumbs like oysters, and is then a very nice dish; or, it may fried without the egg crumbs, in gravy, thickened with little flour, and flavoured with ketchup or Vinegar; or may be fried in Butter, made thicker than for pancakes, eggs beaten with flour, milk, a little salt, pepper, and nutmeg; dip in the tripe, and fry in butter, or fresh dripping of a light brown colour, and serve with a garnish parsley and melted butter, with lemon pickle in it.

Hint 206   Or, it may be Broiled like a steak, buttered, or peppered, etc.

Hint 207   Or, it may be roasted in the following nice manner: — Cut it into oblong pieces, and, having made forcemeat of bread crumbs, chopped parsley, pepper, and salt, with the yolks of two eggs, lay it on the tripe, put the pieces together, roll tightly, and tie; roast it for an hour and a half, basting well with butter; serve it with melted butter, or a little Sharp Sauce.

Hint 208   Or, it may be made into a Pie, there being layers of Ham, or Beef Steaks, in the bottom of the dish, and afterwards filled up with tripe, fricassee fashion.

Hint 209   Or, it may be Curried, by frying with fat, and onions in slices. When these are brown, put in the tripe, which must be previously tender; add a little salt and pepper, with a teaspoonful of Curry Powder over the tripe, a little fried butter to accompany the dish.

Hint 210   Or, Tripe may be Stewed in the Italian fashion: — Cut previously boiled tripe into strips, like ribbon maccaroni. Take a stew-pan, and melt in it three ounces of good butter, in which stew gently an onion, cut very small; mince finely from two to three tablespoonfuls of parsley, and put it in the stewpan; add the tripe. Dust in a quarter of a pound of Parmesan cheese, finely grated, until the butter is of sufficient thickness to form a rich sauce. If more sauce should be required, add a little of the milk and water in which the tripe was previously boiled.

Hint 211   Fried Sausages, or toasted Bashers of Bacon, may be served with boiled tripe, especially when plainly done.

Various Ways of Cooking and Serving Sweetbreads

Hint 212   Sweetbreads should be parboiled, and then thrown in cold water, to make them white and firm. This is called blanching, and it should precede all the other modes of cooking.

They may be Roasted and served plainly, being simply rubbed over with egg sprinkled with bread crumbs, salt, pepper, and chopped parsley, and finished in a Dutch oven. They should be accompanied with melted butter, with or without a little mushroom ketchup.

Hint 213   Or, they may be Broiled, over a slow fire, after being rubbed with butter. Turn frequently, and baste now and then, by putting upon a plate, kept warm by the fire, with butter in it.

Hint 214   Or they may be Fricasseed thus:— Slice them, or dress one or more whole. Thicken some veal gravy with a bit of butter rolled in flour, a little mushroom powder, a little cream, white pepper, nutmeg, and grated lemon peel. Stew these ingredients a little, then simmer the sweetbread in them - about twenty minutes. Serve with sippets of untoasted bread.

Hint 215   Or, they may be Fricasseed (brown) thus:— Cut them in pieces, about the size of a walnut; flour and fry them of a fine brown; pour to them a good beef gravy, seasoned with salt, pepper, cayenne, and allspice; simmer until tender; thicken with flour and butter. Morels, truffles and mushrooms, may be added, and mushroom ketchup.

Hint 216   Or, they may be made into a Pie: — Parboil five or six Sweetbreads; cut them into two or three pieces; stew them ten or fifteen minutes in a little white stock, with some chopped shallot, a bit of butter rolled in flour, some salt, with white pepper, and a good many button mushrooms. Put them into a pie dish, with some asparagus tops, forcemeat balls, and hard boiled yolks of eggs, and slices of fat bacon on the top; cover, and bake.

Hint 217   Or, a Pie of Sweetbreads and Potatoes: — Fry the Sweetbreads a nice brown; boil the potatoes tender, skin, and cut them into square pieces. Brown a bit of butter with flour, and a pint of good gravy, seasoned highly with spice and salt; put in the sweetbreads and potatoes, and let them stew till nearly ready for eating. Lay them in the pie dish, and break down in the sauce the yolks of two hard-boiled eggs, and add it. Cover with a good puti paste, and when the latter is sufficiently baked, the pie may be served.

Hint 218   Or, they may be Stewed with Potatoes:— Boil the Potatoes till the skin can be easily peeled off; parboil the Sweetbreads with them. Skin and cut the potatoes into pieces; and, if the sweetbreads are large, cut them in two the long way; dust them with flour, and fry them a light brown, in butter; then stew them in rather more than a pint of the liquor in which they were boiled. Brown a piece of batter with flour; add it, with a little cayenne, salt, pepper, grated lemon peel, and nutmeg, and a glass of white wine. Just before serving, stir in a spoonful of vinegar, or a little lemon juice.

Hint 219   Or, they may be Stuffed and Stewed. After blanching, stuff them with a forcemeat of fowl, fat and lean bacon, an anchovy, nutmeg, lemon peel, parsley, and a very little cayenne and thyme; when mixed, add the yolks of two eggs, and fill the Sweetbreads, Fasten them together with splinter skewers, and lay them in a pan, with slices of veal over, and bacon under them; season with pepper and salt, mace, cloves, herbs, and sliced onion. Cover close over the fire for ten minutes; then add a quart of broth, and stew gently for two hours. Take out the sweetbreads, strain and skim the broth, and boil it to - half a pint; warm the sweetbreads in it, and serve with lemon sliced.

Hint 220   Cold Sweetbreads (remnants of either of the previous dishes) may be made into nice Croquets. Mince some of the meat, and warm them in some of the sauce, to which has been added a little good stock, and a little cream; when quite cold, form them into balls, or into rolls about two inches long; fry, and serve them with fried parsley in the middle.

Hint 221   Or, as Rissoles:— Take the meat prepared as above. Roll out thin puff paste, enclose the meat in it, brush it over with a beaten egg, and strew over it grated bread; fry to a light brown.

Hint 222   Or, as Scallops:— Cut them into square bits. Stew them in strong gravy till heated through. Fry scallops of bread. Place the meat and bread scallops alternately upon a dish, and garnish with fried parsley.

Hint 223   Sweetbreads, if not served as a separate dish, make a great addition to Ragouts and Fricassees of other meat, cut into slices, or very large dice, with or without truffles, etc. Or, make a good addition to Calf's Head Pie,

Various Methods of Dressing and Serving Kidneys

Hint 224   Kidneys require a longer time to dress, in proportion to their bulk, than any other parts of animals; and beef kidneys, more than those of sheep, lambs, etc. Ox Kidneys may be Fried in the following manner:— Trim, and cut the kidney into slices, dredge them well with flour, and season with salt, pepper, and cayenne; fry on both sides, and as the slices are done, remove them from the pan, and make a gravy with a small slice of butter, a dessert spoonful of flour, pepper, and salt, and a little boiling water; add a little mushroom ketchup, lemon juice, shallot vinegar, or any sauce that will impart a good flavour. Some add to the gravy, at the last moment, a glass of white wine; serve with sippets of fried bread.

Hint 225   Ox Kidney may be cut into small pieces (the harder parts being rejected), and mixed with ox or other heart, and Baked in a pan with potatoes, bacon, etc.

Hint 226   Or, as Scotch Kidney Collops:— Let the kidney be very fresh; cut it in pieces, the size of very small steaks; soak the slices in warm water, and dry them well dust them with flour, and brown them in a stewpan with fresh butter. When browned, pour a little hot water into the pan, a minced shallot, or the white of four young onions minced, with salt, pepper, cayenne, shred parsley, and a little plain or shallot vinegar, or of onion pickle vinegar. Cover the stewpan close, and let the collops simmer slowly for two hours or more.

Hint 227   Veal Kidney may be chopped with veal fat, together with a little leek or onion, pepper, and Salt, rolled into balls, with a little egg, and Fried.

Hint 228   Or may be Stewed:— Make a gravy, and after skinning the kidneys, put them into a stewpan, with the gravy, and a few fresh mushrooms; stew gently half an hour, and garnish with toasted sippets.

Hint 229   Ox, Calves, Pigs and Sheep's Kidneys may be split and broiled;— Cut them in the middle, so as nearly to divide them; run a skewer through them to keep them open, that they may be evenly done; boil gently; season with salt and pepper; rub a piece of butter over, and serve. They can be sent to table on toast, or with any sauce; or upon slices of Broiled Bacon,

Hint 230   Or, they may be Fried, with Champagne:— Cut the kidneys in slices, fry them with salt, pepper, cayenne, parsley, and chives, chopped fine; while frying, and when nearly done, pour in champagne enough to make a sauce. White Wine will do.

Hint 231   Or, they make a capital dish, with Sheep's Tails, or Trotters:— Parboil half a dozen Tails or Trotters in mutton broth. Let them cool, and skim the broth. Split the trotters; brush them, or the tails, with egg, dip them in crumbs, chopped parsley, and a little lemon thyme, and brown them. Have six Kidneys larded and cooked in a Dutch oven, and stew a little boiled rice in. the broth. Serve the rice in a shallow dish, and lay the tails or trotters on it, their toes or points meeting in the centre; place a Kidney between each of them, and, garnish with cut pickles; or with hard eggs cut into halves.

Hint 232   Pigs Kidneys or Skirts may be dressed together thus:— Clean and wash them; cut the Kidneys across, cut the Skirts into small square bits.

Fry to a light brown in beef dripping; brown a bit of butter the size of a walnut with a little flour, and add as much boiling water as may be required for gravy, and an onion chopped fine. Add the meat a little pepper, salt, and mushroom ketchup and let it stew till tender.

Hint 233   Kidneys are variously cooked in Puddings and Pies, to which the reader is referred.

Methods of Cooking and Serving Brains

Hint 234   Any kind of Brains, previously washed, parboiled, the skin being removed, well seasoned with pepper and salt, and a few slices of bacon added to the batter, make a very agreeable dish.

Hint 235   Or, after cleansing the brains in cold water, and then in hot, make them into Brain Cakes:— Free them from the skin and large fibres, and boil them in water, or veal gravy, slightly salted, from two to three minutes; beat them up with a teaspoonful of sage, very finely chopped, or with equal parts of sage and parsley, half a teaspoonful, or rather more, of salt, half as much mace, a little white pepper, or cayenne, and one egg, drop them in small cakes in a frying pan, and fry them in butter of a light brown; add a little grated lemon.

Hint 236   Or, the brains may be Boiled, and beaten to a paste in a mortar, with some chopped parsley, green onions, and chopped mushrooms; work this together with some cream and veal gravy. When properly seasoned, serve with slices of Tongue, glazed, and set neatly round the dish; or, spread it on toast, and divide into convenient pieces.

Hint 237   Cold Brain and Tongue may be converted into a nice Pudding:— Cut the brain in pieces, lay thin slices of tongue in the bottom of the pudding, then add some brain. Season with salt, pepper, parsley, and a little chopped onions; repeat until full; and lay in two hard boiled eggs, in slices; then mix a teaspoonful of flour with a gill and a half of milk or water, and pour in; then close the pudding, and boil one hour, and serve. A little gherkin, cut fine, may be added for flavour.

Hint 238   Ox, Calves', Sheeps', Lambs', and Pigs' Brains, may be made into similar Puddings, with remnants of either Tongues or Cheeks.

Hint 239   Brain Sauces will be found by reference to the Index.

Methods of Serving Marrow Bones

Hint 240   Have them neatly sawed, and fill up the opening with a piece of paste; tie a floured cloth over that. Set the bones in a saucepan, placed upright, keep them covered, and Boil for two hours. Serve upright, with a napkin around, and slips of dry toast.

Hint 241   Or, the marrow may be taken out of the bone, and Spread upon the Toast, with a little pepper and salt sprinkled over it. The toast may be served dry, or may be just steeped in water, with a little butter rubbed over it while quite hot, and after that, the marrow.

Hint 242   Or, the bones may be Baked with Batter, in a deep pie dish, after being cleaned and wiped. Lay them in the dish, and cover them completely with a good batter. Send them to a moderate oven for an hour or more, and serve them in the batter.

Various Methods of Cooking and Serving Tongues

Hint 243   Ox Tongues may be Stewed:— Wash clean, rub well with common salt, and a little saltpetre, or with salt, vinegar, and pounded allspice; let it lie two or three days, and then boil until the skin comes off. Trim the coarse part of the root, but leave on some of the soft part. Put it into a close saucepan, with part of the liquor it has been boiled in, and a pint of good stock. Season with black and Jamaica pepper, and two or three pounded cloves; add a glass of white wine, a tablespoonful of mushroom ketchup, and one of lemon pickle; thicken the sauce with butter rolled in flour, and pour it over the tongue. Or, flavour the liquor with a faggot of sweet herbs, two bay leaves, and a head of young celery sliced; take out the herbs, and season with cayenne, pounded cloves, mixed spices, and a little walnut ketchup. Serve in a deep dish, with the sauce, and a few dressed mushrooms, or small onions.

Hint 244   Or, they make an excellent dish roasted, with the Udder:— Take an Ox Tongue, clean it well, salt it with common salt and saltpetre three days; then boil it, and likewise a fine Udder, with some fat to it; boil the udder apart from the tongue; let both be tolerably tender; let them become cold; then tie the thick part of one to the thin part of the other, and roast the tongue and udder, together. Serve them with good gravy, and currant jelly sauce. A few cloves should be stuck in the udder for those who like the flavour.

Hint 245   Or, they may be baked, with Parmesan Cheese:— Cut a boiled Tongue in very thin slices; put rasped Parmesan in a very deep dish, and lay the slices of tongue over it; continue doing so, until there are three or four alternate layers of tongue and cheese; sprinkle every layer with a little of the stock the tongue was boiled in, and finish with a covering of cheese.

This must be basted with melted butter; put it into an oven, and when the cheese is nicely mellow, serve.

Hint 246 Or they may be Plainly Boiled:— Run an iron skewer through the root of a pickled Tongue; tie some string round the point of the skewer, and fasten it at the other end, to give the tongue the form of an arch. Boil for about three hours; when done, immerse in cold water, and pull off the outer skin. Truss the tongue afresh, in the form of an arch, put it to press, sideways, between two dishes, with a weight on the top, and when cold, trim it smooth; or with a small sharp knife, carve the surface, so as to represent leaves, flowers, or a short motto; glaze it over brightly, and set upon a dish; if cold, put a fringe of cut paper round the root. If hot, serve with a rice border; or, serve upon Spinach, or Mashed Turnip, Or, cold, garnish with veal jellies, from small moulds.

Hint 247 Or, they may be Baked with Bacon and Cow Heel, etc:— Take a baking pan, and put into it a thick slice of Bacon, and cover that with some lean veal, or beefsteak; then put in the Tongue (either fresh or salted), after trimming, curling it round to fit the pan; have ready the flesh of a parboiled Cow Heel, place the pieces over the tongue, and over all another slice of bacon, and beef, or veal. For seasoning, take two teaspoonfuls of pepper, a little powdered ginger and cloves, one bay leaf, one carrot, and two onions sliced; add two wine glasses of brandy or sherry, four of old ale, and a quart of water. Cover well over, and put into a slow oven for three hours; remove the cover, and set a board with a weight on the top until cold; next day, dip the pan in hot water, sufficiently long to loosen the meat, and turn it out. Or, it may first be used hot, and the remainder Pressed for eating cold.

Hint 248 Or, may be Stewed with Vegetables and Dumplings:— Put in a pan, with any suitable proportion of carrots and turnips sliced, some cloves, and small suet dumplings; fill the pan with water, and add a little bay leaf, thyme, or winter savoury; stew in an oven three hours; trim and dish up with the vegetables and dumplings round, putting some of the gravy in a sauceboat.

Hint 249 Or, may be Roasted, and served with Currant Jelly:— Soak a fresh Tongue for two hours, sprinkle salt over it, and drain well in a colander; boil it slowly for two hours; take off the skin, roast, and baste with batter. Serve with brown gravy, and Currant Jelly Sauce.

Hint 250 One large tongue, or a number of small ones, may be Boiled in a Mould:— Trim the Tongues, cutting off the rough part of the roots, and removing the small bones; roll them, tip inwards, to suit the shape of the mould; press down with a mould.

Boil six or seven hours, and stand in the mould until quite cold. Garnish with parsley.

Hint 251   Neat Tongue may be Spiced and Served with Sweet Sauce:— Put the Tongue into boiling water, and take off the skin. Boil the tongue in a braise; cut it nearly in two, and stick it with preserved lemon, and slices and sticks of cinnamon put in a stewpan, a bit of sugar, a glass of wine, and a little gravy; simmer until the sugar is dissolved; put. in the tongue, and let it stew a little time. Dish it up hot with the sauce.

Hint 252   Or Neat Tongue may be Larded: — Having removed the root and gullet of a small Tongue, rub it well with salt; next day, hang it to drain, and wipe it. Let it lie in salt one day; boil it half an hour; blanch and remove the skin; then, having rolled some freshly cured fat bacon in a seasoning of pepper, salt, cloves, mace, cinnamon, and nutmeg, with parsley, knotted marjoram, chives, or shallots, and a little morsel of garlic minced small [these may be varied], lard the tongue all over, except a little space from the root to the tip in the middle, where it is to be divided, braise and glaze as usual, having, after boiling, cut it in two, except at the extremities. Lay it on a dish in the form of a heart.

Hint 253   Pig's and Sheep's Tongues may be Stewed: — Blanch and stew them; make a compound of a dozen and a half small onions, fried whole in butter, with a little minced shallot, ketchup, wine, and seasoning; add a little stock. Stew the Tongues in this for half an hour; skim the sauce; set the tongues on a dish; pour the sauce over them, and surround them with the onions.

Hint 254   When Tongues have been in pickle about a month, they begin to deteriorate. Although not wanted for immediate consumption, the best plan then is, to boil them as usual, and set them by with the skin on; they will thereby keep for a fortnight or three weeks longer, and when wanted may be put in cold water, and gradually brought to a boil. The under fat of the tongue, which is otherwise liable to become rancid, will be preserved in excellent condition by this process.

Hint 255   The Roots of Cold Tongue eat well warmed with Greens; or may be Potted; or serve to make Pea Soup, Stew, or Scotch Kale.

Hint 256   Or Slices of Cold Tongue may be warmed in any kind of Savoury Sauce, and laid in a pile in the centre of a dish, the sauce being poured over them.

Hint 257   The thin Tips of Tongues, if hung up to dry, will grate like hung beef, and make a fine addition to Savoury Omelettes.

Hint 258   The remains of Pickled Tongues are very nice, intermixed, and placed in a pan and pressed, when they will turn out resembling Collared Meat. A little thick jelly may be poured into the pan with them.

Hint 259   Fragments of Cold Tongues may be made into very nice Puddings; refer to that head. For Pickling Tongues, see Pickling.

Various Methods of Cooking and Serving Heads,
Cheeks etc

Hint 260   The heads of the larger animals, commonly used as food, afford a variety of cheap and nourishing dishes, are not adequately appreciated, because the methods of preparing them are little understood. They are not necessarily simple or meagre dishes, but may be made to yield soups, stews, sauces, pies, puddings, etc., of very good flavour. Ox cheek may be Stewed with Vegetables:— Bone the cheek, and steep it in cold water for two hours; then parboil it in water for five minutes; immerse in cold water, drain, and trim it. Break up the bones, and put them at the bottom of a stewpan; place the cheek upon them, and cover with carrot, onion, celery, a faggot of parsley, six cloves, a blade of mace, and twelve peppercorns. Moisten with two quarts of broth or water (if the latter, add some salt); set the cheek to simmer very gently by the side of the fire for about two hours; when done, take it up carefully, and press it between two dishes. Half the broth may be used for preparing some brown sauce, and the remainder boiled down to half a glaze. Next, cut the cheek into twelve pieces of equal size; trim them neatly, and place them in a saucepan with half the thickened broth, or glaze. Ten minutes before sending to table, put the cheek, covered with the lid, to simmer gently until it is warmed through, and then boil quickly over a brisk fire for three minutes; dish up, arrange the pieces in a circle, closely overlapping each other. Fill the centre with Green Peas, or Carrots, or Brussels Sprouts, or Stewed Onions, or Mashed Potatoes, or Turnips, or Cabbage, stewed or plain, or Mixed Vegetables.

Hint 261   Or, Ox Cheek may be Stuffed and Baked:— Cleanse it as for stewing, and boil it gently about an hour. Throw in a large teaspoonful of salt, and remove all the scum as it rises. Take it out, allow it to cool, and separate the meat from the bones, working the knife close to the bones, and avoiding cutting the meat. When the cheek has become cold, put in it a good roll of Forcemeat; skewer up the cheek; bake in a moderate oven an hour and a half. Drain it well from fat, unbind it gently, and send it to table with a little good brown seasoned gravy.

Hint 262   Ox Cheek, either raw, or previously dressed, will make an excellent Toad in the hole, which refer to.

Hint 263   The Liquor, in which an Ox cheek has been boiled, may be made into good Barley Broth; or Beef Brose; or into Cock'a'Leekie, and other Soups, which refer to.

Hint 264   The Fat, skimmed from the liquor in which an Ox cheek has been boiled or stewed, serves very nicely for Puddings, or for Frying, or to make economical Soups, or Stews.

Hint 265   Cold Ox cheek may be Potted:— Cut the meat into small bits, and warm up with a little of the liquor in which the cheek was boiled; season with black pepper, salt, nutmeg, and a little lemon juice, or vinegar; then pour into a mould, and press. Or put it into stoneware shapes or basins, and, when cold, turn it out; garnish with curled parsley, or pickled beetroot, sliced. This is capital for breakfast, supper, or luncheon.

Hint 266   Or, may be Curried; or as Bubble and Squeak; which refer to.

Hint 267   Calf's Head may be Plainly Boiled:— Clean it carefully, and soak it in water, that it may look very white. The whiteness will be improved by rubbing over it a little lemon juice. Take out the Tongue to salt; or, if preferred to send to table with the head, boil and skin it, and dish with the brains round it. Boil the head extremely tender; then strew it over with crumbs and chopped parsley, or melted butter and parsley. The Brains should be cleansed in cold water, and boiled; then mixed with melted butter, scalded sage, chopped very fine, pepper, and salt. When the head is dressed with the skin on, the ears must be cut off quite close to it; it will require three-quarters of an hour, or upwards, of additional boiling.
To boil the Brain, requires from fourteen to sixteen minutes. A Cheek, some delicate Pickled Pork, or curled slices of Bacon, or some Sausages, should accompany calf's head, the head may be rubbed with egg, and sprinkled with breadcrumbs, and brotoned in a Dutch oven after boiling.

Hint 268   Or, Calf's Head may be Boned, and stewed with the Brains:— The head having been boiled until tolerably tender, let it cool, and bone it; replace the brain; lay the head in a stewpan, and simmer it for an hour in rich gravy. About half an hour before it is served, add half a pint of button mushrooms. Thicken the gravy with rice flour, or with flour and butter, and serve plenty of forcemeat balls round the head. A little sweet basil wine, or a few sprigs of the herb, will improve the flavour. But if neither these, nor the mushrooms, are at hand, the rind of a small fresh lemon may be boiled in the gravy, and the strained juice be added when served.

Hint 269   Or, Calf's Head may be Roasted : — Wash and clean it well; parboil it; take out the bones, brains, and tongue; make Forcemeat sufficient for the head, and some balls, with breadcrumbs, minced suet, parsley, grated ham, and a little pounded veal, or cold fowl. Season with pepper, salt, grated nutmeg, and lemon peel; bind it with an egg beaten up; fill the head with it, which must then be sewed up, or fastened with skewers, and tied. While roasting, baste it well with butter; beat up the Brains with a little cream, the yolk of an egg, some minced parsley, a little pepper and salt; blanch the Tongue, cut it into slices, and fry it with the brains, forcemeat balls, and thin slices of bacon. Serve the head with white or brown thickened gravy, and place the forcemeat balls and brains around it; garnish with cut lemon. It will require about an hour and a half to roast

Hint 270   Or, Calf's Head may be Stewed in Sauce. The head being well cleaned, take out the bone of the lower jaw, and of the nose — the latter as close to the eyes as possible; wash the head well in warm water, and let it blanch in some clean water. Prepare a sauce as follows:— One pound of beef suet, and one pound of fat bacon cut small; half a pound of batter, a bunch of parsley, a little thyme, two or three bay leaves, one or two onions, and the juice of a lemon; season with salt, pepper, mace, cloves, and allspice; boil all this an hour in six pints of water. Then tie the head, in a cloth; stew it in the sauce about: three hours, and drain it; take out the tongue, skin, and replace it; serve quite hot, with a sauce made of minced shallots, parsley, the brains minced, some vinegar, salt and pepper.

Hint 271   Or Calf's Head may be Curried: — Prepare the head as for boiling; boil a pound of rice as for curry, and pile it in the centre of a dish. Hare ready a sauce made of two acid apples and four mushrooms sliced, a sprig of thyme, a few sprigs of parsley, a blade of mace, and four cloves. Fry these in two ounces of butter, and, when browned slightly, rub to this a large tablespoonful of curry powder. Stir well in, and add three pints of white sauce. Boil the whole for fifteen minutes; strain into another stew pan, add white pepper, a little cayenne, and salt, and pour it hot over the hash of the head kept warm. Serve the pyramid of rice with the top flattened into a well, in which the cooked brains are to be laid.

Hint 272   For variety, a whole Calf's Head be divided into halves one half be boiled, the other roasted, or baked.

Hint 273   Calves Ears may be stewed for a delicate side dish Take two or four ears, cut off deep and even at the bottom, so that they will stand; clean them well; boil till tender, in milk and water; fill them with a nice Forcemeat; tie them with thread, and stew them in a little of the liquor they were boiled in; season it with pepper, salt, mace, and a small onion minced. Before serving, thicken the sauce with the yolk of an egg beaten in a little cream.

Or, the ears may be filled with a Stuffing of calf's liver, fat bacon, grated ham, bread soaked in cream or gravy, herbs, an unbeaten egg, a little salt, and a small piece of mace. Or, substitute cold chicken for the liver. Or, the ears and stuffing may be rubbed over with egg, and Fried of a light brown.

Hint 274   Calf's Head may be Collared: — Scald the skin of a fine head, and clean it nicely; take out the brains. Boil until the meat separates easily from the bones, and remove the latter. Have ready a good quantity of chopped parsley, mace, nutmeg, salt, and white pepper, thoroughly intermixed; season the meat well with these; lay the parsley in a thick layer, then a quantity of thick slices of good ham or tongue; the yolks of six eggs, boiled hard, stuck in various parts; roll the head quite close, and tie it tightly. Boil it, and proceed as for other collars.

Hint 275   Calf's Head is eminently useful for various Soups, to which refer. The Liquor in which a head has been boiled makes excellent Broth, with or without vegetables, or puree of peas, carrots, turnips, etc., or base for Mock Turtle.

Hint 276   Cold Calf's Head may be Grilled, Curried, Fricasseed, Hashed, Fried as Cutlets, made into Pies, or Patties, etc., or Collared or Potted, to which refer.

Hint 277   Sheep's Head and Pluck may be Stewed:- Split the head into halves, remove the brains, steep the whole in water, and wash them thoroughly. Place the head, heart, and liver in a stew pan, with carrot, onion, a faggot of parsley, some green onions, two blades of mace, a dozen cloves, and a teaspoonful of peppercorns; moisten with a glass of brandy, and sufficient broth or water; add salt; cover the whole with buttered paper, and put the lid on; then set the stew pan on a gentle fire to braise for about one hour and a half. When the head, etc., are done, take them up carefully on a dish. Stain the broth, and, after having divested it of all fat, down one half to a thin glaze, and with the remainder make some brown sauce. The pieces of the head should trimmed, seasoned with pepper and salt, chopped parsley, and two shallots, then rubbed over with beaten egg well covered with breadcrumbs, and placed aside on a dish. The liver and heart should be minced fine, and when the sauce has been reduced to the usual consistency, added to the mince, together with a spoonful of fine herbs, and a little lemon juice. When about to send to table, make the mince quite hot, and turn it out on a dish; place the pieces of the head, previously broiled on both sides, upon the mince. Then pour on some of the thin glaze, and serve. This is a capital dish.

Hint 278   Sheep's Heads may be Boiled: — Before boiling, take out the brains; wash them clean, and free them from the skin.

Chop about a dozen sage leaves very small, tie them in a bag, and let them boil half an hour, then beat them up with pepper and salt, and half an ounce of butter; pour it over the head. When it is taken up, after boiling for two hours; serve it on a tureen, or on a dish with the tongue. Accompaniments as for Boiled Mutton, The liquor makes capital Broth.

Hint 279　　　　Lambs Head and Pluck may be served in a similar way:— scald the head, and take off the hair; parboil it with the pluck; divide the head, and take out; the brains; mince the heart and lights, and an onion; put it into a saucepan with a little gravy thickened with butter and flour; add a little salt and pepper; cover the pan closely, and let it stew an hour. Rub the head with the yolk of an egg beaten, and strew over it finely grated bread, mixed with salt and Pepper, and boiled minced parsley; stick bits of butter here and there, and brown it in a Dutch oven. Cut the liver into slices, and fry it in butter; make the brains into cakes. Serve the head upon the mince, and garnish with the liver.

Hint 280　　　　Sheep's and Lambs Heads may be Grilled, or browned in a Dutch oven. Braised, and Bread crumbed, and served with any kind of Sharp Sauce. They may also be boned for Puddings, Pies, "Toad in the Hole," or may be Boiled, or Baked upon or under Potatoes, with or without Batter, etc.

Hint 281　　　　Pig's Cheek may be Stuffed, Stewed, and Collared:— Take a head cut off deep from the neck; singe it carefully; put a red-hot poker into the ears; bone the head, taking care not to break the skin. Rub , it with salt, and pour boiled cold brine over it, with a large handful of chopped juniper berries, a few bruised cloves, and four bay leaves, with thyme, basil, sage, a head of garlic, bruised, and a quarter of an ounce of saltpetre, pounded. Let the head steep in this for ten days, and turn and rub it often. Then wipe, drain, and dry it, and make a forcemeat for it thus:— take equal quantities of undressed ham, and breast of bacon; season this highly with pepper, and spices, if liked. Pound this meat very smooth, and mix with it some seasoned lard, parsley, and young onions, finely minced. Spread this equally over the head. Roll up and sew it; bind in a cloth, and stew it in a braise made of any trimmings and seasonings left, with stock to cover it. It will take nearly four hours to cook, and will be still richer if larded before it is stuffed. Pierce it with a larding pin 5 if the pin enters easily, it is done. When cool, take off the binding cloth; trim the ends, and serve on a napkin. It will keep a long while.

Hint 282　　　　Or, Pig's Head and Feet may be Soused:- Clean them carefully, and boil them; take for sauce part of the liquor, and add vinegar, lime or lemon juice, salt, cayenne, black and Jamaica pepper; put in, either cut down, or whole, the head and feet.

Boil all together for an hour, and pour it into a deep dish. It is to be eaten cold with mustard and vinegar.

Hint 283   Pig's Ears and Feet may be Stewed and fried;— Boil the ears and feet till the bones of the latter nearly drop out. Cut the ears into long narrow strips, and stew them with a little good gravy, half a glass of white wine, pepper, salt, a pinch of cayenne, and a little mustard. While the ears are stewing, split the feet in half, wet them with the yolk of egg, and dredge them with breadcrumbs; then fry them in some nice lard, to a light brown. Serve them nicely ranged round the stewed ears in a dish. Two sets of feet and ears make a good dish.

Hint 284   Pig's Head may be Pickled and Collared: — Take out the brains, and clean the head well; rub it with two ounces of saltpetre, and a sufficient quantity of common salt. Let it lie a fortnight; turn it every day, and rub it well in the brine; then wash it, and boil it until the bones will come out easily; but care must be taken not to boil it so much as for the bones to drop out. Lay it in a dish, and take off the skin without damage; take out the bones, and peel the tongue. Have ready a large handful of sage, washed and picked, a tablespoonful of thyme, picked from the stalks, and four shallots, chopped very finely. Put the meat to it, and chop it a little, until the bits of meat are about an inch square; put a strainer or thin cloth in the bottom of an earthen pot or pan, large enough to come up to the sides, and cover it. Lay the skin from one side of the head at the bottom of the pot, then the meat and the other skin at the top; or use a tin mould; press it down with a board that will go within the pot or mould, having first covered it with the corners of the cloth that was laid in the bottom of it; set the pot in the liquor again (which must be kept over the fire all the time), and let it boil three quarters of an hour longer; then take it out, set a weight upon the board, and let it remain all night; then take it out, strip off the cloth, and it is fit for use. The Ears may be chopped with the meat, or be put in whole, at a proper distance from each other; or be dressed with the Feet for a separate dish.

Hint 285   Or, Pig's Head may be Collared more expeditiously by boiling it in a pickle consisting of one gallon of water, two pounds of salt, three quarters of a pound of brown sugar, half a pound of saltpetre bruised. With the head may be used the feet, ears, tongue, or a piece of the belly, with some of the sword. The meat should be boiled very tender, until a quill will go through it. Season with pepper, a little mace, cayenne, and salt, the latter if necessary. Place the sword parts round the outer parts of the brawn tin, and fill the tin with meat, pressing it down with a heavy weight.

Hint 286   Or, Pig's Head may be Collared with Cow Heels: — Three Cow Heels to a Pig's Head, to which may be added the feet, ears, and tongue of the pig, and a Neat's Tongue pickled. Cut the meat into pieces, and lay them nicely in the tin. Proceed in other respects as in the preceding directions.

Hint 287   Pig's Head or Cheek may be Baked upon Potatoes, with a little sago and onion stuffing placed in the ears, underneath. Or, may be Pickled and Smoked, as a breakfast relish, or to accompany poultry, etc.

Hint 288   The Liquor in which Pigs' Heads or Cheeks have been boiled or stewed for collaring, will make a good stock for Pea Soup, the remains of a Pigs Head may be used for, Toad in the Hole.

Various Methods of Cooking and Serving Necks of
Veal, Mutton, Lamb, etc

Hint 289   A Neck of Veal may be Stewed:— Lard the best end with bacon, rolled in parsley chopped fine, salt, pepper, and nutmeg; put it into a pan, and cover it with water. Put to it the scrag end, a little lean bacon or ham, an onion, two carrots, two heads of celery, and about a glass of Madeira wine (the latter may be omitted, or any white substituted). Stew it quickly two hours, or till it is tender, but not too much. Strain off the liquor; mix a little flour and butter in a stewpan until brown, and lay the veal in this, the upper side to tile bottom of the pan. Let it be over the fire until it gets coloured; then lay it into the dish, stir some of the liquor in, and boil it; skim nicely, and squeeze orange or lemon juice into it; serve with the meat.

Hint 290   Or, cut off the scrag to boil, and cover it with Onion Sauce, Boil it in milk and water. Parsley and Butter may be served with it, instead of onion sauce. Or, it may be Stewed with whole Rice, small onions, and arid peppercorns, with a very little water. Or, Boiled, and eaten with Bacon and Greens; or, the best end may be either. Roasted, Broiled, or made into Pies.

Hint 291   Neck of Mutton may be dressed as Cutlets, with Mashed Potatoes:— Take a neck, and divide it into cutlets; beat, and trim them neatly; lay them in a pan with some clarified butter, and cover them, until required; meanwhile cut and slice five or six good potatoes; boil them; when done, drain them on a sieve, and stir them well in a stewpan, with a bit of butter, pepper, and salt, and some good cream; rub the whole through a sieve, and put it again in a stewpan warm; then put the cutlets in a moderate fire; turn them till done; add a spoonful of gravy or broth; stir them about till well done; place them round the dish, and put the potatoes hot in the middle.

Hint 292   Neck of Mutton stewed with Bacon, Turnips, etc: — Cut the neck into good cutlets, beat and trim them, and lay them between slices of fat bacon, with the scrag ends and trimmings chopped in pieces, placing some at the bottom, and some over the cutlets, with a carrot, onion, parsley, clove of garlic, peppercorns, and some good strong gravy, just enough to cover them. Let them stew very gently for two hours or rather more. Take the whole from the fire to cool, then trim them very neatly, and put them in a pan. A quarter of an hour before dinner, put them into a gentle oven, with some glaze, a small bit of butter, and a little gravy; cut and fry turnips as for turnip soup put them in a stewpan with a ladleful of good gravy, a little sugar, and salt; stew gently until the sauce thickens; then add a little lemon juice; pour the turnip into the centre of the cutlets, and serve.

Hint 293   Neck of Mutton may be Boiled: — As the scrag end takes longer to boil, some persons cut it off, and boil it half or three quarters of an hour before the rest; however well washed, the liquor will require attentive skimming. When it is time to put the best end in, add cold water to check the heat, allowing an hour and a half, or three quarters, after the second boil. Cut off some of the fat before dressing, which may be made into Suet Dumplings, Peel off the skin when taken up. Parsley and butter, caper sauce, onion, turnips, carrots, spinach, etc., are proper accompaniments to Boiled Mutton in general.

Hint 294   Neck of Mutton may be roasted; or cut into Chops for Cutlets, Hashes, Stews, Pies, etc. The Liquor of the boiled neck furnishes good Mutton Broth.

Hint 295   Neck of Lamb may be dressed the same as Mutton.

Various Methods of Cooking Feet, Heels, Trotters, etc

Hint 296   Skilfully used, Cowheels may be made to supply various nice and economical dishes. After being boiled tender, cut into convenient pieces, egg and breadcrumb them, and fry to a light brown; lay them around a dish, and put in the middle sliced onions fried, or the accompaniments usual for tripe.

Hint 297   Or, Cow heel may be Boiled: — After being scraped and cleaned well, boil gently until tender, with water or milk, onions, and salt, as for tripe.

Hint 298   Or they make a very nice Potted Meat:— cut the meat into small pieces, and add just a sufficient portion of liquor to moisten it; mix with it a tablespoonful of vinegar, with a seasoning of pepper, salt, and mace; put it into a mould, press it down, and turn out when cold. It is usually eaten with vinegar and mustard.

Hint 299   The water they were boiled in will make good Broth, or base for Soup, to which refer.

Hint 300   Cowheels may be used for Jellies, when Calf's feet cannot be obtained; they may also be added to Mock Turtle and other Soups.

Hint 301   Calf's Feet may be Stewed:— Divide a foot into four pieces, and put it to stew with half a pint of water; add a potato and onion sliced, and a seasoning of pepper and salt; let the whole simmer gently for two hours.

Hint 302   Or, Calf's Feet may be Boiled plainly, as Cowheel.

Hint 303   Or may be Fried in Batter, and served with Italian, or any other suitable Sauce.

Hint 304   Or be Braised, and afterwards drained upon a cloth, cut into pieces about two inches square, then pot into a stewpan with some butter, mushrooms, and sauce, and served with a border of Mashed Potatoes.

Hint 305   Or nicely Potted, as follows:— Boil the feet as for jelly, pick all the meat from the bones, add to it half a pint of gravy, and a seasoning of salt, pepper, nutmeg, garlic, shallot, and shred ham; simmer it for half an hour; dip a mould into water; put in a lay of meat, then some pickled beetroot, and some boiled minced parsley; upon this, a layer of meat, and so on until the mould be filled. When cold, turn it out. Or do it in a plainer manner, as the Cowheel; or the Cowheel may be done in this way.

Hint 306   Calves Feet are best for Jellies, and for Broths for invalids. For Jellies, the unboiled feet should be procured from the butcher's; they will make a large quantity of jelly, better in quality than the boiled feet from the tripe shops.

Hint 307   Pigs Feet, after being pickled about ten day, may be gently Braised in common broth, seasoned with carrot, onion, celery, and a faggot of parsley. For this dish, the feet of bacon hogs are best, and they will require about four hours gentle boiling. When done, drain then cut them into halves, and remove the large bones; press them into shape with the hands, and set them in a cold place. When cold, season the pieces with pepper, and salt if required; rub them over with a brush dipped in clarified butter; then roll them in breadcrumbs, and put these on to them with the blade of a wide knife; broil them on a gridiron over a clear fire, turning them frequently until they are warmed through. Serve them with a piquant sauce.

Hint 308　　　　　Pigs Feet may be Pickled and Boiled, and eaten cold as a breakfast, luncheon, or supper relish; may be added fresh to Stews, of Rabbit, Fowl, etc.

Hint 309　　　　　Pigs Petitoes is a dish consisting of the feet and internal parts of small pigs. These may be stewed:— Put them on with a sufficient quantity of water or broth; add a small onion or two, if approved; also four or five leaves of sage, chopped small. When the heart, liver, and lights are tender, take them out, an chop them fine, let the feet simmer the while; they will take from half to three quarters of an hour to do. Season the mince with salt, nutmeg, and a little pepper, half an ounce of butter, a tablespoonful or two of thick cream, and a teaspoonful of arrowroot, or flour; return it to the saucepan, in which the feet are; let it boil up, shaking it one way. Split the feet, lay them round the mince; serve with toasted sippets, and garnish with mashed potatoes.

Hint 310　　　　　Sheep's and Lambs feet may be Braised, the same as Calves Feet.

Hint 311　　　　　Or may be Boiled, and served plainly, and eaten with vinegar and mustard.

Hint 312　　　　　Or may be added to Stews of Rabbits, Poultry, Game, etc.

Hint 313　　　　　Or may be Boiled until the bones can be easily taken out of them, but they must not be removed; then fried in a light batter to a delicate brown, and served with a garnish of fried parsley.

Various Uses of Tails and other Parts

Hint 314　　　　　Ox Tails make an excellent Stew:— Take three tails, divide them at the joints, or, if sawed through the bones, all the better extract will be obtained; place them in a saucepan, and cover them with water; set them upon the fire to stew gently, and clear the scum as it rises; when it boils, put in a little salt, half a teaspoonful of white pepper, and half that quantity of cayenne; eight or ten cloves stuck in two small onions two large or four small carrots, and a good sized bunch of parsley. Let it stew very gently, until the meat is tender, which will take three hours; then strain the gravy from the meat, thicken it, and serve with the tails in a tureen. When the gravy has been thickened, the vegetables may be returned to it or not, according to taste, and it may be sent to table, poured over the tails, or in a separate tureen.

Hint 315   Or, they may be Baked with chopped onions and herbs; each piece should be carefully rolled in flour, and set in a pan, with some of the onions and seasoning; add a pint of water; bake three hours; carefully skim off the fat, and serve.

Hint 316   Or may be Stewed by another process:- Cut a Tail into pieces, and blanch it in boiling water; put it into fresh water, and parboil it; then make a sauce with a spoonful of flour and butter, moistening it in a little of the liquor in which the tail was boiled; put into it the pieces of the tail, with a dozen whole onions from which the outer skin has been taken. Add a glass of white wine, a bunch of parsley and chibbols, a clove of garlic, a laurel leaf, and some basil and thyme, two cloves, salt, and pepper; let them stew gently until the meat and onions are done, taking care to skim well. Put into the sauce an anchovy cut, a teaspoonful of whole capers; place the pieces of the tail in the middle of the dish, and put the onions round and over them; pour the strained sauce over it. Garnish with bits of fried or toasted bread. Of course the mixture of herbs mentioned above may be modified, according to taste or convenience; two bay leaves may be substituted for a laurel leaf, etc.

Hint 317   Ox Tails are employed for Oxtail Soup, and Calves Tails for Chesterfield Soup, to which refer.

Hint 318   Calves Tails may be Stewed:— Clean and blanch them, the same as oxtails, divide them at the joints, and brown them in butter, Or other fine fat. Drain, and stew them in good stock, seasoned with parley, onions, and a bay leaf. Add green peas, or small mushrooms; skim and serve.

Hint 319   A little Bacon, cut into slices, may be added; some Suet Dumplings, very small, previously boiled. The stew may be Baked; it will require about an hour and a half. Six calves tails make a good dish.

Hint 320   A tail or two is very good added to stews of any kind, and cold Fowl, Rabbit, etc., may be warmed and sent to table in the stew of calves' tails.

Hint 321   Calves Tails makes a very nice Curry.

Hint 322   Calves Udders form the basis of a great variety of Forcemeats. The method of preparing them is, to bind them round with twine in the form of a sausage, to prevent them falling to pieces, then boil them in stock. When they are quite soft, they are taken out, and allowed to get cool. The outside should then be pared off with a knife, cut into small pieces, and pounded in a mortar; it should then be rubbed through a wire sieve with a wooden spoon, and allowed to get quite firm and cool before using.

A very nice Stew of Ox Palates

Hint 323   The Palates must be well cleaned, and boiled until the upper skin will come off easily; they should then be cut either into long fillets or square pieces. They should then be stewed very slowly in good thick gravy, and seasoned with cayenne, minced shallot or onion, and a large spoonful of ketchup; or the pickle of walnuts, mushrooms, or onions.

Hint 324   Palates are excellent for breakfast or supper, either served hot, or pickled, and eaten cold.

Hint 325   They may be parboiled, skinned, and cut into strips; first Fry an onion in butter, then add the Palates and a bunch of sweet herbs; moisten then with some well-seasoned stock, and when sufficiently done, add a little mustard.

Hint 326   Or, after having prepared them, and cut them into pieces, put them in a Pickle of lukewarm vinegar, salt, pepper, a shallot, and two bay leaves. When they have soaked in this mixture for about a hour, take them out, and Fry them to a good colour and serve them with crisped parsley.

Hint 327   Or, they may be served with a good Curry Sauce, just before sending to the table, make the curry quite hot, and dish it up with boiled rice.

A very nice Stew of Palates and Sweetbreads

Hint 328   Parboil and skin the Palates, as before; parboil the Sweetbreads with them; cut the palates, and if the sweetbreads are large, cut them in two the long way; dust them with flour, and fry them a light brown in butter; then stew them a portion of the liquor in which they were boiled. Brown a piece of butter with flour; add it, with little cayenne, salt, pepper, grated lemon peel, and nutmeg and a glass of white wine. A little before serving, stir in a spoonful of vinegar, or a squeeze of lemon.

A very Savoury and Economical Dish, commonly
called "Baked Faggots"

Hint 329   Procure Pig's Fry, wash it, and set it upon the fire in a saucepan, with just sufficient water to cover it. Add a bunch of sage, and four or five onion boil ten minutes: take out the meat, and cut in slices; then take out the sage and onion and chop it all finely together. Season with pepper and salt; cut the caul in pieces, and make into balls with the meat, about the size of an ordinary teacup; place them on a tin, and bake in an ordinary oven.

Preserve the water the meat was boiled in, and boil it down to a sufficient quantity to serve as gravy. Plenty of hot potatoes with these afford a very acceptable dish for a family of hearty children; and depend upon it, when the savoury odour announces that dinner is ready, there will be no difficulty in getting them in from the playground.

An excellent Dinner of Lamb's or Pig's Fry

Hint 330   Clean and parboil the lights, liver, sweetbread, and heart; slice, dredge with flour, season with pepper, cayenne, and salt, and fry (with chopped onion and sage, if of pigs) in butter or dripping, with a bit of bacon. The parboiling will take about ten minutes, and some persons omit the Lamb's sweetbread from this part of the process. Before frying, dip the pieces into a batter made of an egg beaten well with a teaspoonful of flour, half a wine glassful of either milk or water, and a little salt and pepper. A few chopped onions or mushrooms are very nice.

Hint 331   Pig's Chitterlings fried with onions are very good. After cleaning, they should be allowed to simmer in a saucepan in salt and water, until tender. Drain and fry as above.

Excellent Black or White Puddings

Hint 332   When about to have a pig killed, previously boil five pints of Grits in milk, or water, until quite soft. While the pig is being killed, save two quarts of the blood, throw a little salt into it while warm, and stir until it gets cold. When the Grits are nearly cold, put with them a good proportion of the inner fat of the pig, cut into pieces the size of a small nutmeg; season with pepper, salt, cloves, and mace, and also parsley, sweet marjoram, winter savoury, pennyroyal, and leeks, all finely minced. Mix them with the grits and fat, and add a sufficiency of the Blood to make it of a dark colour. The skins must be well washed, and when perfectly cleansed, laid in salt and water for several hours. To fill them, tie one end, and turn them inside out; fill them about three parts full, and, tie them of equal lengths or rounds; put them into hot water, and when they have boiled five minutes, take them out and prick them in several places with a large needle; then boil them slowly from half an hour to an hour, according to size. Hang them up to cool and dry.

Hint 333   Rice may be used instead of grits; and four Eggs, well beaten and strained, may be added to the above quantity, and the whole may be boiled in pudding basins or cloths, floured, instead of skins. Crumbs of bread may be mixed with the grits, and in this any pieces of stale bread may be used. These puddings may be kept cold, and when used be warmed whole in a Dutch oven, or be cut into slices, and broiled upon a gridiron, or may be fried.

Hint 334   The blood of Calves, Lambs, and Sheep, may be used in the same manner.

Hint 335   White Puddings may be made in precisely the same way as Black, by omitting the blood and substituting the White of Eggs. Or the following filling may be preferred:— Mix half a pound of blanched almonds, each cut into seven or eight bits, with a pound of grated bread, two pounds of finest suet, a pound of currants, some beaten cinnamon, cloves, mace, and nutmeg, a quart of cream, the yolks of six and whites of two eggs, a little orange flower water, a little fine Lisbon sugar, and some lemon-peel and citron sliced, and half fill the skins. To know whether they are seasoned to liking, warm a little of the filling in a pannikin, and taste. Prick them, as in the previous case, and boil in milk and water. These are very delicious.

A nice Pudding from Cold Calf's or Sheep's Brain and Tongue

Hint 336   Roll out the paste for the pudding; then put a layer of thin slices of Tongue on the bottom, then of Brain; repeat; season each layer with salt, pepper, parsley, and a little chopped onions; continue until full. Then mix a teaspoonful of flour with a gill and a half of milk, or water, and pour in; close the pudding and boil one hour. Two boiled eggs, hard-boiled, and cut in slices, would improve it; and a little gherkin, chopped fine, will vary the flavour.

Hint 337   Puddings may also be made of Ox, Sheep's, lamb's, and Pig's Brains and Tongues in the same manner. Also cold Sheep's Head, Tongue, and Trotters, which will be improved by the addition of sliced Pickled Walnuts.

Hint 338   Puddings are preferable when boiled in a basin or dish, for then the paste retains all the nutriment of the meat, which is otherwise liable to escape. A rather shallow dish is better than a basin when ample time cannot be allowed for boiling.

A Cheap and Savoury Herb Pudding

Hint 339   Of Spinach Beets, Parsley, and Leeks, take each a handful; wash them, and give them a scald in boiling water; then shred them very fine. Have ready a quart of groats steeped in warm water half an hour, and a pound of hog's lard, cut into little bits; three large onions chopped small, and three sage leaves, crumbled very fine; put in a little salt, mix all well together, and tie it closely in a cloth. It will require to be taken up while boiling, to slacken the string a little; and while doing so, the further time required to complete the boiling may be judged of.

A cheap Pudding, to accompany a Goose, and modify
its richness

Hint 340   Half a pound of Bread, soaked in a little boiling milk, and mashed to a paste; when cold, add two or three eggs, a little salt, pepper, marjoram, and thyme, a spoonful of oatmeal, a good handful of suet (may however be omitted), and an onion chopped fine. Spread it in a dripping pan, and bake it under the goose. Very serviceable where there is a large family, and only one Goose among them.

A very Savoury Pudding from Fragments of Bread
and Scraps of Cold Meat

Hint 341   Collect pieces of Stale Bread, and select the crumb (the crust may also be used, if previously soaked); steep this in warm milk, let it stand until well softened. Then strain of the milk; beat up the yolk of an egg, mix it with the bread, and also a bit of butter; put it into a saucepan, and boil until it becomes stiff; let it cool, and then add some chopped parsley, thyme, pepper, and salt; beat up two eggs; mince about one pound of any cold meat, and add all together. Boil in a basin for three hours, and when served, pour a good gravy over it.

Hint 342   It is a great folly for parents to insist upon children eating bits of bread, and other fragments of their meals, under the idea that it is wasteful not to eat the whole of what has been served to them to eat. It is, indeed, waste to make children eat too much, sowing the seeds of diseases, and leading to habits of gluttony. By receipts of the nature contained in our Save-all, not a scrap of anything nourishing need be lost.

A nice Pudding of Sausage Meat, Cold Pork Apples
and Onions

Hint 343   Line a pudding basin with some pudding paste in the usual way; place at the bottom a layer of slices of Apples, half an inch in thickness; then a layer of Sausage meat, or Cold Pork cut small and seasoned; then a layer of sliced onions; then apples, meat, and onions alternately, until the basin is full; season with pepper and salt between each layer; cover with paste; tie in a cloth, and boil. Time, according to size.

A nice pudding of Calf's Feet

Hint 344   Pick the meat of three well boiled and cleaned Calf's Feet; chop it fine, with half a pound of fresh beef suet; grate the crumb of about half a pound of bread; shred some orange peel, and some citron to taste; beat six eggs into a froth.

Mix these ingredients thoroughly together, and add a wine glassful of brandy, and half a nutmeg grated; boil in a cloth for three hours; serve with sweet sauce.

An Excellent Pudding of Pieces of Stale Bread etc

Hint 345   Soak two pounds of dry Stale Bread, or pieces of Stale Toast, all night in plenty of water, with a plate laid on the top of them, just to keep the bread under the water. Next morning, pour off and squeeze out all the superfluous water; then well mash the pieces of bread, and mix with it half a pound of flour, a quarter of a pound of currants which have been cleaned, four ounces of suet chopped fine, a quarter of a pound of moist sugar, and two teaspoonfuls of fresh ground allspice; then grease the inside of a baking dish with a bit of suet, put the pudding into it, and bake it for two hours.

Hint 346   Or it may be tied in a clean floured cloth, set in boiling water, with a plate at the bottom, and boiled for the same time.

An Excellent Savoury Pudding of Cold Potatoes, Mashed, and Cold or other Meat

Hint 347   Mash the potatoes, and rub them through a colander and make it into a thick batter, with milk and two eggs. Lay some seasoned meat in a dish, then some batter, and over the last layer put the remainder of the batter. Bake until nicely brown.

A Savoury or Sweet Dripping Pudding

Hint 348   Six ounces of Dripping to twelve ounces of flour, half the dripping to be well rubbed into the flour, with a little salt; then, with water, work into a stiff paste; roll it out thin, and add the remainder of the dripping, by spreading it thinly over the paste, then fold it over, and roll out again; repeat the process, and then work into a round pudding; put it into a basin, set it in boiling water, and continue to boil for two hours.

Hint 349   This may be eaten with Savoury Gravy; or with a sweet pudding, with Jam, Treacle, or sugar. It is light and inexpensive for a family of children.

Excellent and Economical Puddings from Cold or other Carrots etc

Hint 350   Grate, or pound in a mortar, the red part of two boiled Carrots, and grate also some bread, or pound a biscuit.

Take two ounces of melted butter, the same quantity of sugar, a tablespoonful of marmalade, or a bit of orange peel minced; half a spoonful of grated nutmeg, and four well beaten eggs; mix all well together; bake it in a dish lined with puff paste.

Hint 351   Or an excellent Plum Pudding may be made from Carrots prepared as above, adding the other ingredients as for plum puddings.

An Excellent Family Pudding of Cold Potatoes and Eggs, etc

Hint 352   Having collected the Cold Potatoes left for two or three days, bruise them through a colander with a wooden spoon; then beat up eggs with a pint of good milk, and stir in the potatoes, the proportion of eggs to potatoes should be four eggs to six large or twelve middle-sized potatoes; sugar and season to taste; bake half an hour. A little Scotch Marmalade or any kind of jam or preserve may be used as seasoning; or the pudding may be made a savoury one and eaten with gravy. This is an economical dish, where there is a family of children; but it will be found to be equally acceptable to "children of larger growth," and a nice light dish for invalids and elderly persons.

A Pudding for Hearty Appetites

Hint 353   Take a pint of whole Oatmeal, steep it in milk over night; in the morning, take half a half pound of beef suet, shred fine, and mix with the oatmeal and milk, some grated nutmeg, and a little salt, with the yolks and whites of three eggs, a quarter pound of currants, a quarter of a pound of raisins, and as much sugar as will sweeten it; stir well together, tie it very close, and boil two hours. Melted butter for sauce.

A very nice and cheap Dish — quite a favourite with the Boys and Girls

Hint 354   Boil one pound of good Rice (after being well washed) in plenty of water; when nicely soft, add one ounce of butter, and stir it in; then add one tablespoonful of sugar. The rice should not be boiled in more water than it will absorb. Peel and slice six apples, take out the core and pips; put them in a stewpan with six slices of beetroot, and a pint of water; stew until it is tender and mash them together, with a little butter and sugar. The beetroot is to give a rich pink colour to the apples, and improve the flavour. When done, place the rice on a dish; form a hole in the midst of it, in which is place the mashed apple; have ready for sauce a little cream, butter, and sugar; pour it over the rice, and serve.

Capital Dumplings for a Family of Young Ones

Hint 355   A pound of Flour, a spoonful of Yeast, and a little salt. Make this into a light paste, with warm water; let it lie for nearly an hour; make it into balls, and put them into little nets or cloths. When the water boils, throw them in; twenty minutes will boil them. Keep them from the bottom of the pan, or they will be heavy. Serve with hot milk and sugar for sauce; or a little seasoned stock; or a gravy made by stewing down bones, and seasoned to liking.

Snow Pancakes and Puddings. The cost of Eggs saved in the dearest season

Hint 356   It is not generally known that Snow is a good substitute for eggs, in both puddings and pancakes. Two tablespoonfuls may be taken as the equivalent of an egg. Take it from a clean spot, and the sooner it is used after it is taken indoors the better. It is to be beaten in, just as eggs are, and should be handled as little as possible. As eggs are dear in the season of snow, it is a help to economy to know the above. It is equivalent to a supply of fresh eggs, without the yoke of having to pay for them.

Hint 357   Fresh Small Beer, or Bottled Malt Liquors, serve, also, instead of Eggs.

Hint 358   Powdered Ice will answer as well as Snow, when the latter cannot be obtained.

A very nice Pudding, made from Stale Muffins

Hint 359   Having some Stale Muffins, make a pudding of them in the following manner. Put them into a pot of boiling of water, and let them boil five minutes; not more, or they will be quite soddened; then take them up, and pull them in halves. They must not be cut, or they will become close and heavy. Pour over the halves of the muffins some sweet sauce previously prepared, some apricot jam, or any other kind of preserve. With a knife, put the muffins together again, and spread some of the same kind of preserve on the top of each; over that, pour some more sweet sauce, and serve.

An Excellent Substitute for Pastry for the Dyspeptic

Hint 360   Boil a teacupful of Sago as thick as it can be made to boil, without burning; put about five spoonfuls into a quart basin; then a layer of baked fruit of any sort, sweetened, and fill the basin to the brim with alternate layers of fruit and sago. Set in a cool place for a little time, and it will become solid.

It is best when made shortly after breakfast, and allowed to stand until wanted, to warm either in an oven, over boiling water, or before the fire, with a plate turned over it, for dinner. The sago boils best when soaked in cold water for a few hours before using. Rice may be used in the same way.

Hint 361   Eaten with Mock Cream made as follows, it is delicious:— Pour half a pint of boiling milk on a teaspoonful of arrowroot, well mixed with a small quantity of the milk; stir the mixture well; and have the white of an egg well beaten, and when about half cold, add it, and place the whole over a slow fire until it nearly boils; then strain for use.

A delicate Pudding of the Petals of Primroses

Hint 362   Take of the Petals of Primroses chopped fine, a quart basinful; flour, half a pound; suet, quarter of a pound; a little salt; and mix with water into a pudding. Boil, and serve with melted butter and sugar.

An Excellent Substitute for Plum Pudding, at small Expense

Hint 363   Take four ounces of each of the following ingredients: Suet, flour, currants, raisins, and breadcrumbs; two tablespoonfuls of treacle and half a pint of milk; mix them well together, and boil in a mould for three hours. Serve with wine, or brandy sauce.

To send Boiled Rice to the Table in the Finest Condition

Hint 364   Soak it for seven hours in cold water, to which a little salt has been added. Have a stewpan ready, containing boiling water, into which put the soaked rice, and boil it briskly for ten minutes. Then pour it into a colander, set it by the fire to drain, and serve it up. The grains will be separate, and very large.

Hint 365   Rice should be prepared for Puddings in this way.

An Excellent and Economical Flavouring for Puddings, Custards, etc

Hint 366   When the Hawthorn is in blossom, gather the buds, which are like little white peas, and put them into wine bottles; let each bottle be three parts full, and then fill it with brandy, and seal. It will be ready for use in two months, and supply a delightful flavouring of which one or two teaspoonfuls will suffice for a pudding

Methods of Re-serving Sweets and other Table Delicacies

Hint 367   It is often a matter of great convenience as well as economy, to give a new and presentable form to the remains of Sweet Dishes which have already appeared upon the table; especially because there is frequently a large amount of them left unconsumed after parties.

Hint 368   Calf's Feet Jelly and good Blanc-mange are excellent when melted and mixed together, whether in equal or unequal proportions. They should be heated only sufficient to liquefy them, or the acid of the jelly may curdle the blanc-mange. Pour this last, when melted, into a deep earthen bowl, and add the jelly to it in small portions, whisking them briskly together as it is thrown in. A small quantity of prepared cochineal, which may be procured of a chemist, will serve to improve or to vary the colour when required.

Hint 369   Many kinds of Creams and Custards may be blended advantageously with the blanc-mange, after a little additional isinglass has been dissolved in it, to give sufficient firmness to all. It must be observed that either jelly or blanc-mange must be as nearly cold as it will become without thickening and beginning to set, before it is used for this receipt.

Hint 370   A sort of marbled mass is sometimes made by shaking together in a mould remnants of various coloured Blanc-manges cut nearly of the same size, and then filling it up with a clear jelly.

Hint 371   When a small part only of an open Tart has been eaten, divide the remainder equally into triangular slices, place them at regular intervals round a dish, and then fill the intermediate spaces, and cover the tart entirely with a slightly sweetened and well drained whipped cream.

A nice way of Warming and Serving Cold Plum Pudding

Hint 372   Cut the pudding into thin slices, and fry them in Butter. Fry, also, some Fritters, and pile them in the centre of the dish, placing the slices of pudding around on the outside. Powder all with lump sugar, and serve with pudding sauce in a tureen.

To Serve Cold Rice Pudding

Hint 373   Remove the baked coating of the pudding, and spread the remainder nicely upon a dish. Over the pudding pour a custard, and add a few lumps of jelly or preserved fruit.

A nice way to Serve the Remains of an Apple Tart

Hint 374   Cut the crust into triangular pieces, and arrange them around the sides of a china bowl. Place the fruit next to the pieces of crust; and pour a nice custard into the centre. Should the fruit be deficient, roast or bake a few apples, and place in the centre.

To secure a Constant supply of Savoury and Nutritious Stock, as a base for nearly all Gravies and Soups, simply from Scraps

Hint 375   To accomplish this, the first thing to do is, to set up a good iron "stockpot", which may be obtained from any furnishing ironmonger. The little outlay at first will soon be compensated by the daily contributions of the Stockpot to the wants of the family. It will last for years, and should never be out of use. The Stockpot should, in fact, be regarded as the principal SAVE-ALL, the magic reservoir, as inexhaustible as the conjuror's bottle, and producing as wonderful a variety of compounds. Before describing what may come out of the stockpot, it is obviously necessary to say what should be put into it. And the answer is, that there is nothing in the shape of scraps of meat and bone, that should not, unless otherwise employed, be thrown into the stockpot. For the benefit of the stockpot, horns should not he picked; the stockpot will clean them most effectively, and extract abundant nourishment from their internal parts. In preparing joints of meat for the table, put the trimmings into the Stockpot, Ham, Beef, Veal, Mutton, Lamb, Pork, Bits and Bones of Poultry, Game, in fact, the bones or remains of any kind of meats should go into the stockpot. Eggshells should be put in; they tend to clarify the stock. Crusts of dry Bread may be thrown in; they gather the scum, which should be taken off three or four times a day. Cold Carrots and parsnips, or the remains of onion sauce or gravy; the outside stems of Celery, thoroughly cleaned and cut into small pieces; and all similar substances, should invariably go into the Stockpot, which should always be kept simmering by the fire, the exhausted bones, etc., being removed day by day, as the stock is drawn off.
The Stockpot thus managed will always be ready to supply the groundwork of almost all kinds of gravies and soups A basin of soup, with the addition of a little water, thickening, and a sprinkling of herbs, may be knocked at a moment's notice. Hashes, meat pies, savoury Puddings, and all gravies sent to the table may be enriched thereby. When Stock is alluded to in the recipes given in this volume, the liquor from the stockpot is that which is indicated.
Every furnishing ironmonger knows what a Stockpot is, but the purchaser should observe that the tap should be raised a little from the bottom, in order that the stock may be drawn off without the sediment. The bones and refuse that come from the stockpot will serve for the pig tub; or suffice for dogs and cats, where such are kept, without wasting better food upon them.

Capital Stock for Gravy and Sauces, from a
Ham Bone

Hint 376   When a Ham has been cut to the bone, cut off all the bits of meat that are not rusty, whether fat or lean, throw the rusty pieces into the pig tub, or to the fowls, break the bone in pieces, beat the meat with a rolling-pin, and put the whole into a saucepan with a quarter of a pint of broth or gravy; then cover it, and stew gently, occasionally stirring it well, to prevent its sticking to the bottom. Then strain off the stock, and bottle down in old pickle bottles, to improve gravies or sauces of any description. This is essentially a good "extract of ham" cheaply obtained.

To make a very relishable Soup without Meat

Hint 377   Take two carrots, two turnips, one onion, the trimming of a head of celery, cut into small slices and pieces, and fry with about half an ounce of butter. Let them be fried until they are quite dry, taking care that they do not burn. When in this state, pour from a pint and a half to a quart of boiling water into the frying pan on them; then pour all together into a saucepan, and boil for three or four hours, adding water to keep up the quantity, as it boils away. Capital for invalids, or as a warmer at bedtime for people with bad colds.

Green Peas Soup without Meat

Hint 378   If the peas are good, this will be as nice a vegetable soup as need be sent to table. Take a quart of young green Peas, and divide half a pint from them. Put them on in boiling water; boil until tender, and then pour off the water, and set it by to make the soup with. Put the peas into a mortar, and pound them to a mash; then put them back into the water the peas were boiled in; stir all well together, and then rub it through a hair sieve, or tammy. Boil the half pint of peas, separated from the others, and when done, turn then into the soup, and serve hot.

Hint 379   The same may be made with the liquor in Calf's Head, Calf's Feet, or Tails, or joints of Veal, Mutton, etc., have been boiled.

Pea-leaf Soup, an inexpensive rarity, when Green
Peas cannot be obtained

Hint 380   Take some shallow pans, plant them pretty thickly with dwarf Spanish peas, and set them in a vinery where there is a shelf, and a good heat. When they are about six inches high, and well furnished with leaves, cut them like mustard and cress, for the purpose of making green pea soup.

Boil a small quantity of blue peas, and also boil the cuttings, mix the two, and pass them through a tammy; add this to the usual stock, and you will obtain a green pea soup which for colour, flavour, and body, cannot be surpassed, even by midsummer productions.

Hint 381   A quantity sufficient to serve a party of fourteen (thirteen is an unlucky number!) can be raised at the expense of 2s. 6d. One quart of the strong growing varieties is enough for sowing; and a half pint of any variety of blue peas to boil separately. Mint should not used.

Hint 382   The young leaves of peas grown out of doors will do as well as those raised in glasshouses. The proportions to be used may be thus indicated:— Half a pint of peas; one quart of pea leaves, two small lettuces, and one middle-sized onion. These will supply enough soup for six persons.

Hint 383   When peas first come in, Pea Shells boiled, and pressed through a sieve, with some of the liquor in which they were boiled, are equally good as peas. The young pea haulm is also good for the purpose. One half the quantity of young peas will suffice - for soup, when the shells are used in this manner,

Delicious Asparagus Soup

Hint 384   This is to be made with the points or heads of Asparagus, in the same manner as green pea soup. Let half the asparagus be rubbed through a sieve, and the other cut in pieces about an inch long, and boiled until soft, and sent to table in the soup. To make two quarts, there should be a pint of heads to thicken it, and half a pint cut in.

Hint 385   A cheaper soup, preferred by many, may be made by adding Asparagus Heads to common Pea Soup.

Plain Pea Soup

Hint 386   To a quart of split Peas, two heads of celery, and a large onion, put three quarts of broth; let them simmer gently over a slow fire for three hours, stirring every quarter of an hour, to prevent the peas burning (as the water boils away, add some more); when the peas are well softened, work them through a coarse sieve, and then through a fine sieve or a tammy, wash out the stewpan, and then return the Soup into it, and give it a boil up; take off any scum that comes up, and it is ready. Send them up with Fried Bread and Dried Mint on two side dishes. This is an excellent Family Soup, produced with very little trouble or expense.

Hint 387   The Broth for the above may be derived from a Liquor made from the Bones of Boast Beef, or the water in which Mutton, Beef, Pork, or Poultry has been boiled. A Shank Bone of Ham, the Root of a Tongue, and pieces of a Red Herring are all-good for Pea Stock.

A very Economical Carrot Soup

Hint 388   Clean arid scrape half a dozen large Carrots; peel off the red outside, which alone is to be used for the soup; put it into a gallon stewpan, with one head of celery, and an onion shred to pieces. Take two quarts of beef, veal, or mutton broth, or if you have any Cold Roast Beef Bones, or the liquor in which mutton or beef has been boiled, you may make very good stock for this soup. When you have poured the broth upon the carrots, cover the stewpan close, and set it on a slow fire for two hours and a half, or until the carrots are soft.
Take some pieces of Stale Bread, and grate a large cupful of crumbs; rub it through a tammy or hair sieve, with a wooden spoon, and add as much broth as will make it about as thick as pea soup. Either put it into the soup; or make it hot in a separate stewpan, season it with a little salt, and send it up as a side dish, with some toasted bread cut into inch squares, to be eaten with the soup, according to taste.

Hint 389   To impart a better flavour, the Celery and Onions may be fried to a light brown in butter, before being added to the soup.

Hint 390   Or, put some Beef Bones into a saucepan: with four quarts of the Liquor in which Beef or Mutton has been boiled; add two large onions, a turnip, and a seasoning of pepper and salt; boil the whole for three hours. Have the Carrots ready, prepared as above strain the soup on them, and stew until they are soft then press them through a sieve. If you have Cold Roast Beef or Beef Steak pulp about half a pound in a mortar, add to the soup, and serve very hot.

Rhubarb Spring Soup

Hint 391   Peel and wash about a dozen sticks of Rhubarb, more or less, according to size, and the quantity of soup required; blanch them in water three or four minutes; drain, and put it into a stewpan, with two onions sliced, a carrot, a piece of lean Ham either shred or pounded, and a good bit of butter; let it stew gently over a slow fire until tender; then put in two quarts of good broth, to which add two or three ounces of bread crumbs; boil about fifteen minutes; skim the fat; season with salt and cayenne pepper, pass through a tammy, and serve up with Fried Bread.

Excellent Celery Soup

Hint 392   Cut six heads of Celery into pieces about two inches long, wash them well, drain them on a hair sieve and put them into a stewpan, with three quarts of clear stock. Stew gently for about an hour, until the celery is very tender. Remove the scum, as it rises, and serve with a little salt. When Celery cannot be procured, half a drachm of the Seed, pounded fine, put in a quarter of an hour before the soup is done, will impart a fine flavour. Or a little essence of Celery may be used.

An excellent Soup of Endives Best when they are
Plentiful and Cheap

Hint 393   Trim away the green and outer leaves of about three dozen Endives, which should be thoroughly washed and examined; blanch them in boiling water and a little salt for ten minutes, after which throw them into cold water, drain, and press all the water out. Cut off the roots, and put the endives into a stewpan with four ounces of fresh butter, a little grated nutmeg, salt, and sugar. Stir the endives over a slow fire for about ten minutes with a wooden spoon; then add a ladleful of good fowl or veal broth; simmer gently in an oven, or by a slow fire for an hour, and then pass the endives through a tammy. To the puree thus obtained, add one quart more of broth, and just before sending the soup to table, add to it a pint of boiling cream or milk, and a pat of fresh butter. This is a capital light soup for the autumn season, when endives are full and white.

A very Economical and Agreeable Soup of Lentils

Hint 394   Take one pint of Lentils, soak them in cold water; add six middle-sized onions; two heads of celery; two carrots; one turnip; one quart of pot liquor from boiled Beef, Mutton, or Pork, and one quart of water. Stew the whole slowly, as green peas for soup; pour it all into a mortar, and pound it well or, use lentil powder, as sold prepared; strain through a tammy or sieve, and add one tablespoonful of powdered lump sugar. One pint of lentils will make enough soup for seven persons.

Capital Soup from Goose or Duck Giblets

Hint 395   The Giblets of two Ducks may be reckoned as equal to those of one Goose, Cleanse the Giblets, and parboil them; take the skin off the feet, and crack the bones of the legs; cut the gizzards into quarters, the neck into three pieces; the feet, livers, and pinions into two, and the head also into two, throwing away the bill. Boil them (i.e. two sets of Goose Giblets, or four sets of Ducks,) in a quart of weak gravy soup, with an onion.

Have ready boiling some rich highly seasoned brown, gravy soup; add the giblets, and the liquor they have been boiled in, with some chopped parsley; take out the onion, and thicken the soup with a bit of butter kneaded in flour.

Hint 396   Or, one set of Goose, or two of Duck Giblets will make a quart of healthful nourishing soup. If a large quantity is desired, and there are no more giblets to be had add a pound of Beef, or Mutton, or Bone of a Knuckle of Veal.

Hint 397   Those who are fond of Forcemeat, slip off the skin of the neck, and fill it, tying up the ends; or make some Forcemeat Balls of the Duck Stuffing. These should be put into the soup about half an hour before taking up.

A Capital Soup, made of Old Partridges

Hint 398   Take off the skins of two Old Partridges, that are too "venerable" for roasting; cut them into small pieces, with three slices of ham, two or three onions sliced, and some celery. Fry them in butter until they are as brown as they can be made without burning; then put them in three quarts of water, with a few peppercorns; boil it slowly till a little more than a pint is consumed; then strain it. Put in some stewed celery and fried bread.

Excellent Soup from Cold Hare, or from an Old Hare, that cannot be otherwise Cooked

Hint 399   Chop the Hare into pieces, and break the bones; stew it in say three quarts of water or stock, with one carrot, cut small, a little onion, four cloves, a little pounded mace, some black pepper, and a bundle of sweet herbs; if liked, a bay leaf may be added. While these are stewing, make a dozen or more of Forcemeat Balls, then the Hare is stewed, so that the flesh leaves the bone, strain through a tammy, pick out the bones, etc., and collecting the meat, mince or pound it, with a little butter, add two or three tablespoonfuls of flour, rubbed smooth with a little soup; rub this latter through a hair sieve, into the soup, to thicken it; add a little more water or stock, to keep up the quantity; let it simmer slowly half an hour longer, skimming it well. Put in the meat, with a glass of port wine, and three tablespoonfuls of currant jelly; season with salt; put in the Forcemeat Balls; and when all is hot serve. If there is a good quantity of the Hare Stuffing, it will suffice instead of the herbs.

Hint 400   Rabbit, Partridge, and Grouse Soup may be made from the old animals, or cold remains if in sufficient quantity in the same manner. Smaller quantities may be made, when the fragments are not sufficient for the above.

A gallon of Broth for Four pence: suitable to the
poor, and good enough for the rich

Hint 401   Of Scotch Barley, well washed in cold water, take four ounces; and four ounces of sliced onions. Put these into five quarts of water — the fifth quart to allow for the decrease of quantity by boiling. After boiling gently for one hour, pour it into a pan, and put into the saucepan from which the soup has been poured two ounces of clear beef or mutton dripping, melted suet, or two or three ounces of fat bacon minced. When melted, stir into it four ounces of oatmeal; rub these together into a paste. Now add the Barley Broth previously prepared; at first a spoonful at a time, and the rest by degrees, stirring well together until it boils. For seasoning, use ground black pepper, cayenne, allspice, salt, etc., to taste. Any other vegetables that may be at hand can be added, particularly chips of celery, carrots, leeks, chopped parsley, thyme, herbs, etc.

Hint 402   Stale bread, bits of biscuit, or plain suet dumplings may be added.

Capital and Cheap Soup from Cow Heels

Hint 403   Boil two Cow Heels; cut the meat into moderately small pieces, and set them by separately in a dish; put the trimmings and bones into a stewpan with three quarts of water, together with an unboiled cow heel cut into quarters; add to this, two onions and two turnips, pared and sliced, the red part of two large carrots, two shallots cut in halves, a bunch of lemon-thyme, and two bunches of parsley; set this by the side of a slow steady fire, keep it closely covered, and let it simmer gently six or seven hours, during which take care to remove the fat and scum. When done, strain the liquor through a sieve, and put two ounces of butter into a clean stewpan; when it is melted, stir into it as much flour as will make a stiff paste, add to it by degrees the soup liquor; give it a boil; strain through a sieve; and put in the thinly pared peel of a lemon, a couple of bay leaves, and the meat of the boiled heels. Let it simmer for half an hour longer; add the juice of a lemon, a gill of wine and a teaspoonful of mushroom ketchup, and serve in a tureen.

Soyer's Soup for the Poor; which has been Tasted
and Approved by numerous Noblemen, Member's
of Parliament, and Ladies. Two gallons cost
about Sixpence

Hint 404   Two ounces of dripping; quarter of a pound of meat, cut into pieces one inch square; quarter of a pound of onions sliced thin; quarter of a pound of turnips, cut into small dice; two ounces of leeks — the green tops will do, chopped small; three ounces of celery; three quarters of a pound of common flour.

Half a pound of pearl barley, or one pound of Scotch; three ounces of salt; quarter of an ounce of brown sugar; two gallons of water.

Hint 405   Put the two ounces of dripping into a saucepan capable of holding two gallons of water, with a quarter of a pound of the leg of beef, without bones (the bones may be also put in, or be afterwards used for stews, gravies, etc.)— cut in pieces about one inch square; put in the onions, and then set the saucepan over a fire. Stir the contents round for a few minutes with a wooden or iron spoon until fried lightly brown. Then put in the turnips, celery, and leeks, cut into small pieces. Stir them with the other ingredients over the fire for another ten minutes; then add a quart of cold water and three quarters of a pound of flour, and the pearl barley, mixing all well together; then add seven quarts of hot water, seasoned with the salt, and brown sugar, stirring occasionally until boiling; allow it to simmer for three hours, when the barley will be tender and the soup ready.

A Beef Brose

Hint 406   After any large piece of Beef has been taken out of the pot it was boiled in, skim off the fat with part of the liquor, and boil it in a saucepan. Make a Beef Brose thus: — Have ready in a bowl, Oatmeal that has been toasted brown before the fire. Pour in the boiling liquor, and stir it a little; if too thick add a little more liquor, and send it to table quite hot.

A Capital Soup of Cold Ox-head

Hint 407   This should be prepared the day before it is to be eaten, as you cannot cut the meat off the head into neat pieces unless it is cold:— the day before you want this soup, put half an Ox-Cheek into a tub of cold water to soak for a couple of hours; then break the bones that have not been broken at the butcher's, and wash it in warm water; put it into a pot, and cover with cold water; when it boils, skim very clean, and then put in one head of celery, a couple of carrots, a turnip, two large onions, two dozen berries of black pepper, same of allspice, and a bundle of sweet herbs, such as marjoram, lemon thyme, savoury, and a head of parsley; cover the pot close, and set on a slow fire; take off the scum, and set by the fireside to stew very gently for about three hours. Take out the head, lay it on a dish, pour the soup through a fine sieve into a stoneware pan, and set it and the head by in a cool place till the next day; then cut the meat into neat pieces, skim and strain off the broth. Put two quarts of broth and the meat into a clean stewpan — simmer very gently for half an hour longer, and it is ready.

Hint 408   If you wish it thickened, put two ounces of butter into a stewpan; when melted, throw in as much flour as will dry it up; when well mixed, and browned by degrees.

Pour to this your soup, and stir well together; simmer for half an hour longer; strain through a hair sieve into a clean stewpan, and put to it the meat of the head — stew half an hour longer, and season it with cayenne pepper, salt, a glass of good wine, or a tablespoonful of brandy, if required.

Hint 409   May be served thickened in one Tureen, and send up the Meat in that, — the remainder as a clear Gravy Soup, with some of the carrots and turnips shred, or cut into shapes.

Economical Soup of Ox Tails

Hint 410   Put into a gallon stewpan eight cloves, two or three onions, half a drachm of allspice, the same of black pepper, and three Tails, divided between the joints; some persons fry the tails before they put them into the soup. Cover them with cold water; skim it carefully as long as you see any scum rise. Then cover as close as possible, and set on the side of the fire to keep gently simmering until the meat becomes tender and will leave the bones easily, because it is to be eaten with a spoon, without the assistance of a knife or fork; this will require about two hours when perfectly tender, take out the meat and cut it of the bones in neat mouthful; skim the broth, and strain it through a sieve.

Hint 411   If you prefer a thickened soup, put flour and butter, as directed in the preceding receipt, or put two tablespoonfuls of the fat you have taken off the broth into a clean stewpan, with as much flour as will make it into a paste; set this over the fire, and stir them well together; then pour in the broth by degrees, stirring it and mixing it with the thickening; let it simmer for another half hour, and when you have well skimmed it, and it is quite smooth, then strain it through a tammy into a clean stewpan, put in the meat with a tablespoonful of mushroom ketchup and season it with salt.

A Nourishing Soup of Ox Heels

Hint 412   Procure an Ox Heel undressed, or only scalded (not one that has been already boiled, as they are at the tripe shops, until almost all the gelatinous parts are extracted), and two that have been boiled as they usually are at the tripe shops. Cut the meat off the boiled heels into neat pieces, and set it by on a plate; put the trimmings and bones into a stewpan, with three quarts of water, and the unboiled heel cut into quarters;— furnish a stewpan with two onions, and two turnips pared and sliced; pare off the red part of a couple of large carrots, add a couple of shallots cut in half, a bunch of savoury or lemon thyme, and double the quantity of parsley; set this over, or by the side of a slow steady fire, and keep it closely covered and simmering very gently (or the soup liquor will evaporate) for at least seven hours.

During which, take care to remove the fat and scum that will rise to the surface of the soup, which must be kept as clean as possible. Now strain the liquor through a sieve, and put two ounces of butter into a clean stewpan; then it is melted, stir into it as much flour as will make it a stiff paste; add to it by degrees the soup liquor; give it a boil up; strain it through a sieve, and put in the peel of a lemon pared as thin as possible, and a couple of bay leaves, and the meat of the boiled heels; let it go on simmering for half an hour longer, i.e., until the meat is tender. Put in the juice of a lemon, a glass of wine, and a tablespoonful of mushroom ketchup, and the soup is ready for the tureen.

Hint 413   Those who are disposed to make this a more substantial dish, may introduce a couple of sets of Goose, or Duck Giblets, or Ox Tails, or Calves Tails, or a pound of Veal Cutlets, cut into pieces.

A very Nice Onion Soup

Hint 414   Brown half a pound of butter, with a little flour; take care it does not burn; when it has done hissing, slice a dozen of large onions, fry them very gently until tender; pour to them, by degrees, two quarts of boiling water, shaking the pan well round as it is poured in, and also a crust of bread; let it boil gently for half an hour; season it with pepper and salt. Take the top of a French roll, and dry it at the fire, put it into a saucepan with some of the soup, to soak it, then put it into the tureen; let the soup boil some time after the onions are tender, as it gives the soup a great richness; strain it off and pour it upon the French roll.

Brown Soup, without Meat

Hint 415   Put into a clean saucepan three quarts or more of water, with raspings sufficient to thicken it; two or three onions cut across, some whole pepper, and a little salt; cover it close, and let it boil about an hour an a half; strain it off through a sieve ; then have celery, endive, lettuce, spinach, and other herbs, not cut too small; fry them in butter; then take a clean stewpan that is large enough for the ingredients; put in a good piece of butter, a dust of flour, and keep stirring it until it is of a fine brown, then put in the herbs and soup; boil it until the herbs are tender, and the soup of a proper thickness; put the soup into a tureen, and send it to table; have some fried bread in a plate, and some in the soup, if agreeable.

White Soup, without Meat

Hint 416 Put into a clean saucepan two or three quarts of water, the crumb of a two penny loaf, with a bundle of sweet herbs, some whole pepper, two or three cloves, an onion or two cut across, and a little salt; let it boil covered until it is quite smooth; take celery, endive, and lettuce, only the white part; cut them into pieces, not too small; boil them, strain the soup off into a clean stewpan; put in the herbs, with a good piece of butter stirred into it until it is melted; then let it boil for some time until it is very smooth; if any scum arises, take it off very clean. Soak a small French roll, nicely rasped in some of the soup, and send it to table.

Nourishing Milk Soup

Hint 417 Take two quarts of new Milk, with two sticks of cinnamon, a couple of bay leaves, a very little salt, and a very little sugar; then blanch half a pound of sweet almonds while the milk is heating, beat them up to a paste in a marble mortar; mix them by degrees with some milk. While they are heating, grate the peel of a lemon, with the almonds, and a little of the juice. Then strain it through a coarse sieve, and mix it with the milk that is heating in the stewpan, and let it boil up; cut some slices of French bread, and dry them before the fire; soak them a little in the milk; lay them at the bottom of the tureen, and then put in the soup.

Mock Turtle Soup

Hint 418 Scald a Calf's Head which cut into inch squares; wash and clean them well, dry them with a cloth, and put them into a stewpan, with two gallons of stock gravy, sweet basil, knotted marjoram, savoury, a little thyme, some parsley, all chopped fine, cloves and mace pounded, half a pint of Madeira or sherry; stew all together gently for four hours; heat a little stock gravy with a little milk (one pint), some flour mixed smooth in it, the yolk of two eggs; keep these stirring over a gentle fire until near boiling; put this in the soup, stirring it as you put it in, for it is very apt to curdle; then let all stew together for half an hour, when it is ready to send to table, throw in some Forcemeat Balls and hard yolks of eggs; when off the fire, squeeze in the juice of half a lemon. The quantity of the soup may be increased by adding more stock gravy, with calves feet and ox palates, boiled tender, and cut into pieces.

Excellent and Cheap Pumpkin Soup

Hint 419 Take a Knuckle of Veal and a Knuckle of Ham, in absence of the Veal, use a Calf's Foot or a Cow Heel, or even some Bones; and, in place of the Ham use part of the Hock of Bacon, Cut and chop these up; put them into a two gallon stewpan.

Then add to them two large onions sliced, one carrot, two middle sized turnips sliced, with skin on, the outside leaves of a large head of celery cut into small pieces, one teaspoonful of ground allspice, one tablespoonful of salt, and a piece of butter or marrow the size of a walnut. Place the stewpan on the fire; keep stirring the contents with a wooden spoon, to prevent them sticking to the bottom of the pan, and until there is a kind of white glaze on the pieces of meat; then add, by degrees, one gallon of hot water; peel and take out the seeds of a Pumpkin about six pounds in weight; cut it into pieces, and put it into the stewpan; boil until the pieces of Pumpkin are quite soft; pass as much as possible of the contents of the stewpan through a coarse hair sieve; then boil it again, adding more water if too thick. Season it with a tablespoonful of pounded sugar, a teaspoonful of pepper, and more salt if required. Serve in a tureen, with some fried bread cut the size of dice.

Hint 420   This soup is preferable to soups of the pea kind; it cools the blood, and corrects the acid humours of the body.

Hint 421   In all kinds of soups, where butter is recommended, marrow is preferable, only in larger quantities.

Hint 422   Pumpkins may also be dressed as vegetables by being cut into slices, boiled in plenty of water with some salt in it, drained well when done, and served on some toast, with melted butter made with cream poured over it.

Hint 423   Pumpkins may likewise be pickled by cutting them into slices, and proceeding the same way as for Indian pickles; or they will do to mix with other vegetables for Piccalilli.

Capital Broth of Sheep's Head

Hint 424   The Sheep's head is well worth cooking for broth. To make broth, get a fine head, and scald the wool off the same as the calf's head; then put it into a saucepan with a gallon of water, and let it boil gently for three hours; having put in with the head a carrot and turnip sliced, and an onion or two, the scum should be taken off five or six times, so as to get it perfectly free from grease; take out the head, cut the meat from the bones into squares, and put them into the saucepan again with the liquor, leaving the turnips, carrots, and onions in also; season with pepper and salt, add a little flour to thicken, and serve in basins, with some toast cut into squares in the basin, and a little chopped parsley, fresh.

Hint 425   The Scrag End of the Neck, Shank Bones, or Feet, will make broth as well as the head.

Soup from Calves Tails, commonly called
Chesterfield Soup

Hint 426   Take three gallons of stock gravy, a little whole pepper and allspice, a few sprays of basil and knotted marjoram, some salt and ketchup, three onions, two carrots, and a little celery cut small; it should boil two or three hours, until the vegetables are done to shreds; in the mean time a Roux should be prepared thus:- place half a pound of butter in a confectionery pan, when it is melted, add two pounds of flour, which having thoroughly mixed with the butter, gradually thin by adding some of the stock which has boiled for two hours; when it can be added to the other ingredients, and allowed to boil for half an hour, being kept well stirred to prevent burning. It should then be strained through a hair sieve into an earthen or tin pan. It will require twelve Calves Tails for the above quantity of Soup; they should be separated at the joints, placed in a stew pan, with two gallons of water, and allowed to boil until thoroughly cooked. When, having removed the scum from time to time, they can be added, liquor and all, to the soup; when, having allowed it to simmer for a few minutes, it can be served with a wineglass of sherry or Madeira, in the tureen.

Capital Zests for Cold Meats, Salads, Gravies, etc,
Costing the Merest Trifle

Hint 427   Pour a quart of the best vinegar on three ounces of scraped horseradish, an ounce of minced shallot, and one drachm of cayenne; let it stand a week, and you will have an excellent relish, at a merely nominal cost. Horseradish is in highest perfection about November.

Hint 428   Horseradish Powder should be made during November and December; slice it the thickness of a shilling, and lay it to dry very gradually in a Dutch oven (a strong heat evaporates the essential flavouring oil); when dry enough, pound, and bottle it.

Hint 429   Dry and pound half an ounce of cress-seed (such as is sown in the garden with mustard), pour upon it a quart of the best vinegar; let it steep ten days, shaking it up every day. This will be very strongly flavoured with the cress, and for salads, cold meats, etc., will be greatly liked. The quart of sauce will cost only a penny more than the vinegar.

Hint 430   Bruise half an ounce of celery seed, and add a quarter of a pint of brandy or proof spirit. Let it; steep for a fortnight. A few drops will immediately flavour a pint of broth, and form an excellent addition to Pease and other soups, and the salad mixture of oil, vinegar, etc.

A Capital and Cheap Sauce for Roast Pork, Pork Chops, or Warmed Cold Pork

Hint 431   Well wash and cut up a good sized red cabbage, or part of one; peel an equal weight of apples; slice and take out the cores; put the cabbage and the apples into a stewpan, together with a piece of butter, and very little water; or in lieu of butter, piece of fat bacon; stew them gently by the side of the fire until quite tender; stir and mix well together, season with pepper and salt, and serve with pork as above. The pieces of cold pork should be put in the stewpan and warmed with the sauce.

Hint 432   When pickling red cabbage, take the opportunity of giving this sauce a trial, and it will become a standard dish.

The Best English Substitute for Indian Chutney

Hint 433   Half a gallon of vinegar; three quarts of green Gooseberries, boiled in three pints of the vinegar until tender; one pound of coarse brown sugar, to be made into a syrup with the other pint of vinegar. Then add three quarters of a pound of common salt; quarters of a pound of pudding raisins; half a pound of currants; two ounces of cayenne; two ounces of garlic; one ounce of ground ginger; three ounces of mustard; one grated nutmeg; one teaspoonful of ground mace and one ounce of Jamaica pepper. The garlic and ginger to be well ground in a mortar. All the ingredients to be well mixed with the gooseberries and vinegar. When the vinegar and gooseberries are nearly cold, mash them up and strain through a colander; then add half an ounce of turmeric for colouring.

Hint 434   This resembles the real Chutney more closely than any of the other substitutes.

Hint 435   Some use Crab Apples instead of gooseberries, and shallots instead of garlic. These changes are to accommodate peculiar tastes.

The Economy of "Bastings" — Means of Saving the Consumption of Butter

Hint 436   Well clarified dripping, and the fat skimming's of broths and soups, when fresh and sweet, will baste everything as well as butter, except game and poultry, and should supply the place of butter for common pies, etc., for which they are equal to lard, especially if the clarifying be repeated twice over. If kept in a cool place, it may be preserved a fortnight in summer, and longer in winter.

Hint 437   To clarify dripping, put it into a clean saucepan, over a stove or slow fire; as soon as a scum forms, skim it well, let it boil, and then let it stand until it is a little cooled, then pour it through a sieve into a pan.

Hint 438   After frying, let the spare dripping stand a few minutes to settle, and then pour it through a sieve into a clean basin or stone pan, and it will do a second and a third time as well as it did the first; but the fat in which fish has been fried, must not be used for any purpose than frying other fish.

To make a Nice Fish Cake, from Scraps of
Cold Fish

Hint 439   There are few articles of food more likely to be wasted when cold than fish of various kinds. Take any Cold Fish, and separate the bones carefully. Instead of throwing away the latter, put all of them, including the head, fins, and tail, if any, into a stewpan, with just enough water to cover them, with some pepper, an onion, a faggot of sweet herbs, and a little salt; stew them down, and a nice gravy will be produced. A drop or two of fish sauce, or anchovy, may be added, if approved. Mince the fish, and mix it well with crumbs of bread, cold potatoes, a little parsley finely chopped, and season to taste. Make into a cake with the white of an egg, or a little butter, or milk; egg it over, and cover with breadcrumbs; then fry a light brown. Pour the gravy over, and serve hot. Garnish with slices of lemon, or sprigs of parsley. This affords a capital dish to help out a scrap dinner; or a nice relish for either breakfast or supper.

To prepare a Nice Dish for Breakfast, Supper, or
Dinner, by escalloping fragments of Cold Soles,
Cod, Whitings, Smelts, or other Fish

Hint 440   Take the Cold Fish, separate it from the bones, and cut into small pieces. Obtain oysters, in number proportioned to the quantity of fish. Stew them slowly in their own liquor for two or three minutes; take them out with a spoon, and beard them, if preferred; skim the liquor, and pour it into a basin. Put a bit of butter into the stewpan, melt it, and add as much breadcrumbs as will dry it up, then put the oyster liquor into the pan with the butter and crumbs, and give it a boil. Put the cold fish into scallop shells that have been previously buttered and strewed with breadcrumbs; add a couple of oysters to each; divide the oyster liquor between the different shells, cover with bread crumbs, and drop bits of butter on the top of each; then brown in a Dutch oven. The whole may be prepared at once in a large flat dish, instead of the scallop shells. Those who like a particularly keen relish may add anchovy, ketchup, cayenne, grated lemon peel, mace, or other condiments to taste.

Hint 441   The Muddy Flavour of Pond Fish may be diminished in the following manner: — When the fish has been perfectly cleaned, insert a slice of bread, large enough to fill up the belly, and remove this when the fish is cooked.

A nice Pie from Cold Salmon or Mackerel

Hint 442   Skin the pieces, and remove all the bones. Then pound the fish very fine in a mortar, with mace, nutmeg, pepper, and salt to taste. Raise the pie of paste, as for meat pies, and ornament the sides in the usual manner. Put the salmon in, and cover it, and bake until nicely browned. When it comes out of the oven, take off the top crust, and put in a little melted butter; cut a lemon in slices, and lay over the top; stick in two or three leaves of fennel, and send to table without a cover.

Hint 443   Cold Mackerel may be served in the same way, mixed with cold veal. The sauce to be poured into this, should be made of melted butter, cream or milk, with chopped parsley. Or, bruise the roes of the mackerel, whether hard or soft, with the yolk of white egg; beat up with a little pepper and salt, and some fennel parsley chopped very fine, mixed with thin melted butter.

Fish Stew, that may be eaten either hot or cold

Hint 444   Take three or four fresh Haddocks, Soles, or Plaice; salt the fish very slightly; cut it into pieces, and then prepare a Fish Forcemeat as follows:— Take a little of the raw fish, a little of the liver, and some parsley, a good quantity of breadcrumbs, some allspice, and mix an egg into balls. Have ready a stewpan, in which you have, previously to making your forcemeat, put a large or small onion (according to the quantity of fish) cut in rings; a little parsley, a bit of butter as big as a chestnut, and a quarter pint of water; add cayenne and mace, each a pinch, and ground ginger as much as would lie on a half-crown piece. When this has simmered a quarter of an hour, and your forcemeat is ready, put in your fish, and lay the forcemeat balls on it. Stew gently half an hour have; the yolk of an egg well beaten; add to it the juice of four lemons; beat well together; add thereto a little of the boiling liquor of your fish to prevents curdling, and add this to the fish. One boil up more and it is ready — and a very savoury dish, too.

Cold Fried Soles nicely warmed

Hint 445   Fried Soles will keep very good in a dry place, for three or four days. They may be warmed for the table by hanging them on the hooks in a Dutch oven, and putting them at a distance from them fire, that they may warm gradually.

Hint 446   Or, they may be warmed in good Beef Gravy according to the directions given for Boiled Soles, etc.

*A nice way of serving up any kind of Cold Fish, with
Stale Bread, etc*

Hint 447   Dip a flat dish in hot water, to prevent cracking; smear it with butter, and sprinkle white pepper on it; then a thick layer of stale bread, grated fine. Upon the bread place a layer of Fish, picked from the bones, and divided into small pieces; another layer of bread as before, with a little melted butter, poured over it. Repeat as often as required for the quantity of fish. Smooth the surface with a spoon, and sprinkle slightly with fine bread, mixed with white Pepper. Place it in a Dutch oven for twenty or thirty minutes. A nice dish for any meal.

Hint 448   Cold Mutton may be served in the same way.

*Mackerel preserved when Cheap, to keep until they
are Dear*

Hint 449   Mackerel, being at certain times very plentiful and cheap (especially to persons who live near the coast), may be preserved to make an excellent and well flavoured dish, weeks or months after the season has passed. Having chosen fine sound fish, cleaned them perfectly, and either boiled them, or fried them lightly in oil, the fish should be divided, and the bones, heads, and skins being removed, they should then be well rubbed over with the following seasoning: for every dozen good sized fish, it will be requisite to use three tablespoonfuls of salt, one ounce and a half of common black pepper, six or eight cloves, and a little mace, finely powdered, and as much grated nutmeg as the operator chooses — not, however, exceeding one nutmeg. Let the surface of each fish be well covered with the seasoning; then place the fish in layers packed into a stone jar (not a glazed one), cover the whole with vinegar; and, if it be intended to be kept long, pour salad oil or melted suet over the top.

Hint 450   The glazing on earthen jars is made from lead or arsenic, from which vinegar dissolves poison.

A Capital and Cheap winter dish, called "Winter Whitebait"

Hint 451   Select some of the largest and soundest Sprats, which are in season all the winter, and best in frosty weather. Shake them in flour to remove the scales, then egg them over with a brush; shake them in equal quantities of flour and breadcrumbs, and fry them in boiling fat for three minutes.

Serve them dry on a napkin. Brown bread and butter and a lemon should be set on the table with them, and those who like them "devilled" should add cayenne to suit their taste. A capital first dish for dinner, or a nice relish for supper, and calculated to entice the master home, thus affording a new application of the old adage " throwing out a sprat to catch a mackerel."

To make a new dish for the dinner table of Cold Boiled Soles

Hint 452   If you have saved the Shins of Soles, throw them into salt and water, and scrape and wash them well. Then put them into a stewpan and cover them with water. Add two onions, with two cloves stuck in each, and one blade of mace. Let it boil twenty minutes, and strain through a sieve into a basin. Make the sauce as thick as cream, by adding a little flour; add also two tablespoonfuls of port wine, and one of ketchup; stir these into the sauce by degrees; give it a boil, and pour it over the fish through a sieve. Then having wiped out the stewpan, warm up, and serve hot. Instead of the sauce thus prepared, good beef gravy, mushroom sauce, or white sauce, may be employed.

A nice stew of cold boiled Soles, Turbot, Brill, Plaice, Flounder, or other flat-fish

Hint 453   Slice and bone the Fish, and rub it with a little salt and flour. Have ready some good beef gravy, put the fish into it, and warm very gently. Take out the fish carefully, and lay on a dish. Make the sauce about as thick as cream, by mixing a little flour with it; add two tablespoonfuls of port wine, one of mushroom ketchup; a little cayenne; stir these into the sauce by degrees, give it a boil, and strain it to the fish through a sieve.

To make a nice Relish out of fragments of cold Lobster or Crab

Hint 454   It very often happens, after Lobster or Crab suppers or luncheons, that legs and claws, and portions of the back, are left untouched or imperfectly picked. Collect all the fragments of fish, and put with them two blades of mace, a little white pepper, and salt, and a small portion of butter, and seasoning; the quantities of the latter must be proportioned to the amount of lobster, according to judgment. Put these all together, and beat them into a paste in a mortar. Take earthenware boxes in which potted fish or meats have been purchased, or such small jars or large gallipots as you may have about the house, and fill as many of these with the prepared lobster as you may be able to do.

If there are any solid parts of the tail, which cannot well be reduced to a paste, they may be cut into small pieces, and set in the middle of the pots, and the paste poured over them. When the pots are nearly filled, press down the contents, pour over them a layer of clarified butter, lard, or melted suet fat. This will afford a nice relish for breakfast, luncheon, or supper. If intended to be kept for some time, tie down with pieces of wet bladder.

A very Nice Supper Dish, or Plain Patties of Oysters

Hint 455 Make little round loaves, or take small French rasps; make a round hole in the top of each, and scrape out a portion of the crumb. Put sufficient Oysters into a stewpan with their own liquor, and add to them the crumbs of bread, rubbed or grated fine, and a good lump of butter. Season with white pepper, a sprinkle of cayenne; stew for five or six minutes, and then put in a spoonful of good cream. Fill the rasps or loaves, and cover with the bits of crust previously cut off; set them in an oven for a few minutes, to warm and crisp.

Hint 456 Minced Veal, Lamb, Poultry, Game, etc., may be done in the same way, as for paste patties.

An Excellent Method of Obtaining Oyster Sauce, when Oysters are "Out of Season," and of making it portable to places where Oysters cannot be obtained

Hint 457 Open the Oyster's carefully, so as not to cut them, except in dividing the gristle which attaches them to the shells. Put them into a mortar, and when you have as many as you can pound at once, add about two drachms of salt to about a dozen oysters; pound them, and rub them through a hair sieve, and put them into the mortar again, with as much thoroughly dry flour as will roll them into a paste; roll this paste out several times, and lastly, flour it, and roll it out the thickness of half a crown, and cut it into pieces of one inch square; lay them in a Dutch oven, where they will dry so gently as not to get burned; turn them every half hour, and when they begin to dry, crumble them. They will take about four hours to dry. Pound them, sift them, and put them into dry bottles; cork and seal them. Three dozen natives require seven and a half ounces of flour to make them into a paste weighing eleven ounces, and when dried in powder, six and a half ounces.

Hint 458 To make half a pint of Oyster Sauce from this powder, put one ounce of butter into a stewpan, with three drachms of oyster powder, and six tablespoonfuls of milk: set it on a slow fire, stir it until it boils, and season it with salt.

Hint 459   As a Sauce, this is excellent with Fish, Fowls, or Rump Steaks; and, sprinkled on bread and butter, it makes good Sandwiches.

Delicate Breakfast Rashers from Cold Boiled Bacon

Hint 460   Cut the Bacon into slices, about a quarter of an inch thick; grate over them some crust of bread, and powder them well with it on both sides; lay the rashers on a cheese toaster, and brown them on both sides.

Hint 461   Excellent to accompany Poached or Fried Egg, and for a garnish around veal cutlets, or sweetbreads; or hashed calf's head, or dishes of green peas, or beans.

A Savoury Supper quite Irresistible

Hint 462   If there are no social objections to your eating Onion, try the following: to an omelette of three eggs, add half a good sized onion, mixed almost to a powder, and a tablespoonful of chopped parsley. The shredding of the onion to a sufficient degree of fineness, is the most important thing, as from the short time required to cook the omelette, it would otherwise be insufficiently dressed. The onion should be boiled previously (or partially so), for fastidious tastes; but thereby some degree of flavour and crispness is sacrificed.

Celery flavour for Soups all the year round

Hint 463   At those seasons, or in those places where celery cannot be obtained for soups. Dried Celery Seed will be found to supply an excellent substitute.

Mint and other Vinegars for Culinary purposes

Hint 464   Put fresh Mint leaves into a stone jar, and pour on them a sufficient quantity of the best wine vinegar to cover them. Set the jar in a warm place for fourteen days; then strain through a jelly bag. In the same way may be made Elderflower, Watercress, Basil, Tarragon, and Burnet vinegars. Fifty English chillies, cut or bruised, may be added to either of the above.

A cheap Method of obtaining a Constant supply of Pure Vinegar

Hint 465   Take one gallon of water, half a pound of sugar, half a pound of molasses, and boil them together for twenty minutes; when cool, add a quarter of an ounce of German yeast; put the whole into a jar, and lay a Vinegar Plant on the surface of the liquor.

Cover the jar with paper, keeping it in a warm place, and it will reduce to a very good and wholesome vinegar in about six weeks.

Hint 466   The Vinegar Plant is a minute fungus, forming what is commonly called "the mother of vinegar." A bit of this thrown into the above liquid rapidly increases, and changes the sugar and water into vinegar. The plant will form of itself in the first instance, but this will require a longer time. Afterwards it may be divided and transferred to other quantities of the mixture, to accelerate the process of vinegar making.

Hint 467   Much of the vinegar which is sold in the shops is either malt vinegar, reduced with water, and strengthened with sulphuric acid, or acetic acid, also diluted, neither of which is very acceptable or wholesome.

To obtain Mint Sauce at any season of the year

Hint 468   When Mint is green and plentiful, cut it up fine, put it into empty pickle bottles. Fill the bottles with vinegar, and cork closely. The sugar can be added when required for use. No one can tell the difference of mint so prepared, from that newly gathered from the bed.

Hint 469   For those who like Mint Sauce, the above may be eaten with lamb or mutton chops.

Essence of Game, for serving with Hashed Game
of any kind

Hint 470   Take the remains of any Game, with an equal quantity of Beef and Veal; salt, pepper, mace, nutmeg, cloves, bay leaf, parsley, garlic, shallots, and morela; some white wine, a little vinegar, and the juice of lemons; put into a stewpan; when on the eve of boiling, slacken the fire, and leave the pan on the hot cinders for six or seven hours; pass the sauce through a sieve, and filter.

Hint 471   Pieces of Game may be warmed in a Dutch oven, and be served with this sauce heated, and poured over it.

Hint 472   Capital addition to Game Pies

Hint 473   The remains of Fowls or other Poultry, either roast, stewed, or boiled, may be done in the same manner, with appropriate seasoning, and with onion, parsley, etc., chopped fine.

To obtain Herbs of the Finest Flavour

Hint 474   When Herbs are to be kept for flavouring dishes, it is obviously of the first importance that they should be gathered at the right time, and dried in the best manner.

The seasons when the various herbs are in their primest flavour, are as follows:— Basil, from the middle of August to the middle of September; marjoram, during the month of July; winter savoury, the latter end of July, and throughout August; summer savoury, the same; thyme, of various kinds, during June and July; mint, the latter end of June, and during July; sage, August and September; tarragon, June, July, and August; chervil, May, June, and July; burnet, June, July, and August; parsley. May, June, and July; fennel, the same; elder flowers. May, June, and July; orange flowers. May, June, and July.

Hint 475   Herbs should be gathered on a dry day, before the sun has been long upon them. When intended for reservation, they should be cleaned from dirt and dust, and dried gradually upon a warm stove, or in a Dutch oven. The leaves should then be picked off, pounded in mortar, passed through a hair sieve, and the powders be reserved separately in well stoppered bottles.

Economical use of Nutmegs

Hint 476   If a person begins to grate a nutmeg from the stalk end, it will prove hollow throughout; whereas the same nutmeg grated from the other end, would prove solid to the last. This is because the centre consists of a number of fibres issuing from the stalk, and extending throughout the centre of the fruit. When the stalk is grated away, those fibres, being attached to no other part, loose their hold, and drop out, and a hollow is formed through the whole nut.

Hint 477   A very useful tincture of nutmeg, ready for immediate use, may be made, by adding three ounces of bruised or grated nutmeg to a quart of brandy. A smaller quantity may be made, by observing the same proportions. This will be a very grateful addition to all compounds in which nutmeg is; a few drops will suffice to impart flavour.

The Very Best Curry Powder

Hint 478   Take of coriander seed, three ounces; turmeric, three ounces; black pepper, mustard, and ginger, one ounce of each; allspice and lesser cardamoms, half an ounce of each; cumin seed, a quarter of an ounce. Put these ingredients into a cool oven, and let them remain all night; the next morning, pound them in a marble mortar, and rub them through a fine sieve. Thoroughly mix them together, and keep them in a well stoppered bottle.

Hint 479   For Curry Sauces, steep three ounces of the powder in a quart of vinegar, or white wine, for ten days, and the liquor will be strongly impregnated with the flavour of the powder.

Homemade Cayenne Pepper of superior Flavour

Hint 480   Those who desire to obtain good Cayenne Pepper, free from adulteration and poisonous colouring matter, should make it of English chillies. By so doing they will obtain pepper of the finest flavour, without half the heat of the foreign. A hundred large chillies, costing only two shillings, will produce about two ounces of cayenne — thus the superior homemade is as cheap as the commonest red pepper. The following is the way to make it:— Take away the stalks, and put the pods into a colander; set it before the fire for about twelve hours, by which time they will be dry. Then pour them into a mortar, with one fourth their weight in salt, and pound and rub them till they are as fine as possible; sift through a little muslin, and then pound the residue, and sift again.

*A very useful Household Tincture from Scraps of
Lemon peel*

Hint 481   Fill a wide-mouthed pint bottle half-full of brandy, or proof spirit, and whenever you have bits of waste Lemon rind, pare the yellow part very thin, and drop it into the brandy. This will strongly impregnate the spirit with essence of lemon, and form an excellent flavouring for tarts, custards, etc.

*How to obtain Cheap and Nice Cress all the year
round*

Hint 482   What is so nice and refreshing as to see a plate of really fresh Salad placed upon a table, and dishes nicely garnished with bits of green? " But," you will say, "this cannot be done, parsley not always being in season." It may easily be done, in a manner to supply both salads and ornaments for the table. Take bottles, small baskets, plates, dishes, or any other articles, and cover them with flannel, old pieces of baize, cloth, or other absorbent material. The cloth should be cut out, and sewn, so as to form a perfect shape for the article to be covered. Saturate the cloth with water after the covering is complete, and then thickly sprinkle or press thereon mustard seed, or pepper seed, so as equally pervade the surface, not too thick, nor too, scanty. In a little while, the gluten of the seed will become softened, and fix the seed firmly to the cloth. Set it in a dark and moderately warm place, and moisten it occasionally. After the seeds have germinated, bring them by degrees into the light, and as their strength increases, expose them, as opportunity may occur, to the sun.

You will soon have cress from an inch to two inches long, growing upon an ornamental shape, which may be set upon the table, and the cress cut from it as wanted. This may be done at any season of the year.

An Excellent Pottage made from Pea Shells

Hint 483   Take three quarts of water, in which meat has been boiled the previous day, and after seasoning it to taste with pepper and salt, set it on a fire. Add the shells of half a peck of Peas, and a bundle of herbs, including a good quantity of chives, or sweet leeks, and if possible a sprig or two of tarragon - a small quantity only of the latter will be requisite. When the pea shells arc sufficiently boiled, which can be ascertained by trying a few of them, pour the whole lot through a colander, and when the liquor has been strained off, pound the pea shells and herbs in a mortar, returning them to the colander, and rubbing through what will pass easily. Add now a small cupful of green peas, two lettuces shred rather small, the more stalky the better, provided they are properly blanched, and a couple of sprigs of mint, and you will have a soup which would not disgrace any table, especially if a little fried bread is added, and an ounce of white sugar.

Hint 484   If a thick soup is preferred, a little Flour and Butter or other thickening must be used. It is not necessary to have anything stronger than common broth as a foundation. No one who may partake of this soup, properly prepared, will doubt the wisdom of making the most of what Providence has placed before us.

An Excellent Spring Vegetable, to be had for the Gathering

Hint 485   Young Stinging Nettles supply an excellent vegetable for the table, boiled, and eaten as greens. They grow abundantly, and are not only highly relishable, but very healthy. Wash them thoroughly; drain them; and put them into boiling water, with salt; they will require about twenty to twenty five minutes boiling; they should then be well drained and chopped, and served plain, or put back into the pan, seasoned with a little salt and pepper, and tossed for a minute or two in gravy or butter. This dish may be had throughout five months of the year; for even when the nettles have grown, their tops are tender.

Hint 486   Nettles are everywhere a pest to the farmer; their young shoots being employed for food, in the months of April and May, their propagation will be materially checked, and the nuisance abated.

Hint 487   The young leaves of Mangel Wurzel, dressed in the same way, are extremely good.

Hint 488   Nettles are also good food for Pigs and Cows; and Turkeys may be fed upon chopped Nettles and Docks.

The Stems of the Artichoke

Hint 489   It is not generally known that the Stems of the Artichoke are as good as the part usually eaten, and that their flavour is equally fine. In Italy, their stems are commonly stewed in gravy, like celery, and are considered very good. If they are cut off when the plant is about a foot high, and boiled in salt and water with the lid off, they make a capital dish, having all the flavour of the root.

The Thistle an Edible Vegetable

Hint 490   Almost all the varieties of this plant are edible; but those most commonly used for culinary purposes, are the marsh thistle (Carduus Palustris) and the milk thistle (Carduus Marianus), called also the white or lady's thistle. The stems of the marsh thistle, gathered before the flowers are formed, when stripped of their rind are good, if boiled and eaten like Asparagus. The milk thistle may, when young, be eaten as a salad. The young stalks peeled, and soaked in water, to remove the bitterness, are excellent when boiled. The scales of the cup are said to be equal to artichokes. The root is equally good during the winter and early spring. They are excellent stewed like celery, in good broth or gravy.

The Puffball an Esculent Fungus

Hint 491   The Giant Puffball (Lycoperdon Giganticum), gathered in its fresh and pulpy state, and fried with butter in slices, is remarkable for richness and delicacy of flavour. They should be only seasoned with pepper and salt; or, a piece of butter, with pepper and salt may be put upon each slice, and they may then be baked, in a closely covered pie dish, for about three quarters of an hour. The fungus should be gathered in quite an early stage of growth, and before there is any trace of yellowness in its appearance, for then its flavour is destroyed. The puffball will not keep many hours after it is gathered; but slices may be cut from it as it grows, and thus an increased supply obtained. Slice them half an inch thick; have ready chopped herbs, pepper, salt, etc., as for an ordinary omelette of eggs; dip the slices into yolk of egg and sprinkle the herbs and condiments upon them; fry in fresh sweet butter, and let them be eaten directly they are taken up. They are much lighter and more digestible than egg omelettes, and resemble brain fritters.

Hint 492   The Giant Puffball is very useful for Stupefying Bees, being burnt, and the fumes driven into the hives; only slightly discolours the combs, and the unpleasant scent soon passes off, upon exposing the combs to the air.

An elegant way of serving up Cold Potatoes, with
Spinach or Cabbage

Hint 493   Mash Cold Potatoes, and moisten them with a little white sauce; take Cold Cabbage or Spinach, and chop very finely; moisten them with brown gravy. Fill a tin mould with layers of potatoes and cabbage; cover the top, and put it into a stewpan of boiling water. Let it remain long enough to make the vegetables hot; then turn them out and serve. This forms a very pretty dish for an entree.

Hint 494   Cold carrots and turnips may be added to soups; or may be warmed up separately, and put into moulds and layers, and served the same as the potatoes and cabbage described above.

To Improve Potatoes of Bad Quality

Hint 495   Potatoes are sometimes of very inferior quality, being deficient in starch, on account of the haulm decaying before the tubers are ripe. The method to improve them by cooking is, to peel them, and boil them gently, until nearly done. Then drain the water from them, and put them again upon the fire, submit these to a dry heat; then mash them with a two-pronged fork, instead of a spoon. The fork breaks them into pieces, and allows the water to escape, thus very much improving, what are called "waxy" potatoes.

Hint 496   A piece of lime, the size of a walnut, put into the water in which inferior potatoes are boiled, will improve their quality.

A very Nice and Novel Dish, where Watercresses
are Plentiful

Hint 497   Collect a tolerably large quantity of Watercress; this may be done by children on a holiday, affording them healthful recreation. Lay the cress in strong salt and water, to free it from insects. Pick and wash nicely, and stew in water for about ten minutes; drain and chop, season with pepper and salt, add a little butter, and return it to the stewpan until well heated. Before serving, add a little vinegar, and put around the dish sippets of toast, or fried bread.

Hint 498   The above made thin, is a good substitute for Parsley and butter, as a sauce for boiled fowl.

Hint 499   Watercresses eaten plentifully are excellent for consumption.

Endive may be Cooked as a Dinner Vegetable

Hint 500   Endive forms an excellent vegetable when cooked for the dinner table in the following manner:— Take two good endives, not blanched, separate the leaves, and boil them in two waters, to extract the bitterness. If still bitter, use a third water; ten minutes before they are ready, throw in a handful of sorrel leaves, when soft, take them out and strain them; then put back in the saucepan with a piece of butter the size of a walnut; season with pepper and salt, and add a little of any rich gravy. Shake them well over the fire and serve as hot as possible.

Hint 501   Or, boil the Endive, then put it into cold water; drain the water off, and press it well out; take a good tablespoonful of flour, and a piece of butter about the size of a walnut; mix them well near the fire. Put this mixture with the vegetable, and about a teacupful of gravy or water; add a little salt and pepper, and stew until quite hot, taking care to avoid burning.

Hint 502   An excellent Puree Soup may be made of endive.

Pea Tops used as an Ordinary Vegetable

Hint 503   A delicious vegetable for the table may be obtained by sowing Peas in shallow boxes, at intervals during the winter months. They will come up slowly but strongly. When about five inches high, cut them for use, and boil them in the same way as cabbage is done. Dish up plainly, to be eaten as any ordinary green vegetable.

Carrots with Flavour, and Carrots without

Hint 504   When you are about to boil carrots, do not scrape them; but first brush and then wash them. When cooked, rub off the skin with the back of a knife. The improvement in the flavour is very great, because all the juice has been kept in. The carrot is more affected by the ordinary system of peeling or scraping than the potato, because the former contains a large proportion of sugar, in a soluble form. Those who try this, will learn to estimate the difference of carrots with flavour, and carrots without.

The Rhubarb Leaf as a Green Vegetable

Hint 505   Take the leaf (the youngest is the best) and divest it of the five stems that run to the right and left hand, and up the centre in connexion with the fruit (those stems containing nearly all the fruity qualities of the rhubarb itself).

The leaves should then be placed in boiling water, and kept boiling fast for twenty minutes, after which well press them to exclude all liquor, and with the necessary condiments of the table it will be found a welcome substitute for ordinary vegetable, while its medicinal properties as a mild aperient are upon a par with the rhubarb.

Hint 506   To please the palates of the most fastidious and lovers of Spinach, it may be dished up as that article in the following way:— After boiling and pressing, place it in a saucepan without water, let it simmer for ten minutes with a small quantity of butter, pepper, and salt, and when done it will puzzle some of the finest connoisseurs to detect the difference.

An excellent Pickle of Unripe Codlins, Plums, Damsons, Apricots, Peaches, Nectarines, or other Unripe Fruit

Hint 507   Make a brine of salt and water strong enough to float an egg boil and skim it. When cold, put full grown Codlins into it, which have not begun to ripen. Let them soak three days; then make a fresh pickle, and soak them in it. On the tenth day, take them out, wipe them, and carefully cut out the stalk piece of each whole, so that it can be put in again. Then with a scoop remove all the core and pippins, without piercing through the eye at the other end. Then mix together equal parts of mustard seed and cumin seed, half the quantity of coriander seed, some sliced horseradish, some chillies pounded fine with salt, some Jamaica pepper, some mace, and a few cloves. Fill up the place of the core with this mixture, then put the stalk piece in its place, and tie it with a string. Put a good quantity of the mixture into a stone jar, with a sufficient quantity of vinegar; let it boil, and put in the Codlins whilst it is boiling hot. When cold, cover the jar. Next day, uncover it, and put it into an oven, and keep it there until they are of a nice colour. When cold, close the jar in the usual manner.
Unripe Plums, Damsons, Apricots, Peaches, Nectarines, and all other kinds of Unripe Fruit may be pickled in the same manner, the stones being removed, after soaking in brine, with as little injury to the fruit as possible.

Hint 508   Considerable quantities of these fruits fall from the trees unripe; and, provided they are sound, they are as good for pickling as if fresh gathered. Wash in cold water those that have lain in the ground, previous to putting them into the brine.

Hint 509   When pickles prove too soft, they may be hardened by pouring off the vinegar and boiling with it a large lamp of alum; when cold, it is to be poured back upon the pickles.

A Delicious Pickle of Eggs

Hint 510   Take two dozen of hen's eggs, an equal number of turkeys eggs, and the same number of guinea fowls. Boil them twenty minutes. When cold, take off the shells. Add to them six or eight dozen plovers or pigeon's eggs, also boiled hard and shelled. Have ready an ounce each of cloves and mace, four or five nutmegs sliced, an ounce of whole pepper, two ounces of ginger, half a dozen cloves of garlic, four ounces of salt, and four or five bay leaves. Put the eggs into a stone jar, with this seasoning between them. Then pour over them sufficient boiling vinegar to cover them. When cold, close the jar in the usual way. Let them stand two days; then pour off the pickle, boil it, and return it to the eggs. Repeat this twice, thus giving the vinegar three boilings after the first; each boiling at an interval of two days. Close the jar in the usual manner.

Hint 511   This pickle may be made with Hens Eggs alone, or any other kind of eggs; but a variety of eggs is preferable. pickled eggs, formerly, were much esteemed.

A very nice Substitute for Capers

Hint 512   Put green and freshly gathered Nasturtiums, with the little bit of stalk attached to them, into a brine made of salt and water. Let them stand six days. Then boil some white wine vinegar in a stone jar, with sliced horseradish, a sliced nutmeg, some grains of allspice, a little mace, some pepper, and a handful of salt. Pour it boiling hot over the Nasturtiums.

Hint 513   The Seed Pods of the Radish also make a good substitute for capers.

A very nice Pickle of Crab Apples

Hint 514   Gather the Crabs while they are still very hard, Peel them, remove the eyes, and put them into a brine of salt and water that will float an egg. Let them stand six days, then change them into a fresh brine, in which they must stand six days more. Put them into a jar with a little mace. Boil some double distilled vinegar with some sliced horseradish, a sliced nutmeg, some allspice, and a few cloves, and pour it boiling hot over the apples. When quite cold, put a cork into the jar. Boil the vinegar again every two days for ten days, and pour it each time boiling hot over the apples. When cold, cork and bladder the jar. After three months they will be excellent.

Pickled Vegetable Marrows

Hint 515   Cut the Marrows in thick slices, and salt them twelve hours, and then dry them in the sun; then boil three quarts of vinegar with a pound of the flour of mustard, a good handful of black pepper, a few allspice and cloves, thirty-six bay leaves, and a stick of horseradish cut in slices; boil them all together until the mixture is of the thickness of cream, pour it hot over the marrow, and cover close. Add the above one pound of mustard seed, half an ounce of long pepper, quarter of an ounce of mace, and nine green capsicums, boiled in a pint of vinegar with a teaspoonful of cayenne. The pickle will be fit for use in six months.

An excellent Pickle of Walnut husks

Hint 516   The green outer husks that are removed when walnuts are first making their appearance early in October, make an excellent pickle, superior to the whole walnut. The peels that fall off late in the season, and are turning black, are too old and stringy for pickling. The process of pickling is much the same as that adopted for young walnuts; salt is sprinkled over them to extract the bitter flavour, which is less intense now than when the fruit is unformed. When they turn black, they are ready for the vinegar and the spice. The very best vinegar should be used pickles.

An excellent Vinegar from Gooseberries

Hint 517   To every quart of moderately ripe Gooseberries, add three quarts of water, and bruise the fruit well; stir Up the whole, and let it stand for twenty-four hours, then strain it through a canvas bag. One pound of brown sugar must be added to every gallon of the liquor, which being well mixed up, should be put in a cask or other vessel to ferment.

Hint 518   Raspberry Vinegar is made in the same way, and will be found very useful in families.

Hint 519   Weak Vinegar may be strengthened by allowing it to freeze; the watery portion congeals first, and may be removed; the portion that remains will be found to be greatly increased in strength. This, of course, can be done conveniently only in the winter time, when, if the vinegar of pickles is found to be weak, it may be improved. Vinegar may also be improved, when its flavour is not good, by the addition of aromatic or pungent substances, such as Chillies or Tarragon.

An excellent Method of Pickling Salmon, so that it will keep good Twelve Months

Hint 520   Cut the fish across into slices about an inch and a half or two inches thick. Then rub over each piece with the following Seasoning: — Pound an ounce of mace, one of Jamaica pepper, one of cardamom seeds, half an ounce of allspice, and a drachm of cloves. Mix this with half a pound of bay-salt, and two grated nutmegs. Add also a little powdered bay leaf, and a very small quantity of dried and pounded mint. Rub this seasoning well into every piece of Salmon, then cover each piece with beaten yolk of egg, and strew seasoning over again. Fill a small frying pan half full of olive oil and fry one piece of salmon at a time until it is of a rich yellow-brown colour. As each piece is fried, put it upon a hair sieve. When all are fried, let them drain until they are quite cold. Then put at the bottom of a stone jar a small bit of fennel, and a little sprig of tarragon. Upon these a layer of pieces of salmon; on these a bay leaf, another little branch of fennel, and another small sprig of tarragon; then repeat until all the salmon is laid in. Fill the jar with vinegar, an inch above the fish, and over this pour a thick surface of olive oil.

Hint 521   This is a rare but not an expensive preparation; and, as it will keep a long time, and supply a capital zest for breakfast, luncheon, or supper, it is worthy of being tried.

A Savoury Relish of Pickled Sprats

Hint 522   Take off the heads of a number of small Sprats, and wash the bodies well. Strew a quantity of salt over them, and let them lie in a pan all night. Take them out next day, and wipe them well. Then put into a stone jar, or an iron saucepan, a quantity of vinegar in proportion to the quantity of sprats. If the vinegar is in a stone jar, put it into an oven to boil; if in an iron vessel, place it over the fire. Put into the vinegar, a bunch of parsley root, some tarragon leaves, a sprig of thyme, one of marjoram, an onion stuck with cloves, and four or five shallots. Let the vinegar boil with these herbs, then strain it into another stone jar, and let it get cold. Meanwhile, have ready some wide mouthed pickle or anchovy bottles. Put a layer of sprats at the bottom of each bottle, then a bay leaf, then a pinch of salt, a grain or two of allspice, and a few peppercorns; then another layer of sprats, until the bottles are full. Then fill them with the vinegar when it is quite cold. Cork the bottles, put bladder over the corks, and sealing wax upon the bladder.

Hint 523   Smelts pickled in the same way are excellent.

A Savoury Pickling of Oysters

Hint 524   As soon as the Oysters are opened put them into a stewpan with their liquor, and place them over a brisk fire. Do not let them boil; but the moment they become white and firm, take them out, and carefully move the beards. Then strain the liquor into a stone jar with double its quantity of white wine vinegar, one quarter of its quantity of mushroom ketchup, five or six shallots, two cloves of garlic, a couple of bay leaves, some leaves of tarragon. Put this into an oven for three quarters of an hour, then take it out and let it stand until it is cold. In the meantime, mix a spoonful or two of powered loaf-sugar with an equal quantity of salt, and sprinkle the mixture over the oystcrs. When these are quite cold, put them carefully into a jar with a handful of peppercorns, the same quantity of grains of allspice, a bunch of bay leaves, and a few leaves of tarragon. When the vinegar is quite cold, pour it upon the oysters, cork the jar, and tie bladder over the cork.

Hint 525   The pickle liquor may be boiled up occasionally, allowed to cool, and poured over the oysters again; this will tend to preserve them.

Hint 526   A spoonful of this liquor will be a great addition to any plain Hash, or common Ragout.

Hint 527   Muscles and Cockles may be pickled in the same manner, but neither of these should be kept long.

To Restore Salt Pork that is Tainted

Hint 528   In warm weather, the brine upon pickled pork frequently becomes sour, and the meat tainted. Boil the brine, skim it well, and pour it back on the meat boiling hot. This will restore the pork, even when it is much injured.

Hint 529   In summer the sooner meat is salted after it is killed, the better. In winter it will eat shorter and tenderer if kept a few days, until its fibre has become set and short. Pork requires a longer time to pickle than Beef,

An excellent Marmalade of Carrots

Hint 530   Take any number of Carrots (those of the months of September and October are the best), wash them thoroughly in cold water, cut off the tops and tails, and wipe the carrots clean. Cut them into pieces about two inches in length, dividing the whole circumference into four parts. If the carrots are large, and into three or two if they are small, taking care to throw away the part that is decayed.

Put these bits into a pan, with as much water only as will prevent the bottom of the pan from burning its contents. Cover them close, and let them stew over a moderate fire until they are very tender. Mash them thoroughly, and pass them through a hair sieve. Then prepare and clarify a syrup, using for every pound of pulp, a pound of sifted sugar and half a pint of water. Clarify, and boil until it adheres to the spoon. Put in the pulp, boil it, evaporating the moisture, until it forms a thick marmalade.

Hint 531   This will keep for two years or more; and it is strongly recommended as a confection for the breakfast table. It is excellent for persons of scorbutic habit.

Preserve of whole Strawberries

Hint 532   Strawberries ripen and decay very fast, and are often destroyed for the want of some easy means of using them. Take an equal weight of fruit and pounded loaf sugar; lay the former in a large dish, and sprinkle over them half the sugar. Give the dish a gentle shake, in order that the sugar may reach the wide part of the fruit; next day, make a thin syrup with the remainder of the sugar, and add one pint of red currant juice left from last year's preserves, to every three pounds of strawberries. In this simmer them until sufficiently jellied. Choose the largest strawberries, not over-ripe. Very nice served in thin cream, in glasses.

An Excellent and Cheap Jam of Blackberries

Hint 533   To every pound of the fruit, add half a pound of coarse sugar, and boil for three quarters of an hour. A silver or wooden spoon should be used for stirring it, as iron spoils the colour. This is a plain homely method, so cheap and easily managed, as to be practicable in every cottage. There is no fruit more salutary for children than blackberries.

Hint 534   A portion of fine loaf sugar may be used, an equivalent quantity of the brown being withheld.

Hint 535   Some persons consider a lemon flavour imparted to the jam an improvement. The rind and juice of one lemon will be sufficient for twelve pounds of jam.

Hint 536   It is to be regretted year after year, to witness the excessive profusion of their own fruit, neglected by the poor in rural districts, when, for the trouble of gathering it, which might in fact be made a pleasure to the children, and a trifling outlay for a few pounds of brown sugar, delicious treats for the winter meal could be procured. No costly, preserving pans, no charcoal fires are required; a homely saucepan will answer every purpose.

Windfall Pears, slightly damaged are excellent for
Baking

Hint 537   Most keeping Pears, such as the Beurre Rance, Easter Beurre, Swan's Egg, Chaumontel, and St. Germain, are excellent when baked without any addition; the juice forms a rich syrup, without sugar. They require merely to be wiped clean and put into a dish; if heaped up, so much the better. In this way, wind fallen fruit, otherwise useless, may be turned to good account. The Marie Louise Pear is a first-rate one for stewing.

A Capital Apple Jam, that will keep Five Years, to
be made in Plentiful Seasons

Hint 538   Take a wide jar, and fill it not quite full with water; cut the unpeeled Apples into quarters, de-cores, but collect the pips, bruise them, and put them into the jar with the apples. Tie paper over it, and put it into a moderately hot oven. When quite soft and cool, pulp the apples through a sieve, with a wooden spoon. To each pound of fruit, after pulping, put three quarters of a pound of crushed sugar; boil it gently until it will jelly. Put it into jars, and tie over with bladder. If to keep for a short time, less sugar will do.

PART 2

INVALUABLE HINTS

How to save Half your Coals, and obtain Better Fires
than under the old system

Hint 539   Before lighting the fire in the morning, thoroughly clean out the grate; lay a piece of thick paper, cut to the form and size of the grate, at the bottom; pile up fresh coal, nearly as high as the level of the top bar; the pieces should be about the size of small potatoes or walnuts, but this is not absolutely necessary; the larger lumps should be laid in front, the smaller ones behind; then put a liberal supply of paper, or shavings, and sticks, on the top, and cover the whole with yesterday's cinders, adding a very little coal. Thus, it will be seen, the fire is to be lighted at the top. The results will be not only satisfactory, but astonishing. The fire lights up at once, without further trouble. The centre of the fuel soon catches, and the inferior strata of coal ignite. The fire spreads downwards, and the smoke is forced to pass through the upper layers of burning coal; the consequence is, there is perfect combustion, the great volume of gas and smoke usually sent off from fires, and which consists of the most combustible part of coal, being thoroughly consumed, and yielding heat. A fire so made will go on burning for six, eight, or even ten hours, without poking, without adding fresh coal, or any attention whatever. There is little or no smoke, and the fire gives out a pleasant and uniform glow. One fair trial of this system will satisfy everybody; and the servant will soon find that it will not only save her master an incredible quantity of coals, but that it will also save her a vast amount of trouble: the bell will be rung less frequently for the coalscuttle, and the hearth will not require sweeping so often; the fire, if properly made, will never require to be relighted during the day; there will be no soot flakes on the furniture, and so little even in the chimney, that the services of the sweep will seldom be required.

Hint 540   It will sometimes be necessary to loosen, or stir slightly the upper part of the fire, if it begins to cake; but the lower part must not be touched, otherwise it will burn away too soon.

Hint 541   The above method of lighting fires, is best adapted for parlours, drawing rooms, libraries, and offices, where the fires are not required for cookery.

Immediately after being lit, as the heat is developed more gradually than in the old method of under lighting. Deep grates are best suited for the new system.

Hint 542   Fires upon this plan may be regulated to the temperature of the weather, and to the number of hours they are required to burn. For instance:— when the weather is very cold, and the fire requires to be lit early and kept up until late, put a much deeper layer of coal in the bottom — quite up to the top bar; when the weather is mild, etc., then lay the coals only up to the second bar from the top, and so on.

Hint 543   When you have tried this experiment a few times, and are fully satisfied with it, have pieces of Sheet Iron, cut to fit the bottom of your grates, instead of the paper. This will save the trouble of cutting the papers daily, and the sheet iron will last an indefinite time.

Another Important Saving in Coals

Hint 544   Preserve the coal ashes which are usually thrown away worthless. When you have a sufficient quantity, add to them an equal amount of small coal from your cellar, and then pour on a little water, and mix it with a shovel. The best way is, instead of throwing the ashes into the ash pit, to throw them on one side in cellar, where they may be easily mixed with the coal dust. Use this compost at the back of your fire, or for placing on the top of the fire, as in Hint 539. It will burn brightly and pleasantly; only a little dust will remain unconsumed; and thus the trouble of sifting will be saved.

Clear and Economical Fires for Cookery, etc

Hint 545   If you live near a depot where coke can be procured, you can obtain no cheaper fuel. By making your fire. as directed in Hint 539, and replenishing it with bits of coke, you will find that the cost of fuel will be less than one half; thus if your winter's consumption amounts to six tons of coals at £1 a ton, you in one winter save £3, and have every reason to, thank "The Family Save-All" for giving you so valuable a hint.

Cheap Fuel, Very Useful where Coals are Dear

Hint 546   One bushel of small coal, or sawdust, or both mixed, bushels of sand, one bushel and a half of common clay. Let them be mixed together with water, like ordinary mortar; the more they are stirred and mixed together the better. Make them into balls or with a mould, make in the shape of bricks; pile them in a dry place, and when they are hard and sufficiently dry, they may be used.

Hint 547　　　　A fire cannot be kindled with them; but when the fire is quite lighted, put them on behind, with a coal or two in front, and they will be found to keep up a strong and more lasting heat than any fuel of the common kind.

Economical Method of Storing Coals

Hint 548　　　　When coals are shot down into a cellar through the circular aperture, they form a conical heap under it; and as is always the case with loose materials, the largest pieces roll farthest down, on the outside of the heap, the smallest occupying the top. Were the coals to be used from this heap as it is formed, the result would be that all the large pieces of coal would be taken first, and towards the last there would only be small coals. To prevent this, a person, called a trimmer, is sent by the coal merchant, whose business is to mix the small and large together properly, by throwing the whole intermixed into the end of the vault. But unless the trimmer be looked after, he is very apt to neglect doing this properly. He should therefore be requested to thoroughly mix the coal, that the large and the small may be consumed together throughout the supply.

An Invaluable Hint, by which the Labour of Washing may be greatly diminished

Hint 549　　　　Pour upon half a pound of soda two quarts of boiling water, in an earthenware pan; take half a pound of soap, shred fine; put it into a saucepan with two quarts of cold water; stand it on a fire until it boils; and when perfectly dissolved and boiling, add it to former. Mix it well, and let it stand until cold, when the appearance of a strong jelly. Let the linen be soaked in water, the seams and any other dirty part rubbed usual way, and remain until the following morning. Get your copper ready, and add to the water about a pint basin full of the above preparation; when lukewarm put your linen, and allow it to boil twenty minutes. Rinse it the usual way, and that will be all that is necessary to get it clean, and keep it a good colour.

Hint 550　　　　The above Hint is invaluable to housekeepers. But, in the same sense as "a nod is as good as a wink to a blind horse," no benefit can be derived from the above without trying it!

A Nightcap, made in a moment, costing nothing, and admirable for Railway Travellers

Hint 551　　　　Take your pocket handkerchief, and laying it out the full square, double down one third over the other part. Then raise the whole, and turn it over, so that the third folded down shall lie underneath. Then take hold of one of the folded corners, and draw its point towards the centre; then do the same with the other, as in making a cocked hat, or a boat of paper.

Then take hold of the two remaining corners, and twisting the hem of the handkerchief, continue to roll it until it meets the doubled corners brought to the centre, and catches them up a little. Lift the whole and you will see the form of a cap, which, when applied to the head, will cover the head and ears, and, being tied under the chin, will not come off. Very little practice will enable you to regulate the size of the folds, so as to suit the head.

Ends of Candles converted into Night Lights

Hint 552   Supposing a few night lights to be wanted in places where they cannot be procured, they may be made from the ends of candles in the following manner. Collect a few old pillboxes; make as many fine cottons as you have boxes, and wax the cotton with beeswax; cut them to the requisite lengths, and fix them in the centre of the boxes, through a pin hole in the bottom. Melt the grease (if mixed with a little wax the better) and fill the boxes, keeping the cotton in a central position while the grease cools. When set to burn, place in a saucer, with sufficient water to surround the bottom, about the sixteenth of an inch in depth.

The Turkish Bath upon a small scale

Hint 553   Place the patient upon a large cane-bottomed chair, and tie a large blanket around his neck, so as to completely envelope the chair and his body; underneath the chair, place a saucer full of alcohol (spirits of wine) and set a light to it. The space within the blanket will soon be filled with hot air, and a profuse perspiration will be produced.

Hint 554   A similar bath may be produced by substituting for the alcohol, a simple invention lately set on foot by Price's Patent Candle Company. It consists of a flat tin saucer, filled with the purest stearine, and having a dozen wicks, supported by tin tubes.

Hint 555   This is good for rheumatic affections; or to prevent chills resulting in serious colds. The patient, after enduring the perspiration for some time, until he begins to feel it oppressive, should be rubbed thoroughly dry, and be put in a warm bed, between blankets.

Beds for Poor Persons

Hint 556   Beech leaves are recommended for this purpose, as they are very springy, and will not harbour vermin. They should be gathered on a dry day in the autumn, and be perfectly dried.

Hint 557   The chaff of newly-thrashed oats also forms wholesome spring beds.

Hint 558   Very luxurious and refreshing beds are in universal use in Italy, consisting of an absolute pile of mattresses, filled with the elastic spathe of Indian corn; but the beds made of beech leaves are not a whit behind them in all desirable qualities, while the fragrant smell of the leaves is quite refreshing.

Hint 559   Feathers, when put into beds in an imperfectly cured state, are unhealthy to persons sleeping upon them. Old feather beds, on which dirt and disease have long lingered, are commonly bought, and the feathers mixed, and sold as new, often causing sickness and death in families.

An Effective Method of Airing Beds and Bedding

Hint 560   Fill a stone bottle holding from one to three gallons with boiling water, securing the cork by tying it down safely with several thicknesses of stout linen, to prevent either moisture or steam from escaping; place it in an upright position upon the mattress, surrounded by bolster and pillows, and over these place the bed with the feathers, as far as possible, immediately round the bottle, leaving it uncovered to allow dampness to pass off. The bottle will support great warmth forty-eight hours in severe weather, and the water need not be replenished, except in special cases.

An invaluable French Receipt for Inveterate Coughs,
costing little more than the trouble of fetching the
ingredients

Hint 561   Collect two dozen garden snails, and add to these the hind quarters of two dozen stream frogs, skinned. Bruise them together in a mortar, after which, put them in a stewpan with a couple of turnips chopped small, a little salt, a quarter of a ounce of hay saffron, and three pints of spring water. Stir these on the fire until the broth begins to boil, then skim it well and set it by the fire to simmer for half an hour; after which it should be strained by pressure through a tammy cloth, into a basin for use.

Hint 562   This broth, from its soothing qualities, often counteracts successfully the straining effects of a severe cough, and alleviates more than any other culinary preparation, the sufferings of the consumptive.

Cure for a Cold which costs Nothing

Hint 563   Persons attacked by the form of cold commonly called "influenza," will find a wonderful efficacy in this simple remedy — abstaining from all liquid food — until the symptoms of febrile excitement, watering of the eyes, and sneezing abate.

The remedy has been tried and found efficacious in many instances within the knowledge of the writer; and it was originally recommended by high medical authority.

The Potato Remedy for Rheumatism

Hint 564　　　　We have heard it asserted by half a dozen of our personal friends that a raw potato, carried habitually in the trousers pocket, is an effectual preventive of rheumatism. Our witnesses have all tried it — tried it long — speak of it confidently — once laughed at the notion themselves — have been laughed at in turn — but are, nevertheless, free from rheumatism, and claim to have "the laughing side."

Apples recommended to Gouty Persons

Hint 565　　　　Apples contain a large proportion of sugar, mucilage, and starch, in which are combined those acids and aromatic principles, which, to persons in the habit of eating animal food, serve to prevent its putrefactive tendencies, and act as cooling tonics and antiseptics, and promote digestion. To those constitutions having a tendency to gout, a walk before breakfast, and the mastication of a good Ribston pippin, would materially aid in preventing attacks of that disease.

Debility in Children Prevented by a Simple
Precaution

Hint 566　　　　A very frequent cause of depressed vital power, is the sleeping of children with aged persons. Dr. Copeland was consulted about a pale, sickly, thin boy, about four or five years of age. He appeared to have no specific ailment, but there was a slow and remarkable decline of flesh and strength — what his mother very aptly termed a gradual blight. Upon enquiry into the history of the case, it proved that the child had been very robust and plethoric up to his third year, when his grandmother, a very aged person, took him to sleep with her; that he soon afterwards lost his good looks, and that he had continued to decline progressively afterwards, notwithstanding medical treatment. He was treated with simple tonics, change of air, etc., and directed to sleep apart from the aged person — the recovery was rapid.

Hint 567　　　　The explanation is a physiological one, connected with the abstraction of vital energy from younger body. Young females married to very old men suffer in a similar manner, although seldom to so great an extent.

How to secure the greatest Treasure for the Chest

Hint 568　　　　A great deal has been said and written upon eating, and drinking. Now for a few words upon a still more important subject, breathing. Most persons, and especially females, contract an imperfect mode of breathing. They suppress the action of the chest, and contract a habit of short quick breathing, not carrying the air more than half-way down the chest, and scarcely expanding the lower portions of the lungs at all. Take a sponge, and hold one half of it under the compression of the hand, then dip the rest in water, and afterwards press the water out into a glass or basin; note the quantity; afterwards dip the uncompressed sponge into the water, notice how much more it will absorb; this will very well illustrate the relative action of the restricted and the unrestricted lungs. Children that run about in the open air, and in no way laced, breathe deeply and fully in the lower part of the chest, and in all parts of it; so also with most outdoor labourers, and persons who take much exercise in the open air. The more exercise we take, especially out of doors, the larger the lungs become, and less liable to disease. In all occupations that require standing, keep the body erect. If at table, let it be also erect, and with this view, tables and desks should be high. If only a few minutes daily were devoted to the practice and exercise of deep breathing, it would prove a real blessing to every one adopting it.

Avoid Arsenical Green Paper Hangings

Hint 569　　　　A preparation of arsenic being used generally in the manufacture of green paper-hangings, the air of a room of which the walls are covered with these papers, is liable to be charged with the fine dust of the poisonous arsenite of copper. Those who inhabit the rooms are liable to breathe this dust, and to suffer in the lungs, eyes, nose, and throat, by local irritation. Glazed papers are less objectionable than unglazed.

Hint 570　　　　From a room thus papered, 450 grains of dust were carefully collected. One hundred and fifty grains of the dust were tested, and enough metallic arsenic was obtained from this quantity to coat about ten square inches of copper foil, in addition to a piece of copper gauze.

An excellent Filter that casts nothing

Hint 571　　　　It is assumed that in every house may be found either a tin or earthenware funnel, and a bit of sponge. Tear off a bit of the sponge, and place it in the narrow bottom of the funnel, and this simple apparatus will answer every purpose of a filter. If the funnel and sponge are not already at hand, they may be procured for a few pence.

The very best Wash for Cleaning and Promoting Growth of the Hair

Hint 572   Take of distilled vinegar, two ounces; salt of tartar, two drachms; spirit of lavender, half an ounce; spirit of rosemary, one ounce; spirit of nutmegs, half an ounce; essence of the essential oil of almonds, one drachm; essence of violets, one drachm; pure spring water, twenty ounces. Mix, and bottle for use.

Hint 573   It is not only the best wash for cleaning and strengthening, and promoting the growth of the hair, but it is a cooling and refreshing perfume.

A simple Method of Catching and Destroying Flies

Hint 574   Take some jars, mugs, or tumblers, fill them half full with soapy water; cover them as jam pots are covered, with a piece of paper, either tied down or tucked under the rim. Let this paper be rubbed inside with wet sugar, treacle, honey, or jam — in fact anything sweet, and it must have a small hole cut in the centre, large enough for a fly to enter. The flies settle on the top, attracted by the smell of the bait; they then crawl through the hole, to feed upon the sweet beneath. Meanwhile the warmth of the weather causes the soapy water to ferment, and produces a gas which overpowers the flies, and they drop down into the vessel. Thousands may be destroyed this way, and the traps last a long time.

Ale or Beer brewed in a Tea kettle

Hint 575   The art of Brewing, it has been well remarked by Cobett, is very similar to the process of Making Tea. If you put into a teapot a handful of malt, and fill the pot with hot water. Not quite boiling, and continue adding water and pouring it out until it becomes tasteless, the strength of the malt will thus be extracted just like the strength of the tealeaves. This malt tea boiled with a few hops, and when cooled to about blood heat, having a little yeast added to it to make it permanent, will produce a quantity of ale or beer, according to the strength of the ingredients. Apply this, which is the whole art of brewing, to the making of a larger quantity, and you cannot be out. A peck of malt, and four ounces of hops, will produce ten quarts of ale better than any you can purchase, and for this purpose all you require is a large tea kettle and two pans. For a larger quantity, you must have a mash-tub and oar, a sieve, and two coolers, a wicker hose, a spigot, and fawcit, with two nine gallon casks. These will cost about £2 new; and you may brew four bushels of malt with them, and, allowing four pounds of hops, this will yield nine gallons of the best ale, and nine more of excellent table beer.

Hint 576   Malt Liquor or Cider may be prevented from becoming sour by adding four pounds of toasted bread to every hogshead. This has been tried with complete success. When stale or hard, it may be restored by covering a large piece of hard toasted bread with mustard (made with water only), cutting it into square pieces, and putting it into the cask.

Hint 577   Sour Beer may be restored by putting equal quantities of wine, pounded chalk, and burnt shells into a linen bag, and suspending the bag from the bung-hole, replacing the bung. Or, drop into the cask, by very slow degrees, a small quantity of carbonate of soda, or of salt of wormwood, and then bung up. The beer will be restored in twenty-four hours, if not very bad.

To make Cottage Beer

Hint 578   Take a quarter of a peck of good sweet Wheat Bran, and put it into ten gallons of water, with three hands of white hops; boil the whole together, in a pot or copper, until the bran and the hops sink to the bottom. Then strain it through a hair sieve, or a thin sheet, into a cooler, and when it is about lukewarm add two quarts of molasses, or three pints of very thick treacle. As soon as the molasses or the treacle is melted, pour the whole into a nine gallon cask, with two tablespoonfuls of yeast. When the fermentation has subsided, bung up the cask, and in four days it will be fit for use.

Hint 579   Table Beer if drawn off into stone jugs, with a lump of white sugar in each, and securely corked, will keep good for several months.

To make Perry

Hint 580   Let the Pears be perfectly ripe, but take care that the cores have not become rotten; after gathering and cleaning off the stalks, the fruit should be laid in a heap to mellow, from fourteen to twenty days. Next, remove it to the press or mill, and squeeze out the juice between a haircloth, from whence the liquor runs into a vat, and from this is removed to casks, which must stand in the open air, or in a very cool place, with the bung holes open. The pulp is then to be washed in hot water. Some add a fourth part of this to three-fourths of the pure juice, but the prime makers confine themselves to the juice, putting the rinsings into separate casks. This perkin makes a pleasant beverage for present use, but it will not keep long. The fermentation is accomplished by mixing a pint of new yeast with a little honey and flour warmed, and the whites of four eggs. Put this in a bag of thin muslin, drop it in the cask, and suspend it from the bung hole by a string, taking care that it does not touch the bottom of the vessel. If it works kindly, the liquor will have cleared itself in five or six days, and may be drawn off from the lees into smaller casks, or bottled.

Those who mix the perkin with the Perry, find it necessary to strengthen it in the proportion of a gallon of French Brandy, dissolved in three pounds of sugar candy to a hogshead of Perry; but this is unnecessary with the pear juice.

Hint 581   When brandy is added, the cask should be immediately stopped close, and remain so for five or six days. In bottling, take care that the liquor does not reach within an inch of the cork; or the bottle will burst.

Hint 582   You must watch the liquor, whether in casks or bottles, and if any hissing noise should be perceived, the bungs should be removed for a day or two; after this has subsided, they may be beaten down, and the casks stowed in a dry place.

Hint 583   In winter, Perry requires to be kept warm and free from frosts or draughts of air. In summer, the vessels or bottles containing it, must be moved to a cool place, otherwise they will burst.

The Best Method of Cider Making

Hint 584   As soon as the Apples are ripe, collect them in heap on the grass; by no means house them, or the cider will inevitably be musty. After they are ground and pressed, pass the liquid through a flannel bag to strain off any bits of skin or core that may have passed through the hair cloths; put it at once in the casks; do not touch it until it has done fermenting; then put in the bungs. Any addition is injurious; and the sulphuring of casks cannot be recommended.

Spruce Beer

Hint 585   Provide sixteen gallons of water, boil half of it, Then put the other half into a barrel; pour the boiling water, on the other, and to the whole add six tablespoonfuls of Essence of Spruce, and sixteen pounds of treacle. When sufficiently cold, add half a pint of yeast, and roll the cask about, or shake it well. Keep it in a warm place for two days, with the bung open; by this time the fermentation will have subsided sufficiently for bottling. Bottle it, or put it in stone jars, well corked, and it will be fit for use in a week. Another method is to add eleven gallons of boiling water to ten of cold water; to this put thirty pounds of molasses and one ounce and a half of essence of spruce. Work with yeast, and bottle as above.

Hint 586   If you wish the Beer to be white, use refined sugar instead of molasses.

Hint 587   Spruce is a powerful antiscorbutic, and should be used freely by persons who have a tendency to that affliction. It is also a diuretic. It is, however, too cold for some stomachs.

The Best Ginger Beer

Hint 588   White sugar, twenty pounds; lemon or lime juice, eighteen ounces; honey, one pound; white ginger, bruised, twenty- two ounces: water, eighteen gallons. Boil the bruised ginger in three gallons of water for half an hour; then add the sugar, the juice, and the honey, with the fifteen gallons of water reserved. Boil and strain. When cold, add the white of an egg, and half an ounce of essence of lemons. Allow it to ferment in the usual way. Then in about four days bottle it, and it will keep for months.

Hint 589   Inferior or smaller qualities may be made by altering and reducing the ingredients.

A Healthful but "Small" Beer from the Sprouts of Nettles, with Sugar, etc

Hint 590   Take half a gallon of the sprouts of nettles, and boil them in one gallon of water; strain, and add half a pound of sugar, or treacle, with a little ginger. When nearly cold, ferment with yeast, and bottle tight. It will be fit for use in a few days, and is very purifying and cooling to the blood.

A nice Table Beer from Treacle

Hint 591   Boil for twenty minutes four pounds of molasses, in from five to six gallons of soft water, with a handful of hops tied in a muslin bag, or a little extract of gentian. When cooled to eighty degrees, add a pint of fresh beer yeast, or from four to six quarts of fresh worts from the brewer's vat. Cover the beer with blankets or warm cloths. Pour it from the lees, and bottle it. Sugar may be substituted for molasses.

Hint 592   This is a cheap wholesome beverage. A little ginger may be boiled in it half an hour, instead of hops if preferred.

Parsnip Wine — the best of Homemade Wines, if properly made

Hint 593   The Parsnips ought to be solid, firm, compact, and taper in form, not forked and divided into several parts. Four or five pounds of such roots, whether purchased or produced in the garden, will be required for every gallon of the wine. They must be placed in a tub of water, be soaked until the dirt in them becomes quite loose, and then be thoroughly brushed, until every particle of dirt be washed away. They must not be scraped, but any black, spongy, or decayed portions may be cut away. The roots being cleaned, take off the leaves and so much of the top as may appear green.

Then split the roots into four parts, by two even cuts, and divide these into pieces three inches long. Put the water into a boiler, add the proportion of parsnips as above stated, but allow for the waste of water by boiling, by putting, say eight gallons of water, though only six gallons of wine are to be made. Bring the liquor to a boil, and continue the boiling during three or four hours, or until the roots are tender throughout. Try them repeatedly with a fork; but it is indispensable that they be not bruised, or rendered pulpy; remove the cover of the boiler slightly aside, to allow the pungent odour of the parsnip to escape. The boiling being complete, strain it through a hair sieve into a tub, but observe the precaution not to produce turbidity by bruising the roots; add immediately three ounces of powdered white argol, and stir the whole for some minutes, promote the solution, and then introduce eighteen or twenty pounds of good loaf sugar. When this is dissolved, the liquor remain uncovered until it be reduced to seventy, or at least, to seventy-five degrees on the thermometer. Fermentation must be produced by the aid of yeast, and subsequently treated in the manner usual with other wines.

Wine from the Leaves of the Vine

Hint 594 The leaves may be taken at any period from vines which are not expected to bear fruit. In other cases, they may be obtained from the summer prunings; the tendrils are equally useful. Forty or fifty pounds of such leaves being introduced into a tub of sufficient capacity, seven or eight gallons of boiling water are to be poured on them, in which they are to infuse for twenty-four hours. The liquor being poured off, the leaves must be squeezed in a press of considerable power, and being subsequently washed with an additional gallon of water, they are again to be submitted to the action of the press. The sugar, from twenty-five to thirty pounds, is then to be added to the mixed liquors, and the quantity made up to ten gallons and a half.

Hint 595 To secure a full bodied dry wine, the proportion of the leaves to the sugar should be the greatest that has been named, in order to provide a sufficiency of leaven, or fermenting vegetable principle, to subdue and convert to vinous alcohol all the sugar that is introduced. Fifty pounds of leaves to thirty-five pounds of sugar will work well, and produce ten gallons of strong wine, that will improve by keeping two years in the wood, and two years more in bottle. The process of fermentation, and subsequent treatment, is the same as in case of other wines.

Hint 596 It must be remembered that July being the season for pruning vines most freely (and all the tender young shoots, tendrils, and leaves, are equally suitable), the heat of the weather will be great, and therefore the processes must be conducted in an airy room, or cellar, not affected by the sun.

The Best Receipt for Elder Wine

Hint 597   Take twelve gallons of soft river water, forty-eight pounds of raisins, fourteen pounds of Lisbon sugar, twelve quarts of Elder juice, three quarts of juice of sloes, and half an ounce of isinglass; mix all together; when this has stood two months, or until it is fine, draw it off into a clear cask, and add six pounds of loaf sugar and three quarts of brandy. Bottle it in the April following, and keep it two years before drawing the corks. This is in the opinion of many persons equal to Port. Smaller quantities may of course be made, by observing the above proportions.

Hint 598   When Sloes are not procurable, an equivalent quantity of Damsons, or any small Black Plums, softened by heat, and put with the chopped raisins, will do as well, and give that roughness which Elder juice is deficient in.

Rhubarb Wine

Hint 599   In the month of May, when Rhubarb is green, the stalks of the leaves should be used in the following proportions:— Five pounds of stalks are bruised in a suitable vessel, to which is added one gallon of spring water. After lying in mash three or four days, the liquor juice is poured off, when to every gallon of this juice three pounds of loaf sugar are added, and allowed to ferment for four or five days in a suitable vat; as soon as the fermentation has ceased, the liquor must be drawn off into a cask and allowed to remain until the month of March, when all fermentation will have finished; it must then be racked off, and more loaf sugar added. In the month of August a second crop will be ready to gather, and may be applied to this method of making wine.

Coltsfoot Wine

Hint 600   To one gallon of Flowers, put four gallons of boiling water; let it stand until cold, then strain it through a sieve, and put three pounds of loaf sugar to every gallon. Boil it until the scum has done rising, then put it into a tub; and when nearly cold, put in the peelings of one lemon and one Seville orange to each gallon, with a little yeast. Let it stand three or four days to work, then put it into a cask with the oranges and lemons. Stop it close, and let it stand three months, then bottle it off, and put a lump of sugar into each bottle.

Hint 601   A quart of brandy is the proper proportion of spirit to each gallon. Put the brandy into the cask, and then pour the wine upon it.

Cowslip Wine

Hint 602   To one gallon of water add one gallon of pips, three and a half pounds of loaf sugar, and three lemons. Boil the sugar and water half an hour and skim it well. Put the pips and lemons (which must be sliced) into the cask next day and pour the liquor to it. Work it with a little yeast upon a toast or crust of bread; stir it well once a day for a fortnight, then put it in the brandy and stir it up. A bottle of brandy is sufficient or twelve gallons.

The Best Method of Making Tea

Hint 603   When tea is made out of the room, its volatile and essential properties are frequently dissipated, before it comes to the table. It is not the bitterness, but the fragrance of tea that is refreshing. The tea should be wetted, or steeped, before the larger quantity of water is added. But if the tea and the pot are both warmed dry, before any portion of the water is added, a stronger infusion will be obtained. Put the tea dry into the empty pot; then place the pot before the fire or on the hob, or still better on the hot plate of an oven, until the tea is well heated, but not burned; then pour upon it the boiling water, and a fragrant infusion will be immediately produced.

Hint 604   Whether tea should be boiled or not, depends in some measure upon the constitution and inclination of the consumer. If it is generally found to be too exciting, and if also a full and slightly bitter infusion is preferred the tea should he hailed a few minutes, because boiling dissipates the volatile extract which disturbs the nervous system, and develops by solution the bitter principle, which acts as a good stomachic.

The Leaves of the Holly an agreeable addition to Tea

Hint 605   The leaves of the common holly possess, in a high degree, be properties of Chinese tea, but they are too strong and oleaginous to supply an agreeable infusion by themselves. The use of tea may, however, be greatly economised by an admixture with them. The leaves should be dried, and roasted as brown as the rust of well-baked bread; let them then be crumbled into small bits, and a pinch of these be added to each brewing of tea.

A Salubrious Tea of Agrimony

Hint 606   Put fresh gathered leaves of Agrimony into a coffee roaster, along with three round pebbles to act as stirrers.

At the end of a quarter of an hour a native tea will be produced, possessed of all the qualities of green tea. This beverage is particularly adapted for people who live poorly, and imperfectly digest their innutritious food; it is also recommended against dysentery.

A Method of Making Coffee to the Greatest Perfection

Hint 607   Sometimes the yolks of eggs only are used, the whites being thrown away. Lay the whites upon a plate, cover them with another plate, raised a little, so as to allow evaporation to go on, and yet keep them free from dirt. Set them in a warm place, and the water from the whites will gradually evaporate, leaving a mass of yellowish, shining, brittle matter, that will scale off by the touch. This substance is positively the best for clarifying coffee, and it may be kept in a bottle for any length of time. When the whites of eggs, in their ordinary state are used, they form unsightly masses of coagulated albumen, that either obstruct the spout of the coffee pot, or escape in lumps into the cups. The way to use the dried egg powder is to throw it into the water before it is poured on to the coffee.

Hint 608   A very small quantity will answer the purpose.

Hint 609   The addition of a teaspoonful of port wine to a cup of Coffee greatly improves its flavour.

Very nice Tea Custards

Hint 610   Put two large teaspoonfuls of Green, and one of Black Tea, into a pint and a half of boiling milk. Add to the milk while boiling, half a pint of cream. When the mixture has acquired an approved tea flavour, take it from the fire, and strain it. Take care not to leave the tea too long in it, otherwise the custards will be too bitter. Having strained the milk, put it again on the fire with a little salt, and sufficient pounded loaf sugar to sweeten it. Add the yolks of ten eggs, and stir until the custard is thick enough. Serve in glasses.

Excellent Coffee Custards

Hint 611   Boil a pint and a half of milk with half a pint of cream. When boiling, throw into it hot, an ounce of whole coffee which has just been roasted, in a small frying pan if you have no roaster. When the milk has acquired the flavour of coffee in an approved degree, take it from the fire, and strain through a hair sieve. Put it on the fire again with a little salt, and two ounces of pounded loaf sugar, or more, if approved; then add the yolks of ten eggs beaten, and stir over the fire until thick enough. Put into glasses.

Very nice Chocolate Custards

Hint 612   Rasp three ounces of Spanish chocolate, which has the vanilla favour. Melt it in the smallest possible quantity of water. Put a pint and a half of milk over the fire with half a pint of cream, and let it boil: then add powdered loaf sugar to your taste, and a little salt. Meanwhile, beat up the chocolate, with a little of the milk as it boils, and mix it well. Pour it into the boiling milk, which must be kept in brisk motion. Add the yolks of eight eggs well beaten. Keep stirring in chocolate until sufficiently thick. Serve in glasses.

The Strawberry Leaf a Substitute for Green Tea

Hint 613   In some parts of Germany, they gather the Strawberry Leaf and also the Flowers when young, and after selecting and clearing them (without the use of water), they are dried in the air in a shady place, out of reach of the sun. To these leaves the appearance of green tea is given, by pinching off the stalks, warming them over the fire, rolling them while in a flexible state, and then drying them. In this condition the substitute for tea is ready for use, and being prepared in precisely the same manner, the difference it is said, can hardly be distinguished.

Improving Tainted Butter

Hint 614   Butter, either fresh or salt, possessing a very disagreeable effluvium or flavour, may be rendered perfectly sweet by the addition of a little carbonate of soda. The proportion to be used is, two drachms and a half of carbonate soda, to three pounds of butter. In making fresh butter, the soda is to be added after all the milk is worked out, and it is ready for making up.

Hint 615   The unpleasant smell is produced by acid, which, being removed, the alkali disperses at the same time the disagreeable flavour. This acid is generated by peculiarities in the constitutions of some by the condition of certain fodders, or by the length time cream is kept before being churned; but, often, by the dairy utensils not being kept thoroughly clean.

Tainted Butter restored by Chloride of Lime

Hint 616   This operation is extremely simple and practicable, it consists in beating the butter in a sufficient quantity of water, in which put twenty-five to thirty of chloride of lime to two pounds of butter. After having mixed it until all its parts are in contact with the water, it may be left in it for an hour or two, afterwards withdrawn, and washed in fresh water.

Hint 617   The chloride of lime, having nothing injurious in it, can with safety be augmented; but it will generally be found that twelve or fourteen drops to a pound of butter are sufficient. Butter, the taste and odour of which were insupportable, has been sweetened by this simple means.

To Prevent Butter Tasting of Turnips

Hint 618   The week previous to giving Cows Turnips, when churning, save a couple or three quarts of Buttermilk; the earthen pot in which the cream is usually collected should be scalded, dried, and put before the fire to make it hot; when hot, put the buttermilk into it, in order to make it sour; the morning and evening cream to be put to it, and then kept until churning. A small quantity of saltpetre is then put into the cream. The same quantity of buttermilk to be saved every time after churning, and the same process repeated. The turnips to be well cleaned, tops and roots cut off; and no decayed parsnips to be given to the cattle on any account.

Hint 619   When Swedish Turnips are used, a pinch of powdered saltpetre thrown into the pan, when the milk is strained after milking, will prevent any unpleasant taste in the butter.

Method of Preserving Butter for Years

Hint 620   Pound together one part of fine lump sugar, one of nitre, and two of the best salt. After the butter is taken from the churn, it must be completely freed from the milk, so that not a drop remains. Then mix, and thoroughly incorporate with the butter, the previous mixture in the proportion of an ounce of the powder to a pound of the butter, avoirdupois weight, and press the butter when so salted into wood vessels, or vitrified jars, but on no account into glazed pans. Butter so salted will not be fit for use until it has stood three weeks; it then possesses a rich marrow flavour, which no other mode of curing will impart to it. With proper care it will keep for years, and exhibit all the qualities of fresh butter.

Hint 621   Butter when too Salted may be restored by patting into a churn in the proportion of a quart of milk to a pound of butter, and a small piece of annatto; churn them together for an hour, and proceed as for fresh butter.

Economy in Butter and Cheese

Hint 622   In Germany the people of the humbler classes economise their butter, and render it more nutritive, by incorporating with it a certain quantity of potatoes.

The process is to dress them by steam, then mash them with pestle or roller, mix them with the cream, and churn all together. The butter comes as usual, and is made up in the ordinary manner, and salt is added to preserve it.

Hint 623   The addition of Potatoes to Cheese renders it not only more nutritive, but more easy of digestion. When the milk is set or curdled, and has been drained from the whey for some hours, then take well dressed potatoes, put them into a copper colander, and force them through the holes, and then knead up the potatoes with the curd. When they are well mixed together, allow the mass to remain untouched for two or three days. Then work it up again, and put it into the moulds or vats commonly used.

How to obtain the Largest quantity of Milk from a Cow

Hint 624   There is a very considerable difference in the results of good and bad milking. If every drop of milk in the cow's udder be not carefully removed at each milking the secretion will gradually diminish in proportion to the quantity left each day behind. This fact is well established; and it is to be accounted for on philosophical principles, as well as being borne out in practice. Nature creates nothing in vain; and the secretion of milk in the cow only suffices to replace the quantity consumed daily — the milk left behind in the udder is reabsorbed into the system, and consequently the next milking will be so much less in quantity. But another reason why every drop of milk should be taken away, is to be found in the well known fact that the last milk is doubly as good as the first; hence, if not removed, there is not merely equal, but double loss.

Hint 625   Cream cannot rise through a great depth of milk. Therefore, if milk is desired to retain its cream for a time, it should be put into a deep narrow vessel; but if it be desired to free it almost completely of cream, it should be poured into a broad flat dish, not much exceeding one inch in depth.

Zinc Pans should Not be Used in the Dairy

Hint 626   The acid of milk forms with zinc a salt which is poisonous. It operates by causing vomiting; but though the solution of it may not be strong enough to produce that effect, it is very injurious to health, if frequently repeated. Zinc butter-churns were for some time used from a supposition that they increased the quantity of butter by some galvanic effect; but they were found to make the food so dangerous and unwholesome that they have been generally discontinued.

To Prevent Milk from Turning Sour in Warm Weather

Hint 627   In Paris the milkmen are in the habit of employing a little sub-carbonate of soda or potash. This, by combining with and neutralising the acetic acid formed, has the desired effect, and keeps the milk from turning as soon as it otherwise would. The salt that is thus formed — viz., the acetate of soda or of potash — is not at all injurious; and as pure milk does contain a small quantity of this salt, it is difficult to pronounce upon the addition of any alkali, except there should be some in a free or uncombined state, which does not exist in milk. The addition of a little carbonate of potash will break down the curd that is beginning to form, in consequence of souring.

To Destroy Mites and Jumpers in Cheese

Hint 628   Pour on each side of the Cheese ravaged by these insects, a coat of melted Mutton Suet boiling hot. This application will not only arrest any further destruction by the mites, but also prevent the too rapid decaying action of the air.

Hint 629   The American Method of Preserving Cheese is as soon as the cheese is sufficiently dried, to cover it with folds of paper pasted on, so as completely to exclude the air.

Uses for Eggs not Commonly Employed

Hint 630   Seabirds' eggs, especially those of the Sea Gull are good when boiled hard and eaten with pepper, salt, vinegar, and mustard. When eaten in a soft state, they have a fishy taste. Rooks' Eggs are as suitable as Plovers' for Salads. The eggs of the Lapwing and Ruff are excellent food.

Hint 631   The Thin Membrane found immediately inside the shell of Eggs is excellent for covering slight cuts, as on the chin when shaving, or abrasions of the skin upon any part of the body. The membrane may be saved, when boiled eggs are eaten, and allowed to dry. When wanted for use, it will only be necessary to steep it in warm water for a minute or two.

How to Eat an Egg with Satisfaction!

Hint 632   What! Mean to insinuate that, after all these years, we don't know how to eat eggs properly? Never mind, don't be above taking a hint. By the usual mode of introducing the salt into a boiled egg, it will not incorporate with the egg; the result is, you get either a quantity of salt without egg, or egg without salt. In order to make the two mix properly, after cutting off the top of the egg, put in a drop of water, tea, coffee, or other warm liquid that may be on the table.

Then add the salt, and stir. The result is far more agreeable — the drop of liquid is not tasted.

Bad Eggs are often purchased for want of Judgment

Hint 633 The safest way to try them is, to hold them to the light; forming a close focus with the hand. If the shell when viewed thus, appears to be studded with small dark spots, they are doubtful. If you see no transparency in the shells, they are fit only to be thrown away. The most certain test is to try them by the light of a candle. If quite fresh, there are no spots upon the shells, and the eggs have a bright yellow tint.

Hint 634 Newly laid eggs should not be eaten until they have been laid about eight or ten hours; because the white is not properly set before that time, and does not obtain its delicate flavour.

Hint 635 Never boil eggs for salads, sauces, or any other purpose, more than ten minutes; and when done, place them in a basin of cold water to cool.

Hint 636 For making plum puddings. Ducks' eggs are more economical than those of fowls. They are larger in size, and richer.

To distinguish the Sex of Eggs

Hint 637 There are two classes of poultry keepers — those who want female eggs only, to rear hens for the sake of their eggs, and those who want male eggs only, to produce cocks and capons for the table. There is only one outward sign which can be regarded as indicating the sex of the egg: it is this, that eggs containing the germs of males have generally wrinkles on their smaller end; while female eggs are equally smooth at both extremities.

Surprise Eggs for Parties

Hint 638 Separate in different vessels the yolks and whites of a sufficient number of Fresh Eggs. Stir any quantity of yolk together, from half a pint to a pint or more. Put this into a bladder, tie it up in a round form, and boil it hard. Then put this boiled yolk into another and a larger bladder, into which pour the whites, keeping the hard yolk as much in the middle as possible. Tie the bladder in an oval form, and boil until the white is quite hard. An immense egg may thus be formed, which, at a large dinner party, will surprise every one, and may be used in a large dish of salad.

Best and Simplest Way to keep Eggs Fresh

Hint 639   The reason that eggs become musty and bad, is in consequence of the action of the air upon the yolk. Those who are so unfortunate as to meet with a stale egg at breakfast will almost invariably find that the yolk lies at the side. The most proper and simple way to preserve eggs fresh is simply to turn them frequently. It is well known that a sitting hen daily turns her eggs. The readiest way of turning them is, to have an egg preserver, made of wire, with squares of a size to receive medium eggs turned on end. The eggs may then be turned singly every day; but for those who have to do with large numbers of eggs, receivers might be made which could be turned frequently, without trouble or injury. Of Limewater, Bran, Sand, and Scalding, the last named is the next best plan to that of daily turning.

Hint 640   We have frequently known not only that eight or ten eggs, after having been broken into a basin, have been thrown away, because the very last that was added proved putrid; but also that, owing to the carelessness of a cook, a valuable pudding has been spoiled by the admission of an egg that was musty. To prevent this, a cup should be used to break each egg into, before it is put into the basin in which they are all to be beaten.

Eggs Cheap and Fresh in Winter, and Poultry for the Spring

Hint 641   The person who wants to make up a good egg basket, had better obtain half a dozen undersized or discoloured pullets, of the March and April broods, the price of which should not exceed 15s. or 21s. for the set. A game-cock would be a capital companion, but is not absolutely necessary. The birds should be got home about the middle of September, about which time eggs begin to get dear. They should be kept clean and warm, and be fed twice a day thus:— in the morning, as much good barley as they will eat; in the evening, a mixture made with hot water in which meat has been boiled or dishes washed, of barley meal and pollard, barley meal and boiled potatoes or mangel wurtzel, or meal and fresh grains, will be the best of suppers. Meal is too expensive to be given alone, but mixed with cheaper food to give bulk, it is excellent. Green food and lime rubbish are necessary, but need not add to the expense. The six or seven fowls may be very well fed for one shilling a week. From September to February (about twenty weeks), they will produce about 350 eggs, and this will amply repay the sovereign expended in food. The Pullets should be killed for the table in February, and will be worth the prime cost.

Hint 642   The manure for the garden will be an additional profit.

A good Family Brown Bread, unfermented

Hint 643   Fermentation by yeast, is obtained at the cost of a portion of the flour, which is converted into gas, the bubbles of which, becoming fixed in the bread, render it light. Every bubble that rises on the surface of what is called "the sponge," represents a few grains of flour, escaping in the form of gas. To avoid this loss, a system of making unfermented bread has been introduced. A capital and economical bread may be made upon the non-fermenting plan, in the following manner:— Three pounds of wheat meal; half an ounce of muriatic acid; half an ounce of carbonate of soda; water enough to produce the proper consistency.

Hint 644   For white flour, four pounds of flour; half an ounce of muriatic acid; half an ounce of carbonate soda; water, a quart.

Hint 645   The way of mixing is as follows:— First mix the flour and soda well by rubbing together in a pan, using a wooden spoon perfectly dry for the purpose; then pour the acid into the water, let it dissolve, and mix thoroughly by stirring.

Hint 646   Four pounds of wheat meal, worked in this manner, will produce seven pounds nine ounces of excellent light bread, which will keep moist longer than fermented bread, and be found far more sweet and digestible.

Hint 647   The object of putting muriatic acid into bread is as follows:— If vinegar be poured upon chalk, a bubbling and boiling takes place. Any acid poured upon a carbonate will produce a similar bubbling. When, therefore, the bicarbonate of soda, which contains a large quantity of carbonic acid, is mixed with the flour, and muriatic acid is poured upon it, an effervescence takes place, which rises the bread, and dispenses with the use of yeast. This is the principle of what are called "baking powders."

Hint 648   Precaution - Dr. Normandy mentions that arsenic is frequently present in muriatic acid, and that this impurity, when present in the acid, remains in the bread. To avoid this liability to evil, tartaric acid may be used; in which case it will be only necessary to read tartaric acid instead of muriatic acid in the foregoing instructions.

Hint 649   Buttermilk, kept until sourish, may be used instead of the chemical acids. The bread made from it has a richer taste than that made from muriatic acid, or tartaric acid, and soda.

Every Man his Own Miller, One-third of the Cost
of Bread Saved. Pure Bread, without Alum, and
with all its nutritive parts retained

Hint 650   Where a family is large, and the consumption of flour considerable. Families should be supplied with hand flour-mills, by which the saving in the cost of bread will be found to amount to nearly one-third. The price of a mill is about £4 10s., which will be saved in a single month, where the consumption is large. To grind twenty pounds of wheat, occupies a boy, or a servant, about twenty minutes. Hand flour-mills can be obtained at the machinery department of the Crystal Palace, or at 266, High Holborn. There are mills which grind and dress the wheat at one operation. The saving in the cost of bread, and the preservation of health by the disuse of alum, and adulterated flour, are matters of great importance.

Hint 651   The old system of "setting a sponge," that is putting the yeast and salt, with a small quantity of warm water, into a pit in the middle of the flour, and leaving this small quantity to rise, is a bad plan; and upon this system the batch will always be uncertain. By incorporating the whole mass, the bread will be undeviatingly good and light. Fermentation should be disseminated throughout.

Excellent Bread of Rice, when Wheat is Dear

Hint 652   Take one pound and a half of Rice, and boil it gently over a slow fire, in three quarts of water, about five hours, stirring it, and afterwards beating it into a smooth paste. Mix this while warm into two gallons, or four pounds of flour, adding at the same time the usual quantity of yeast. Allow the dough to work a certain time near the fire, after which divide it into loaves, and it will be found, when baked, to produce excellent white bread, very acceptable to children.

To Make Good Bread from Sprouted Wheat

Hint 653   Take, say four or five stones of flour, and boil it as many hours in a bag; place the bag on a drainer over a tub until the next day; then with a wooden mallet pound the flour in the bag until it crumbles rather small; after that, roll it fine with a rolling pin on the table. Then make the bread as usual.

Hint 654   By these means excellent bread has been made of wheat, every sheaf of which had sprouted and to improve which various remedies were resorted to in vain: hands could not make, the oven could not bake a loaf; ten or twelve hours in a hot oven did not set the dough. More excellent bread, cakes, and pickles, than damaged flour prepared as above will produce, were never eaten.

Hint 655   The following mixtures form excellent Household Bread:— 1. Half maize and half barley, with a leaven of wheat flour, one-fifth of the total weight 2. Half wheat flour and half maize. A more agreeable and healthful bread cannot be obtained. 3. Half oatmeal and half barley, with a leaven of wheat flour, rather more than one-fifth. 4. Equal parts oatmeal and wheat flour; excellent. 5. Barley flour, with one-fifth its weight of wheat leaven; bread white and well tasted. 6. Barley and rye, or barley and wheat in equal quantities; this last is equal to the best bread of wheat flour alone. 7. Buckwheat, with an equal quantity of barley or rye, and one-fifth of wheat leaven; or, still better, with one-half of wheat flour. 8. In general, potatoes may serve, when they are dry, for one-half, and when fresh or new, for two-thirds, and oven for four-fifths, in the fabrication of household bread. This last quantity of four-fifths is the greatest that has ever been employed with advantage to uniform success, when used with a wheaten leaven of one-fifth of the total weight.

Hint 656   Sprouted Wheat is Good for Seed; it will germinate as freely a second time, as at first.

Capital Pudding from Spoiled Breads or Fragments

Hint 657   Take the bread of a "sad" or "heavy" loaf, or crusts and other fragments, soak them in hot water, stirring, pressing, and pouring off — repeating this if necessary; then put the soaked bread into the pudding bag, and by twisting very tight, and pressing it under a board, get out as much of the water as possible. Then mix this pressed bread with milk, sugar, and spice (as powdered cinnamon and nutmeg), and add flour enough to bind it into a proper consistence. Then put it into the pudding bag for boiling. It is a simple, economical, and wholesome pudding for children, and it is best eaten with syrup of fruit.

Other Uses for Stale Bread

Hint 658   A Very nice dish, called Turkey Pie, may be made from pieces of Stale Bread. Put the pieces into a saucepan with some boiling water poured over them, let them simmer by the fire until saturated, then put salt and pepper to taste, and add a little butter.

Hint 659   For Puddings from Stale Bread, Suet should be used instead of eggs.

Hint 660   Crusts of Bread may be grilled for Soups. Put the crusts upon a small wire gridiron over hot cinders to crisp. When done, wet the inside with top fat, and sprinkle a little salt over them, and slip them into the tureen; or crisp them over a furnace, wetting good stock.

Hint 661   For Cheese, pull rough pieces from a loaf, or broken parts, soak them in warm water; take them out and let them drain, until they remain just moist, then brown them in an oven or before the fire.

Economy of Yeast

Hint 662   In places where yeast cannot be readily obtained, a little may be made to go a long way, in the following manner. Knead the first supply with the usual proportion of water and flour into a piece of dough about the size of a large teacup, then leave it to rise; and when risen as much as usual when put into the bread tins, add as much flour again, and water enough to knead it with. Knead it, and leave it as before, and again add flour and water in the same proportions. The only difference necessary is, to have the water a little warmer than usual — "as hot as the hand can bear." The bread thus made, with a deficient quantity of yeast, according to the usual method, will be as light as usual.

A Healthful Substitute for Alum in Bread

Hint 663   Water saturated with lime produces in bread the same whiteness, softness, and capacity of retaining moisture, as results from the use of alum; while the former removes all acidity from the dough, and supplies an ingredient needed in the structure of the bones. The best proportion to use is five pounds of water saturated with lime, to every nineteen pounds of flour. The way to saturate water with lime is to drop into it stones of quicklime, stir, until the whole is slack, let the lime settle, then strain off the clear water, and it is fit for use. No change is required in the process of baking; the lime most effectually coagulates the gluten, and the bread becomes light.

Hint 664   Dr. Muspratt, of Liverpool, in his "Chemistry as applied to the Arts and Manufactures," article "Bread," strongly recommends the use of lime water.

Excellent and Economical Paste for Pies and
Cakes, with Potato Flour

Hint 665   A very nice paste for meat or fruit pies may be made with two-thirds of wheat flour, one-third of the flour of boiled potatoes, and some butter or dripping; the whole being brought to a proper consistence with warm water, and a small quantity of yeast added, when lightness is desired.

Hint 666   This will also make very pleasant cakes for breakfast, and may be made with or without spices or fruits.

Capital Luncheon Cake, that will keep Six Months,
and save the trouble of frequent Making

Hint 667   Take two pounds of flour, one and a half pound of treacle, half an ounce of ground ginger, quarter of a pound of sugar, quarter of an ounce of ground caraway seed, and candied lemon peel, cut very small. Mix all well with the flour; warm the butter, and mix with the rest; then warm the treacle; dissolve in a little boiling water a large teaspoonful of carbonate of soda, and stir it well into the treacle; add to the other ingredients; work all well together, and bake in a buttered tin two hours, in a rather slow oven. Wives whose husbands are professional men, having frequently only time to take a snack and a glass of sherry in the middle of the day, will win admiration by making these cakes, and sending them to their husbands' offices.

Chopped Thistles an excellent Food for Cattle

Hint 668   Thistles, commonly regarded as one of the Farmer's pests, may be rendered subservient to farm economy, by being chopped as food for cattle. Girls and boys may be employed to gather them with hooked knives; they should be chopped when gathered in quantity, and may be given, either green or dried, to cattle. In this way horses will prefer them even to tares or oats; and they will look well, and be as thoroughly up to their work as when kept upon the best of food. We thus find that the contemned donkey is not an ass, because he eats thistles!

Hint 669   The simplest and best time for destroying thistles is after they have made their growth, and just before they show flower. Immediately after heavy rain, set a labourer to work, with a pair of strong harvest gloves, and pull them up, with as much root as possible, for which a slow steady pull straight up is required. If in a field of corn, let the labourer begin on the outside land; as he pulls up the thistles with his right hand, let him place them under his left arm, until he has got as many as he can well convey to either end of the field. From whence they may be carried and chopped for cattle.

"Food for Cattle" equal to any of the Patented
Compounds, at one-fourth the Cost

Hint 670   The best compound for fattening beasts, and keeping sheep in a growing and healthy condition during the winter months, is one part beans or peas (if old, the better), one of linseed (which is preferable to oil-cake, as it contains all the oil), one barley, and one wheat, mixed and ground together. A small quantity of some warm condiment, as turmeric, may be added. This food is to be given dry with the cut turnips to the fattening beasts, to be moistened by their saliva.

The quantity given to sheep should be at the rate of half a bushel to hundred sheep, merely sprinkled over the turnips as a condiment, just as we use pepper. Even this small quantity will be found to have a remarkable effect. The condiment provokes appetite, and is consequently found useful to cattle which for fattening purposes are being highly fed, and to hard worked horses, tempting them to eat when, from sheer exhaustion, they would scarcely be inclined to do so without something to entice them. It thus supplies the place of the "cordial ball," which is sometimes given with the same object in view.

Hint 671   Boiled Barley is an excellent mash for Horses and Cows that are troubled with costiveness, as it corrects their bowels without medicine (an object of great importance), and is both cheaper and more efficient than bran mashes. Boiled Barley is also a very nourishing supper for old horses; it ought to be mixed up with oat seeds or oat dust, and the water it is boiled with could also be mixed with it.

Hint 672   Dry Barley doubles in measure when boiled, so that, when joined with the dust or seeds, one peck of barley will be produced from about one-fourth of a peck of barley; and this, considering the strength of the substance in connection with the cost price, will be found much cheaper as a support to the animal, than fine or coarse barley dust, or sharps, shellings or bran.

Hint 673   It has also been found on trial that boiled barley, when mixed as above, and given to Cows, is productive of more milk than the usual food; but when given to Cows, it ought to be boiled amongst more water than for Horses, and the kine will benefit by drinking the surplus water, after it is cooled to the heat of new milk. In no case whatever should either the Barley or water be given hotter than new milk, and care should be taken that it be consumed before getting sour. The evil of giving it too hot is apparent by its occasioning swellings in the upper part of the mouth, especially of Horses, rendering them unable to chew hay or corn.

Hint 674   When Wheat a little damaged can be got cheap, it is often bought up for feeding Cows and Horses. As it is a stronger substance than barley, and not good for either of these animals when raw, it ought to be well boiled, and should not be mixed with dust, but with Oat seeds, or small cut Hay or Straw, in order to keep it loose in the stomach of the animal, which renders it more digestible and wholesome.

An Economical use for Coal Ashes in Pig Feeding

Hint 675   Pigs will devour small coal ashes greedily, especially when feeding upon store food, raw vegetables, and the "swill" of the house.

In the absence of coal ashes, burned clay, or brick dust, is a good substitute. It is notorious that coal dealers, whose pigs have access to the coals, are generally successful feeders. Those who find that their pigs, when shut up do not progress favourably, will do well to try this plan. A score of fat pigs will consume a good-sized basket of burned clay and ashes daily. Young sucking-pigs are very fond of nibbling and eating coal ashes. The fact itself is invaluable, though we may not be able to explain the reason. Dogs often eat grass, and vomit afterwards; and it may be that, as pigs are naturally root grubbers, a provision has been made by nature for the reception of earthy particles into their digestive system. In their domesticated state they are deprived of this, and hence the good of ashes, burnt clay, etc., just as sand is good for cage birds.

Potato leaves as Food for Milk Cows

Hint 676   Norwegian farmers collect Potato Leaves, and lay them on frames and fences, or any other places where they may be dried with facility; when dried, they are kept for making cooked mashes for milk cows. A good handful of them is put in a vessel for each cow, and hot water poured over it; it is then left to stand covered until next day, when the leaves and juice are given to the cows. They yield more milk on this meal.

Fattening Turkeys and other Domestic Fowls with Charcoal

Hint 677   The fattening of Turkeys and other Fowls may be greedy accelerated by mixing with their food a proportion of powdered charcoal. The following is the result of a careful experiment:— Four Turkeys were confined in a pen, and fed on meal, boiled potatoes, and oats. Four others of the same brood were also at the same time confined in another pen, and fed daily on the same articles, but with one pint of very finely pulverized charcoal mixed with their meal and potatoes. They had also a plentiful supply of broken charcoal in their pen. The eight were killed on the same day, and there was a difference of a pound and a half each in favour of the fowls which had been supplied with the charcoal, they being much the fattest, and the meat greatly superior in point of tenderness and flavour.

Hint 678   Onions are an excellent preventive and remedy for various diseases to which domestic Poultry is liable. For gapes, and inflammation of the eyes, throat and head, onions are almost a specific. Fowls, especially chickens, may advantageously be fed with them twice or three times a week. The onions should be finely chopped, and a little corn meal added.

Use for Rotten Wood

Hint 679   Dry Rotten Wood, being thrown into a pigsty, the hogs will eat and fatten upon it. Not only is it a good aliment for these animals; but they preserve better health by its use, than when kept without it.

Hint 680   Pigs should be early taught to eat slowly, for the advantage of the pig, as well as of the owner. Nothing is easier. Give the weaned pig, at six or eight weeks old — in a clean trough — half a teacup of dry shorts or bran, and after his dry food is all eaten, give his drink, and increase the dry food according to the age and appetite, until three months old; then add one-half Indian meal for two months, and then dry Indian meal, until fattened sufficiently. This plan has been followed for five years with decided success.

Usefulness of the Goat

Hint 681   Goats' milk is, except sheep's, the richest produced by domestic animals. It yields more butter and cheese than that of the cow. Asses' milk is the poorest, and is only suitable to the debilitated stomachs. Goats' milk boiled with rice makes excellent puddings. Goats require little or no management or care; they will do well on almost any kind of vegetable food; they browse freely on furze, brambles, thistles, and other wild vegetation. In wild and rocky situations, especially where furze and whin abound, they produce a great deal of excellent milk, and thrive to perfection where no other animal would be half as useful. By the simple plan of coupling to milk goats together, like dogs, they may be prevented from leaping fences, and getting out of bounds. A good milk goat will yield about two quarts of milk a day, and will require milking twice a day.

Hint 682   The flesh of the goat comes into season as the deer, from July to November; they furnish tallow of excellent quality, little inferior to wax candles; the gigot and loin are the best parts; the haunches not so good; but a pasty of any part of the flesh is better than mutton, and very little inferior to venison.

An excellent use for Sawdust, where it is plentiful and Straw may be scarce

Hint 683   Sawdust forms an excellent bedding for Horses during the summer months, and does wonders for the feet and legs; but it is necessary to rake it over with an iron rake, and to pick out the feet night and morning. It should also be turned over with a shovel every five or six days, as it becomes hard. The best plan is, to rake the dung with the sawdust; it becomes dry and pulverizes quickly, and is free from any offensive smell.

Brown beech sawdust is better than white pine; it is cheaper, free from turpentine, and supplies a strong and excellent manure for the flower or kitchen garden.

Hint 684   The drains may be covered with sawdust, as it is absorbent, and will not stop the drainage. The wet and soiled surface over the drains should be raked off daily, and a little fresh added. When the sawdust becomes much discoloured and hardened, it should be taken away altogether for manure, the floor underneath swept, and three or four wheelbarrows of fresh sawdust put on. This will not require to be done very often.

Hint 685   It is equally well adapted for stalls, looseboxes, cow houses, and forms also excellent lying for Dogs, keeping them much cleaner, and freer from infested coats, than when upon straw.

Hint 686   It is not so good for Fowls, but answers for pigs; and, in the winter time should be mixed with straw in all cases.

Sawdust for Blanching Celery

Hint 687   Celery in very retentive and damp soils may be blanched and preserved from rot and frost until a late period, by being earthed up with sawdust; it will keep wonderfully fresh, and the frost will not penetrate far through the surface to the hearts; slugs and insects generally will not attack it underground, and the heads will be found solid, clear, crisp, and well flavoured. The mixed sawdust of pits may be used; it has been found that sawdust of resinous trees does not affect the flavour of the celery.

To Prevent the Growth of Butttercups, to the Injury of Grass

Hint 688   Geese are very fond of the plant, and the goslings eat the flowers and seed vessels, thus preventing the plants seeding; while the old geese scoop up the roots, biting off the leaves and rootlets. They eat the bulb with much relish, and if kept in sufficient numbers, in proportion to the ground, they will very soon root up every buttercup. Thus the geese may be fed, and the pastures at the same time improved.

A Hint for the Sporting Season

Hint 689   Newly ground Coffee, sprinkled over Game will keep it sweet and fresh for several days. Clean the game; that is, wipe off the blood, cover the wounded parts with absorbent paper, wrap up the heads, and then sprinkle ground coffee over and amongst the feathers or fur, as the case may be; pack up carefully, and the game will be preserved fresh and sweet in the most unfavourable weather.

Game sent open and loose cannot, of course, be treated in this manner; but all game packed in boxes or hampers may be deodorised as described. A teaspoonful of coffee is enough for a brace of birds; and in this proportion for more or for larger game.

Hint 690   Fresh ground coffee may be used with advantage in a Sick Room; a few spoonfuls should be spread and exposed on a plate.

Hint 691   Burned by a red hot iron, it is a safe and pleasant fumigator.

Advantages of Salting Wheat in the Mow

Hint 692   Most farmers know the effect of salting rather green hay, when it is put into the mow. But few have even thought of or practised Salting Wheat. It is worth a trial. Commence on one side, placing the sheaves in regular layers, with the butts outside, tramping heavily on the butt of each, as it is laid down. Place the next layer with the tops lapping about halfway over the first, care being taken to keep the heads or tops uppermost. When the entire space of the mow is covered in this way, sprinkle common ground salt over the mow on the top of the layer, at the rate of four quarts to every twenty dozen sheaves of wheat – a greater proportion of salt if the sheaves are large. During the sweating, the salt is dissolved and absorbed by the grain and straw. The effect has been found to make the grain brighter, and bring a better price per bushel than that which has not been salted. Millers say that the yield of flour is larger and whiter. Cattle eat the straw freely; and the salt is an effectual remedy against the Barn Weevil.

To Prevent Horse's Feet Balling with Snow

Hint 693   Soft Soap, brushed into horses' hoofs, will prevent their feet balling with snow, but its effect does not last long. Or melted Suet poured into the hoof. A simple and certain preventive against balling is Gutta Percha, about the thickness of leather used for shoeing. Cut it so as to fit tightly the inside of the shoe and hoof, by heating it in hot water. It can be placed in, or removed, by letting the feet stand in a pail of hot water; the flat surface leaves no corners for the snow to stick in.

Hint 694   The same application of Gutta Pertha is very good for horses with tender feet, on stony roads, in the summer time.

Hint 695   Another and more perfect plan for Preventing Balling and Slipping, is to have three screw holes in the shoe, one at the apex, and the others at the heel.

Screw steel wedges tightly into these holes, the shoe and sole being covered by strong leather or Gutta Percha previously, which the screws will keep in place, holes having been made to admit the screws. A horse thus protected may gallop with safety on snow or ice. The screws may be taken off when not wanted, as the shoe is an ordinary one, with three holes in it.

To Increase the Produce of late Peas, Scarlet Runners, and Kidney Beans

Hint 696   Take care not to allow a single pod to ripen or grow old; pluck them carefully; the object being to prevent the plant from maturing any part of its fruit, which prevents more pods, being formed with the plants standing for seed. The plants thus being deprived of their first fruits, will continue to make effort to produce more young, and these will keep up a continuous supply for the table. If in dry weather, a drenching with the watering pot (avoiding wetting the leaves or stem) will be found to produce immediate good effects. And if care is observed not to tear the stalks, leaves, or tendrils, when gathering the young pods, five or ten times the quantity of young peas or beans may be obtained for the table.

Hint 697   To obtain Early Scarlet Runners:- at the end of the autumn, cut off the tops of the old plants a few inches above the ground when they are dying off; take up the roots, and keep them in dry sand during the winter, out of the reach of frost, but in a cool dry place. (The roots must not be eaten, as they are noxious.) At the end of February, or early in March, plant them in a frame without any heat, and in a few weeks they will sprout; if the sun should be powerful, shade with evergreens for a few days; the same protection will serve against frost. In this way the first dish of beans may be obtained twenty days, or more, earlier than by the usual method; they will bear plentifully throughout the season, and run less to wood than those that are sown.

Method of Preserving Growing Fruit Damaged by Tits, Wasps, etc

Hint 698   In many instances the finest Pears, Apricots, etc., are pecked by Tits, or gnawed by Wasps; the holes thus formed are then acted upon by air and rain, and the fruit decays. In such cases it is an effective plan to fill the holes as soon as possible with a little plaster of Paris and water; this excludes the air and rain, without injuring the flavour of the fruit, and it entirely arrests decay.

Hint 699   A Hawk stuffed, with expanded wings, affixed by a string, and attached to a long thin rod fixed horizontally to the top of a tree, will scare away birds from fruit trees over a considerable space. A live Hawk, kept in a cage near the same spot, will, by occasional noises, greatly increase the effect.

The Best Method of Destroying Weeds in Roads and Walks

Hint 700   Apply clean dry agricultural Salt by the hand; and where the weeds are strong, then let there be the more liberal application. Choose a hot day, in preference to wet or stormy weather. By going over the roads twice a year — in March and September — the weeds never get very strong; and there is no other plan of extirpation of weeds upon a large scale so efficient as this. By this way of cleaning roads, you do not disturb a single stone; and the harder the road the fewer the weeds, and of course so much better travelling.

Hint 701   The salt should be applied early in March, so that it may be thoroughly washed in before the sun has too much power, otherwise a white crystallization will be left on the gravel under the drying influence of the sun. Boiling water and salt does not prove nearly so efficacious as dry salt, when used at a very early period of the year.

Hint 702   Waste Salt, from the bacon-curer's, is very afficacious for the purpose; the effect is always greatest when it lies upon the ground a few days, before being dissolved by the rain. Salt is not only useful for clearing the surface, but also for consolidating the walks; it greatly improves their appearance, and renders them more comfortable for walking.

An Effective and Easy Method of Destroying Wasps in their Nests

Hint 703   Between nine and ten o'clock in the evening, having previously marked the localities of the nests, take a can of Gas Tar, and pour a little into the entrance of the nest, then stuff in a pellet of dry grass, and pour some more gas tar over it. If the hole happens to be in a wall, dip a piece of tow or cotton in the gas tar, and stuff it into the hole. It is well to go round again in a day or two, to see if the wasps have been destroyed, as they sometimes find a second opening, through which they communicate with the nest. When this happens, the process must be repeated at the new outlet.

Hint 704   Wasps may be diverted from attacking fruit, by having sugar placed in the forks of the branches. Half a pound of sugar is sufficient for a large fruit tree.

An Excellent Dye from Horse Chestnuts

Hint 705   The Horse Chestnut affords a permanent valuable dye for muslin, cotton, etc., is little known, but may be relied upon. The dye varies from a sort of buff to dull nankeen, according to the degree of ripeness of the fruit.

When about the size of a gooseberry, cut the whole fruit into quarters, and steep it in soft water, with just enough soap to tinge it. When deep enough for use, pour off the clean water. In all cases, the water must be cold; if boiled, the dye is of a more dingy colour. The colour from the whole fruit is buff – not unlike that of anotta. The husks only, when the fruit is nearly or quite ripe — not cut, but broken up and steeped in cold water, with a tinge of soap as above – yield a dye which will be more or less bright according to the degree of ripeness of the husk. If cut, the knife stains the husks, and the colour is not so good.

Best Method of Making Flour from Horse Chestnuts

Hint 706   Grind the nuts, and mix with the pulp of carbonate of soda in the proportion of one or two percent at the utmost, and then wash the produce until it is perfectly white. One pound of carbonate of soda will purify one hundred pounds of horse chestnuts, and produce sixty pounds of flour fit for bread, as the salt removes the bitter principle of the nut.

Hint 707   When Horse Chestnuts are ground into powder, the bitter principle is easily extracted by repeated washings in cold water; after which a wholesome, and nutritious starch remains, which has all the good qualities of arrowroot.

A Novel way of killing Magpies upon Farms, where they are found to Destroy Eggs

Hint 708   It is a well established fact that magpies will allow women to approach them, though they are exceedingly shy of men. When you wish to shoot them, put on a lady's cloak and bonnet, conceal the gun, and walk towards the birds, but not in a direct line. This, though a laughable stratagem, will almost invariably be found to succeed.

Hint 709   Some keepers entice magpies near them, by concealing themselves, and imitating the cry of an ensnared hare, or of the bird itself. The latter is done by placing the lips on the back of the hand, and drawing in the breath with a smart chirp. These plans succeed admirably.

A superior Method of taking Honey from Bee Hives, without killing the Bees

Hint 710   Pour two teaspoonfuls of Chloroform onto a piece of rag, double it twice, and place it on the floorboard of the hive, which must be lifted for the purpose, the entrance hole being carefully secured. In about two and a half minutes there will be a loud humming, which will soon cease.

Let the hive remain in this state for six or seven minutes, making about ten minutes in all. Remove the hive, and the greater number of the bees will be found lying senseless on the board; there will still be a few clinging between the combs, some of which may be brushed out with a feather. They return to animation in from half an hour to one hour after the operation. This plan possesses a great superiority over the usual mode of brim stoning, the bees being preserved alive; and over the more modern plan of fumigation by puffball; it is far less trouble, and the honey does not become tainted with the fumes. The expense is three pence per hive.

A certain Remedy for the Potato Disease

Hint 711   The Potato Disease may be said to have perplexed the wisdom of our profoundest philosophers, and to have baffled the skill of practical men. It has, however, been recently demonstrated by microscopical examination, that the malady which has so seriously affected a very important article of food, is due to the deposition by the atmosphere of a minute Fungus, which, taking up its habitation first upon the leaf and the haulm of the potato plant, propagates with astonishing rapidity, and rapidly finds its way to the tubers, and destroys them. Having, at first, without a knowledge of this remedy, tried successfully an experiment which we have since found to entirely accord with it, we are anxious to make known our experience, so that others may profit by the result.

Hint 712   Last season, we departed from the old system, so far as the greater part of our crop was concerned, and pursued the following plan: we planted the potatoes in double rows, instead of single, the two rows occupying about a foot in width, a foot of vacant space remaining on the outside of each row; they were planted upon the level ground, and hoed up at the usual time.
When the haulm had reached its full growth, or about the 1st of July, we turned it over right and left towards the vacant spaces, by adding earth between the rows, and pressing down the haulms, so as to prevent their erect position, and to allow the rain falling upon them, instead of descending direct to the roots, to fall upon the vacant spaces.
The kind of potatoes upon which we experimented, were Regents and Flukes. Of the former we planted one portion upon the old system, and a larger portion upon the new; the Flukes were all planted upon the new system. The soil consists of clay, — about as bad a description of land as can be devoted to the growth of a potato crop.
The result was, that the Regents, planted upon the new system, turned out to be a good crop, while those upon the old plan were a complete failure, although grown upon a part of the same plot of ground, and planted at the same time from the same seed. The Flukes produced an excellent crop, not two in a hundred being bad; while our neighbours, for miles round, without exception, lost their crops.

Hint 713   The efficacy of this system has been proved, not alone by our own experience, and that of several others who have tried it, but has been attested by the following curious circumstance:— A, gentleman, who had planted a bed of potatoes, having a number of planks which he required to be put out of the way, but not knowing how to dispose of them, allowed them to be thrown down upon a part of the potato bed. Upon removing the planks sometime afterwards, and digging the ground, fully expecting to find that the potatoes which had been covered and pressed down by the planks were completely destroyed. He found, to his surprise, that those which the planks had lain upon were in excellent condition, while those which had been exposed in the ordinary manner were diseased. The laying down of the planks had, in this instance, effected the turning over of the haulms, and sheltered the potatoes from wet; and the result was as good as if the system we have recommended had been carried out by design.

Method of Improving Seed Potatoes

Hint 714   Keep back some seed potatoes for six to seven weeks; after the usual time of planting, say until the last week in June, or the first week in July, and then plant and cultivate them as with stock potatoes. They will grow until the frost withers the haulms, when they should be dug. As they have not had time to mature, they will be quite small – not more than an inch to an inch and a half; but they should all be carefully collected, and kept safe from frost through the winter, and planted at the usual time of planting in Spring. One of the small potatoes being sufficient for seed in each hole. The result will be large-sized, sound, mealy potatoes, as the plan has proved by actual trial.

How to Grow Large Potatoes

Hint 715   To improve the size of potatoes, whether planted with large or small, whole or even cut tubers, when the plants are only a few inches high, let the roots be reduced by pulling them up to one, two, or at most three of the strongest. The tubers will consequently be fewer, and very much larger, also in measure nearly all fit for the table or market.

Hint 716   Growers may assure themselves of the efficacy of this method, by first experimenting upon a few rows.

Remedy for Frozen Potatoes

Hint 717   In the time of frosts, potatoes that have been affected thereby, should be laid in a perfectly dark place for some days after the thaw has commenced. If thawed in open, they rot; but if in darkness, they do not rot; and they lose very little of their natural properties.

Hint 718   The water in which potatoes have been boiled is excellent for Chilblains. The feet or hands should be bathed in the water as hot as can be borne. It will afford immediate relief, and prevent breaking.

Potatoes Slightly Diseased, Preserved by Peat Charcoal

Hint 719   When potatoes are slightly diseased, sprinkling Peat Charcoal among them instantly stays the rot, takes away the bad smell, and renders them sweet and wholesome food. Potatoes may be kept in this way for two years, and when planted the third they will produce a good crop. The charcoal will also prevent the sound potatoes from being infected by the ones.

Hint 720   The charcoal need not be lost; it may be mixed with other manures when the potatoes are removed.

*Means of Doubling a Crop of Potatoes, without
increased expenditure*

Hint 721   A double crop of potatoes may be obtained by pursuing the following course: When the potatoes have come to maturity, take off the loose earth carefully, without disturbing the old stem; pick away the tubers that are fit for immediate use; be careful not to disturb the main stalk, then cover over the small ones that are left, and add a little more earth. In about two months after, the later crop will be more productive than the first.

Advice and Precautions respecting Fires

Hint 722   Be careful to acquaint yourself with the best means of escape from a house, both at the roof and on the ground. The father of a family should make himself familiar with the means of outlet to the roof, and with the best way of passing thereon to the adjoining premises.

Hint 723   On the first alarm, reflect before you act if in bed at the time, wrap yourself in a blanket or bedside carpet; open no more doors or windows than are absolutely necessary, and shut every door after you.

Hint 724   There is always from eight to twelve inches of pure air close to the ground. If you cannot walk upright through the smoke, drop on your hands knees, and thus go on. A wetted silk handkerchief, a piece of flannel, or a worsted stocking drawn over the face permits breathing, and, to a great extent, excludes smoke.

Hint 725   If you can neither make your way upwards or downwards, get into a front room. If there is a family, see that they are all collected here, and keep the door closed as long as possible, as smoke always follows a draught.

Hint 726   On no account throw yourself, or allow others to throw themselves from the windows. If no assistance is at hand, and you are in extremity, tie the sheets together. Having fastened one end to some heavy piece of furniture, let down the women and children, one by one, by tying the end of the line of the sheets round the waist, and lowering them through the window over the door, rather than over the area. You can then let yourself down, when the helpless are saved.

Hint 727   If a woman's clothes should catch fire, let her roll herself over on the ground; if a man be present, let him throw her down, if necessary, and wrap her in a rug, coat, or anything at hand.

Hint 728   Bystanders, the instant they see a fire, should run for a fire escape (or to the police station, if that should be nearer), where a jumping sheet is always held.

Hint 729   On the first discovery of a fire, it is of the utmost consequence to close, and keep closed, all the doors, windows, and other openings.

Hint 730   It may often be observed, after a house has been on fire, that one floor is comparatively untouched, while those above and below are nearly burnt out. This arises from the doors on that particular floor having been closed, and the draught directed elsewhere.

Hint 731   If the fire appears serious, and there are fire engines at a reasonable distance, it is best to await their arrival, as many buildings have been lost from opening the doors, and attempting to extinguish fires without adequate means.

Hint 732   If no engines are within reach, it is well to keep a hand pump. If that is not to be had, the next best thing is to collect as many buckets outside the room on fire as can be obtained, keeping the door closed; then creep into the room on the hands and knees (if the heat and smoke are considerable), and throw water as nearly in the direction of the fire as possible, keeping the door closed, while more water is being collected.

Hint 733   Raking out the fire before going to bed is a dangerous practice. It should be allowed to go out. A fireguard should be placed before every fire so left.

Hint 734   Children should be early taught to press out sparks that may fall upon their clothing; and throw themselves down when their clothes become ignited.

General Precautions against Fires in Farms, etc

Hint 735   Forbid the use of Lucifer matches, smoking, the firing of guns, or any other unnecessary use of fire or combustibles in or near the rick-yard, or near to any wooden outbuilding on the farm.

Hint 736   Keep the rick-yard, and especially the spaces between the stacks and ricks, clear of loose straw.

Hint 737   Place the ricks in a single line, and as far distant from each other as may be convenient. If hay-ricks and corn stacks are placed alternatively, the former will check the progress of the fire from stack to stack.

Hint 738   When a steam threshing machine is to be used, place it on the lee side of the stack or barn, so that the wind may blow the sparks away from the stacks. Have the loose straws frequently cleared away from the engine; and keep two or three pails of water nearby; and see that the ash pan is kept full of water.

When a Fire breaks out in a Farm Yard

Hint 739   Do not allow the rick or stack which may have taken fire to be disturbed; let it burn out, but make every exertion to press it compactly together, and as far as practicable prevent any lighted particles flying about.

Hint 740   Get together blankets, carpets, sacks, rugs, and other similar articles; soak them thoroughly in water, and place them over and against the adjoining ricks and stacks, towards which the wind blows.

Hint 741   Having thus covered the sides of the ricks adjoining that on fire, devote all your attention to the latter.

Hint 742   Press it together by every available means. If water is at hand, throw upon it as much as possible. If engines arrive, let the water be thrown upon the blankets etc., covering the adjoining stacks, and then upon the stack on fire.

Hint 743   Among the numerous hands who flock to assist on these occasions, many do mischief by their want of knowledge, and especially by opening the fired stack and; scattering the embers.

In order to obviate this evil, place your best man in command over the stack of fire, desire him to make it his sole duty to prevent it being disturbed, and to keep it pressed and watered.

Hint 744   Place other men, in whose steadiness you are assured, to watch the adjoining ricks, to keep the coverings over them, and to extinguish any embers flying from the stack on fire. In order to effect this, it is most desirable that there should be ladders at hand, to enable one or two of the labourers to mount upon each stack.

Hint 745   If the ricks are separated from each other, and there is no danger of the fire extending to a second, it is of course desirable to save as much of the one on fire as may be possible. That, however, is not unfrequently accomplished by keeping the rick compactly together rather than by opening it.

Hint 746   Send for all the neighbours blankets and tarpaulins; these are invaluable; they are near at hand, and can be immediately applied.

A simple Fire Escape

Hint 747   Drive a strong staple into the upper part of the window frame of any sleeping or other room, and provide two blocks, with two or three pulleys in each. Put a strong rope through each pulley, of a length sufficient to reach the ground. Provide also a strong sack about four feet deep, into which fix a wooden bottom, and a few hoops, to keep the sack open.

Hint 748   Should a fire happen, let the hoop of the upper block be hung to the staple; the person to be saved should stand upon the wooden bottom of the sack, draw the sack up around him, and hang the string of the sack on the hook of the under block, and then any one person may, with ease and safety, let down a whole family one by one, and at last lower himself down, by holding the rope in his hand, and letting it out by degrees.

Hint 749   In cases of fire, it is very difficult to manage Horses, The best way is, to blind them with cloths, and back them out. Putting the saddle or harness upon their backs will sometimes divert their attention from the alarm, and induce them to leave the stable.

Hint 750   To extinguish Chimneys on Fire, throw on the fire, salt, or flour of sulphur. Block up the fireplace with wet rugs or a carpet.

To Prevent Injuries and Deaths from the Ignition of Clothing

Hint 751   Messrs. Johnson & Sons, 18a, Basinghall Street, London, have experimented upon the Tungstate of Soda, and succeeded in producing a refined preparation of it, which may be employed to render the most delicate of fabrics non-inflammable, without the slightest risk of injury to their whiteness, texture, or colour. One penny worth of this preparation, used with the starch in getting up a muslin dress, will render it certainly non-flammable. The only caution necessary to be observed in the use of this preparation is, that it should not be employed for those parts of clothing which infants are liable to suck.

Hint 752   An ounce of Alum dissolved in the last water used to rinse children's dresses, will render then non-inflammable, or so slightly combustible that they would take fire very slowly, if at all, and would not flame.

Hint 753   It ought also to be generally known that all ladies' light dresses may be made fire proof at a trifling cost, by steeping them, or the linen or cotton used in making, in a diluted solution of Chloride of Zinc. We have seen the finest cambric so prepared, held in the flame of a candle, and charred to dust, without igniting.

Economical Hints Respecting the Management of Poultry

Hint 754   Give them plenty of Cayenne with their food; it is useful before and during the whole of moulting time; and let them have the free use of salt during the whole year. They should likewise have access to green food. Allow them also occasionally bacon rinds and scraps of salt meat.

Hint 755   Consider all bottoms of bottles, as lees of port wine, of elderberry, of all homemade wines, odd heel taps of porter, ale, or spirit, as the perquisites of the poultry. A quarter of a pint of a compound made of such remains, diluted with water, may be occasionally mixed with the food of a dozen fowls.

Hint 756   Poultry should also be allowed to peck bones, and any scraps of meat and bits of fat, and be allowed to drink any waste milk, to which a little meal may be added.

A Radical Cure for the Croup in Fowls and in Pheasants, even when the disease is very bad

Hint 757   Take one pennyworth of blue vitriol (sulphate of copper), and dissolve it in a teacup of hot water.

When cold, put it into a bottle, and add one penny worth of each of the following ingredients: spirits of hartshorn, spirits of lavender, and tincture of myrrh. To use it, take a drop on a wood skewer, and drop it into the nostril of the bird; if a very bad case, a little may be dropped into the opening in the roof of the mouth.

Hint 758　　　　The pale colour of the yolks of eggs arises generally from a deficiency of green food. Let fowls have plenty of grass, or other green food, and the yolks of their eggs will become deep coloured, and the fowls improve in health.

Hint 759　　　　A dust bath of sand, wood ashes, and sulphur, in the poultry yard will prevent fowls from being infested with lice. The houses of the fowls should be whitewashed with lime once a year.

The best Season to commence Pig-keeping

Hint 760　　　　The month of September is the best to commence Pig-keeping. The age at which a pig should be bought, is from three to four months. The gardens in September are full of refuse vegetables: and the commons supply fern, which should be dried and ricked for litter during the winter. The gleaners have left the fields, and in many places, by paying a trifle, a pig may be allowed to run amongst the wheat stubble, which will materially assist the progress of fattening, by laying a good foundation before commencing the stall feeding. Acorns and Beech nuts fall soon after this time, and the pig or pigs may be driven to where they lie, or they may be picked up by children, and carried to the pigs.

Hint 761　　　　The best mode of Fattening Pigs is to combine roots, meal, and any milk slops attainable. The value of roots for pig feeding stand relatively thus:— Ist, Parsnips; 2nd, Mangold; 3rd, Swedes; 4th, Carrots. The comparative value of meals thus:— 1st, Barley; 2nd, Oats; 3rd, Indian Corn; in addition to the various dressings from Wheat, such as Pollard, etc. Some use damaged rice. These things should be mixed, the roots boiled, mixed with meal, and given warm. Feed three times a day.

An Economical Food for Sporting, and other large Dogs

Hint 762　　　　Indian Meal, mixed with potatoes and greaves, is a cheaper and better food for dogs than greaves and dog biscuits; oatmeal, or bread raspings. They may be kept upon this in first rate condition at the rate per head of sixpence a week. There is a foreign greave cake, which may be procured of oilmen in many parts, which is very good; it consists of the pressed meat of the buffalo, costs rather more than one penny per lb., and will keep perfectly good for years.

Useful Employment of Soot

Hint 763   Peas may be preserved from destruction by Mice by sowing Soot with them; and when the peas come up, if soot be sprinkled over them while they are damp, Sparrows will not touch them. Soot is also invaluable for Carnations and Tulips in any ground where Wireworms are abound. It is not only a destroyer of insects, but a rich manure.

The best Posture during Sleep

Hint 764   Dr. Franklin recommends the limbs being placed so as not to bear inconveniently hard upon one another; as, for instance, the joints of the ankles; for though a bad position may at first give but little pain, and be hardly noticed, yet a continuance of it will render it less tolerable, and the uneasiness may come on during sleep, and may disturb the imagination. In cold weather the arms should be under the clothes, and above them in the warm; and care should be taken not to fold them round the head. It is imprudent to hide the head almost entirely under the bedclothes. We ought to sleep with our mouth shut; as, besides other inconveniences attending a contrary practice, the teeth are liable to injury from it; for the air continually passing in and out between them, hurts, and by degrees renders them less firm in their sockets; it also tends to consume, unnecessarily, the moisture of the mouth and throat, consequently they become too dry, which is always unpleasant, and in cold weather may occasion sore throats.

To Cultivate Water Cresses in the Garden

Hint 765   About the early part of March, procure a handful or two of healthy plants, rooted out of a brook. Prepare two small beds of good loamy soil, and cut the plants into lengths of about three or four inches, preferring those pieces which have the appearance of a little white root attached, and plant them with a small dibble, nearly up to the tops, in rows about eight inches apart, and six inches between the plants, watering them well, and shading them with mats supported on sticks just above the plants for a few days.

Hint 766   Keep the beds damp by watering nearly every day. By the next month they will be so much grown that you may nip off the tops, and supply a good plate every day in the week.

Hint 767   When the tops are first gathered, the plants will throw out side shoots in abundance, and soon cover all the bed; and during the spring and summer will produce so abundant a crop that there will be some difficulty in keeping them down by gathering.

To Cultivate the Cranberry

Hint 768   This agreeable fruit may easily be cultivated. It grows, naturally in low boggy places, or on wet moors amongst the bog moss. This moss rising gradually above the level of the water, forms, as the lower parts decay, a bed in which the Cranberry flourishes and bears fruit abundantly. To cultivate it near home, we must imitate the situation in which it grows wild. To accomplish this, fix upon a situation near to a supply of water, then dig out the common soil four inches, and fill up the place with bog earth; raise this peat six inches above the level; then form a trench round the bed a foot or sixteen inches wide, puddling it at the side next the common soil and at the bottom with clay. Keep this trench full of water. Place the cranberry plants in the raised bed a foot apart every way; they will soon run over the whole surface, and bear plenty of fruit. The water should be frequently changed, or it will become foul. Should there be a small lake, or even a large one, near at hand, an excellent cranberry bed must be made near to the side. All that would be required would be to form a low flat island with a peat earth surface, the cranberry plant put in at a proper distance, and kept clear from weeds. A small extent of space would yield a large supply of fruit. If the island were eight yards long and four feet wide, it would be quite large enough to supply a moderate family.

Hint 769   This fruit may be grown in a bed of peat one foot deep, sunk an inch or two below the general surface, and during dry weather to be flooded with water occasionally. Thus treated, they will fruit to a middling extent. The former method is, however, the best. The American berry, on the account of its size, is the best for cultivation.

Asparagus Grown as an Underground Esculent

Hint 770   Throughout Holland, no Green Asparagus is grown; the heads and stems are white throughout, and are tender and of excellent flavour. The asparagus is never allowed to appear above the surface of the ground; a slight protuberance in the soil shows where the plant is rising, and by this index a practised eye knows when it is fit to cut. In proportion as the stem rises above the soil, it hardens, both above and beneath; thus in England we get only half the plant, while in Holland they utilise the whole.

To obtain Mushroom Spawn

Hint 771   It is often to be met with in manure heaps, and in fields, particularly where hay ricks have been made, and the old thatch and bottoms have been thrown up into a heap, to decay for manure. It smells just the same as the mushroom.

In heaps of manure that have been thrown out of an old cowshed, where horses and cows run for shelter; and in the sweepings of horse mill walks, thrown into a heap in some dry corner, and allowed to lie for three or four months undisturbed, plenty of mushroom spawn is likely to be generated.

Hint 772 If horse droppings, mixed with sand and loam, in equal parts, and partly dry, is placed in boxes or large flowerpots, with a small bit of good spawn in it three inches below the surface, all jammed in as solid as it can be done, and put in any heated structure, the whole bulk will very soon be found to be the best spawn, if kept dry for five or six weeks.

To prevent Slugs from attacking Celery, Care against Frogs

Hint 773 Dust slacked lime liberally in and over each plant. This preventive will be attended by unvarying success.

Hint 774 It is a good plan upon the approach of Frost to cover Celery with long, loose, dry litter. If snow falls before the covering of litter is laid on, no matter; it is itself a warm covering, and the litter may be laid over the snow.

A Method of Estimating the Weight and Growth of Live Pigs

Hint 775 A tape or string should be passed under the belly close to the forelegs, and brought up over the shoulders in a straight line. The circumference thus ascertained is the gauge; thus, a pig measuring forty-eight inches as described, will weigh fourteen stones of fourteen pounds to the stone; and every inch of increase in circumference will increase a stone in weight, supposing the pig to be in good condition, and of moderate size. A good pig when feeding should gain an inch per week, until he ceases to gain; but he may cease for a week, and be making inward fat.

Which Pays Best, Pork or Bacon?

Hint 776 Fresh Pork is 4½d. per pound, pays better than when just out of salt at the same price, because pork loses in salt at least three-quarters of a pound for every stone of fourteen pounds, besides the cost of the salt. But Bacon, dried and sold at 7d, per pound, will pay best of all, and will fetch at least 1d. per pound more on the whole.

What is the best age for a Hog to be put up to
Fatten, with a view to Profit

Hint 777　　　All pigs require to finish their growth, before they are put up to fatten, as, if not fully grown, growth arrests the fatting. The Suffolk pigs take nine months to grow, and then they are fit to fatten. Their food should consist first of Peas, and a small quantity of Turnips. As soon as it is perceived that the hogs are getting fat, then peas only, and they should at this time be ground. They should be fed from five to six times a day, having small quantities only at a time. The rule as to quantity is, one bushel of peas, or peas-meal, to every stone of pork, or six pecks of barley-meal.

Hint 778　　　Barley meal is an excellent fattening food; warmth, cleanliness, even to scrubbing with warm water every week, and feeding four times a day at regular intervals, are great aids to fattening.

The Best Method of Curing Bacon

Hint 779　　　As soon as the Hog is quite cold - the day after killing, it should be cut into halves, and rubbed with a mixture of salt and saltpetre; twenty-eight pounds of salt being required for a hog of ten score pounds, mixed with an ounce of saltpetre, pounded, for every score pounds of pork. The sides should be laid upon a stone floor, and for the first week turned daily, and some of the salt mixture rubbed in; but for the second and third weeks the turning and rubbing need be repeated only every second day; at the end of the three weeks it will be sufficiently salted.

Hint 780　If the bacon is not immediately required, the salted pieces should be put on edge in a bin, and salt put between them so that they cannot touch, and salt should also be heaped over them, so as to exclude the air, and to keep the next tier of sides from touching them. If the sides are placed flat they become too salty. They should be taken out for smoking (making into bacon) as required, and thus they quite escape that rustiness which will occur in bacon which is stored for any length of time.

Hint 781　　　To convert the Pork thus salted into Bacon the sides must be taken out, the salt wiped from them, and they should then be hung by hooks fixed across the roof of a brick built room, made so high that the lower end of the side of a hog is about eight feet from the floor. If nearer the floor, the heat would melt the fat. On the floor a little sawdust should be lighted and kept smouldering constantly, day and night, for ten days, which is long enough for the side of a hog weighing ten score pounds.

The door of the smoking room should be closed, but there must be a hole through the wall on a level with the floor to admit air enough for keeping the sawdust burning, and the only escape for the smoke should be through the tiles, for it is the confinement of the smoke about the pork which so soon baconizes it.

Hint 782   A most important point is the quality of the sawdust; oak, elm, and birch are best. We ourselves prefer that of the oak; and there are two other points not to be forgotten:— Firstly, the sawdust cannot be too old or too dry; and secondly, no fir, larch, deal, nor other sawdust containing turpentine must be used, or it will spoil the bacon.

Hint 783   Bacon, Hams, and Fish may be smoked on a small scale, by driving the end out of an old puncheon, or large cask. Invert it over birch or juniper branches, on a heap of oak sawdust, in which a bar of red hot iron is plunged. Hang the Bacon, Harris Tongues, or Fish on sticks fixed across the cask, and cover well to consume the smoke, allowing very little air to enter below.

Hint 784   Pyroligneous acid may be employed as a substitute for smoke. The plan is to add two tablespoonfuls of the acid to the pickle for a ham of 10lbs. or 12lbs; and when, taken out of the pickle, previous to being hung up, it should be painted over with the acid by means of a brush. The same mode answers equally well with Tongues, requiring a little more acid on account of the thickness of the integuments. Upon dried Salmon it answers admirably; brushing it over once or twice has a better effect than two months smoking in the usual way.

A Scale of Proportions, etc, for Lovers of "Home-Brew"

Hint 785   The following practical scale will be found of great utility to persons brewing their own malt liquors. The quantities may be varied, but the scale will in all cases prove an unerring guide.

Strong Ale

Quantity to be brewed	-	50 gallons
Water required	-	94 gallons
Malt	-	4 bushels
Hops (if the beer is to be kept over twelve months)	-	4 lbs
Hops (if required for keeping over six months)	-	3 lbs
Barm for working	-	1 quart
Heat of water for first mash	-	170 degrees
Heat for second mash	-	180 degrees
Time for water to stay on each mash	-	3 hours
Time the beer must be boiled each time	-	2 ½ hours
Quantity of beer to begin working	-	5 gallons
Proper heat to set the beer To work	-	65 to 70 degrees

Times for brewing, October to March.

Table Beer

Quantity to be brewed	-	50 gallons
Water required	-	85 gallons
Malt	-	3 bushels
Hops	-	2 lbs
Barm for working	-	3 pints
Heat of water for first Mash	-	170 degrees
Heat for second mash	-	180 degrees
Time for water to stay on First mash	-	3 hours
Ditto on second mash	-	2 ½ hours
Ditto for boiling beer each Time	-	2 hours
Quantity of beer to begin The working	-	5 gallons
Proper heat to set beer to Work	-	80 degrees

Times for brewing, when wanted.

Economy of Fuel in Heating Ovens

Hint 786   In heating an oven, a much smaller amount of time and wood is consumed, if care is taken that every part of the floor of the oven is, in its turn, kept quite clear of wood and ashes: it should be kept as clean as it can be scraped. The heaped up embers prevent the free circulation of hot air over the floor. Heated as suggested, the oven will yield loaves as crisp at the bottom as the top; whereas if this precaution is neglected, you may have many loaves well baked in all parts except the bottom, which will be soft and tough, and to which every particle of ashes left on the floor will have adhered.

Another Method of Finding Wasps nests, and Destroying the Wasps

Hint 787   Melt any quantity of Brimstone in a flower saucer; have any kind of rags, such as bits of worsted stocking, flannel, or carpet, four or five inches in length, and two inches wide, and dip them well in the melted brimstone. Make enough of these matches, for they will keep any length of time.

Hint 788   The next thing is to find the nests, which may be unfailingly done as follows:— Suppose the fruit they are attacking should be situated in a confined place between buildings, then take a portion of the fruit and place it in a convenient open space where you can command a clear view; they will soon find it out; take your stand close by, and wait until several flights have been taken, carefully marking their direction, and if they do not all go one way, know for certainty there is more than one nest then, to find them, go in a straight line according to their line of flight, and it is an unerring rule to find them. A close observer can pretty well determine the distance of a nest in this way: first, suppose the ground inclines downward in their line of flight, and from their starting point they partake of this inclination - you may conclude the nest is between you and the next rising ground. Secondly, if their inclination is the reverse of this, rest assured the nest is beyond the valley lying between you and the rising ground beyond.

Hint 789   Having found the nest, take one of the prepared brimstone matches, a lighted Lucifer, and spade, and, above all, the house bellows. Then, within a short distance of the nest, light the match at one end, wait a little until it is well lighted, then, place the lighted end at the hole, and directly apply the bellows, blowing the burning brimstone steadily into the nest, pushing the match inward towards the hole as fast as it is being consumed, until the whole is blown into the nest. At the commencement of this operation a dismal humming noise is heard, but only for a few seconds, when all is hushed in death. No matter how strong the nests are, so much may be accomplished in two minutes.

This being done, dig out the nest, and, if not wanted for any purpose, smash it with the back of the spade, and the work is complete without a sting; for not one will escape to tell the tale. This had better be done after dark.

Liquid Glue — Useful for various Household Repairs

Hint 790   Take a wide mouthed bottle, and dissolve in it eight ounces of best glue in half a pint of water, by setting it in a vessel of water, and heating until dissolved. Then add slowly two and a half ounces of strong aqua fortis (nitric acid), stirring all the while. Keep it well corked, and it will be ready for use at any moment.

Hint 791   This preparation does not gelatinise, nor undergo putrefaction nor fermentation. It is applicable for many domestic uses, such as mending china, repairing cabinet work, etc.

Waterproof Leather Boots that will resist the Severest Weather

Hint 792   Take half a pint of linseed oil, and half a pint of Neat's foot oil, and boil them together. When the boots to be waterproofed are dry, and free from dirt, rub them well with this mixture before the fire; until completely saturated; set them by for two or three days, after oiling the first time; and after using, wash them clean from dirt, and oil when dry; or upon the feet, before going out.

Hint 793   The bottoms of dress boots may be made impervious to wet or snow, by the same mixture.

Best Method of Destroying the Gooseberry Caterpillar

Hint 794   Put into a boiler as many bucketsful of water as you require (one bucketful will do for twenty trees); add one pound of soft soap, and one ounce of ground black pepper for each bucket. Let the water boil, and then put out the fire, and let it stand until cool. A bunch of twigs from the Birch, about twice the size of ordinary birch rod, must be used to beat up the preparation, and to dash it over the bushes. If possible, every leaf should get some; to effect which, the Lancashire, or the goblet way, of training is most favourable. Once, perhaps, in five years they may require a second dressing, a fortnight or three weeks after the first. The time for applying it is generally about the middle of April. When the first set of leaves are out, look carefully over the bushes, and you will see here and there a leaf with a round hole in it, the size of a mustard seed to that of a split pea. On looking at the other side of the leaf, you will see the young brood, four or five in number, about the tenth of an inch long. Choose a day for the work when it is likely to keep until the lather is dry.

Best Bait for Black Beetles and Cockroaches

Hint 795   One teaspoonful of sugar; two of beer; one ditto of crumbs of bread; mix these together, and put it in the ordinary trap, which should have a fresh supply every night.

Hint 796   The parings of cucumbers thrown about the floor will destroy them.

Method of Destroying Ants

Hint 797   These prolific creatures may be driven away from particular haunts by sprinkling guano in their runs. They may be destroyed by pouring ammoniacal gas water in their runs and nests. They may be exterminated in meadows by the following simple method:— cut off the hillocks with a sharp spade, leaving a little mould to form a basin; then pour in strong ammoniacal gas liquor. Either of these plans will be found effective.

Effective Method of Destroying the Turnip Fly

Hint 798   Take road dust, soot, and a small proportion of guano; mix them together, and sow them along the rows in the middle of the day. In a short time the flies will disappear.

Hint 799   A little sulphur may be used instead of guano. Some prefer to apply it in the night, when the ground is wet with dew. These remedies are invaluable.

Methods of Exterminating Insects and Worms Injurious to Farm Crops, etc

Hint 800   For the Wireworm, destroy the beetles by hand-picking. They will chiefly be found upon nettles, hemlock, fool's parsley, etc. The eggs are deposited in pastures, clover layers, and fallows. When they appear, have the pastures eaten close by sheep. Give a top dressing of quicklime two parts, soot three parts, salt two parts. Roll in early spring, after this dressing.

Hint 801   Or sow Soda broadcast. This is an excellent remedy, and is effective also against the Green Fly, Encourage Frogs, Toads, Newts, Robins, Blackbirds, Thrushes, Fowls, Ducks, etc., the latter especially should be turned into infested fields.

Hint 802   For the Turnip Fly, add to every twenty pounds of seed half a pint of Linseed Oil, taking care to have it well mixed; add one pound of the flour of sulphur every morning; have the whole rubbed between the hands, to get the seed in a proper state for drilling.

The drill man must be appraised of what seed he has to use, otherwise he will not drill a sufficient quantity, as the sulphur will choke the cups; this, of course, must be looked to.

Hint 803   Or, pour a quart of Spirit of Turpentine on every six pounds of seed, rubbing it through the hands, and leaving it to dry.

Hint 804   Or, supposing the Fly to be developed, dust gas-lime over the crop, in proportion of half a barrel an acre, along the line of turnips.

Hint 805   For the Black Caterpillar, employ women with long twigs to dash the caterpillars from the plants, let them then trample as many as they can with their feet; let the women be followed by a man with a scuffler, set so as to cover the space between the plants. Twice or thrice going over will clear them. Where this cannot be done, hand-gather them.

Hint 806   Young Ducks will be the best for this work. Put water in the field for them, and let them be watched by a boy.

Hint 807   For the caterpillars of the White Turnip Butterfly and indeed all large caterpillars, no remedy surpasses hand-picking, and the aid of Ducks.

Hint 808   For the caterpillars of the Diamond-black Moth, and Leaf Mining Caterpillars. Dust with quicklime early in the morning, while the leaves are covered with dew. They drop to the ground by their silken thread when the plant is agitated, and therefore a bush harrow should be sent over the land, immediately preceding the duster, to bring the insects to the ground, and in contact with the lime. The process should be repeated if necessary.

Hint 809   Young Ducks will be found very useful; but when these are sent into fields of plants of which they are fond, they should be very young, indeed should not have lost their down. They will not then feed upon the plants, but upon the caterpillars.

Hint 810   For the Bean Fly, take a small portion of orpiment, mix it with equal parts of sulphur and asafoetida, and wrap all in a quantity of soft paper, made into touch-paper by being steeped in a solution of saltpetre, proceed to the field, and place this all in a shovel; get into the situation which will take the wind from you across the field; hold the shovel close to the ground, and gradually move about until the whole field has had the benefit of the effluvia.

Hint 811   Or the soft parts of the beans upon which the flies congregate may be cut off by women.

The growth of the beans will even be improved by this treatment, independently of the advantage of getting rid of the pest.

Hint 812 For the Green Fly, or Turnip Plant Louse, fumigate as previously. Or the following is excellent for the Green Fly and the Turnip Fly. Take an old sack, and rip it open, nail it to a pole, the thickness of a pitching fork handle, leaving the pole about eight inches at each end longer than the sacking. Then have one side smeared with gas-tar, and let two men — one at each end of the pole draw the sacking, the tarred side downwards, regularly over the field, letting it sweep the ground, carrying it at an angle of about forty-five degrees, fresh tarring with a brush every "bout," or more often if required; on examination, you will find great numbers of flies sticking to the tarred sacking. Repeat the operation, once a day, for four days; once going over a field will not prevent the destruction of a crop; it must be persevered in, according to the strength of the fly, and the state the land is in. But the remedy is certain, if persevered with.

Hint 813 For the Grubs and Worms that destroy Mangel Wurzel, the most effective remedy is sprinkling powdered quicklime in the drills, between the plants, and suffering it to be slacked by the natural action of the atmosphere. Fresh slacked lime, freely dug into the land previous to sowing, and the steeping of the seeds, as already described, will probably be also found useful in some cases; and when the pest makes its appearance on the leaf. Fumigation may be resorted to with effect.

To prevent Foxes Running off with Poultry — Hints about Badgers, Hedgehogs, Moles etc

Hint 814 As, for the love of sport, it is deemed dishonourable to trap, poison, or shoot Foxes, it may be well to make known that the depredations of these marauders may to a great extent be prevented by surrounding the coops or pens of fowls with nets. Foxes have a great dread of nets, and will seldom return to premises where they have found themselves slightly entangled in their meshes.

Hint 815 The nets should be fixed upon sticks, not too firmly driven in the ground, but hanging rather loosely. A net hung against the Poultry house door in the night is a good protection.

Hint 816 Badgers are rather the friends than foes of the Farmer. They eat earthworms, snails, and any kind of worm, or insect they can lay hold of. They should, therefore, rather be protected than exterminated. Hedgehogs are equally useful; and they destroy a very troublesome weed - the plantain, beneath which they burrow.

Hint 817   The following is an efficacious method of Killing Moles:— Take a quantity of fresh worms, put them in a wooden box, with a small quantity of carbonate of barytes in powder, and let them remain for an hour or two; then find out the runs where the Moles leave the faeces for the land, lay in every run five or six worms, and continue doing so as long as the worms are taken away by the Moles.

Hint 818   It has been suggested that the increase of wireworms has resulted from the indiscriminate destruction of Moles. Where the latter have been spared, the former have been kept down.

To Prevent Injuries to Trees by Rabbit – Best Method of Trapping them

Hint 819   Mix common cold tar with equal portions of cow dung and lime, and with a brush smear the stems to the height of about thirty inches from the ground. The repetition of this treatment annually will eventually preserve the trees from their attacks.

Hint 820   The best mode of taking Rabbits is by means of the trap. For this purpose, dig a pit in the run most commonly frequented, and have it considerably wider at the bottom than at the top; across this lay a board, so nicely balanced upon a central pin, that the weight of the Rabbit is sufficient to bear it down at the extremity, while, as soon as the weight is removed, the board will resume its former position. Numbers may be taken by this method.

To Prevent the Depredations of Rats, etc, in Corn Stacks, — Field Mice, etc

Hint 821   Take one pound of nitre, and one pound of alum; dissolve them together in two quarts of spring water; get about a bushel of bran, and make a mash thereof, putting in two pints of the above liquid, and mixing all together. When you build your stacks, every second course, take a handful or two of the mash and throw upon them until they come to the easing.

Hint 822   For Field Mice, bore holes in the ground to the depth of twenty inches, letting the holes be wider at the bottom than the top; drop into these holes some favourite food, and they may be captured in enormous numbers.

Hint 823   Or drop into their holes, and natural haunts, pellets of the Phosphoric Paste recommended for destroying rats.

To Destroy Rats and Mice

Hint 824   Melt a pound of lard with a gentle heat in a bottle or glass flask, plunged into hot water; then add half an ounce of phosphorus, and one pint of proof spirit; cork the bottle securely, and as it cools shake it frequently, so as to mix the phosphorus uniformly with the lard. When cold, drain off the spirit which will serve another time, and thicken the mixture into a paste with flour. Put this paste on pieces of bread into the places infested with rats.

Hint 825   This is poisonous to Poultry etc., and should be put out of their reach into the holes.

Hint 826   When handling Phosphorus, take care to keep it wet with water, that it may not ignite with the heat of the hand; and guard against bits of it getting under the fingernails.

Hint 827   The Phosphor Paste may be purchased ready made at most chemists; or they will prepare it to order.

Hint 828   Poisoned Wheat, now generally sold, is very effective for the destruction of Mice, and also small birds.

Hint 829   A less dangerous method of getting rid of rats is, to strew pounded potash in their holes. The potash gets into their coats, and irritates their skin, and the rats desert the place.

Hint 830   To prevent rats dying in their holes and becoming offensive, poison them by mixing half a pound of Carbonate of Bart with a quarter pound of lard. It produces great thirst, the rats leaves their holes to drink, and are unable to return.

Various Methods of Destroying Insects in Gardens, Hothouses, etc

Hint 831   To keep down almost every description of Insect injurious to the Gardener and Horticulturist, an effective plan is to employ Children in the summertime to destroy the moths. The destruction of every female moth before the deposition of eggs, may be fairly calculated to prevent the existence of some thousands of Larva's, and thus the races will be kept down.

Hint 832   The Bed Spider may be banished from Hothouses and Greenhouses, by the simple process of cutting off the infected leaf. A leaf once attacked soon decays and falls off; but then the animals remove to another. By carefully pursuing this amputation, plants will become remarkably healthy.

Hint 833   The Red Spider may also he destroyed by a wash of quicklime, adding to it a quantity of sulphur vivum; with this wash, brush over the flues of the house; a fire rather stronger than usual should be kept up for a few days after the operation; the fumes will be then so effectual, that scarcely any spiders will be found alive.

Hint 834   An excellent Method for Destroying the Red Spider, Scale, Thrips, and Green Fly, is the following:— where there are but a few plants infested with either kind of insect, take a one-light frame and place the plants infested about four inches apart, and then procure from one to two gallons of green laurel leaves and well bruise them, immediately place them between the pots and close the frame with the least possible delay, taking care to keep the frame airtight; at the expiration of one hour take out the plants infested with red spider and green fly and it will be found that the insects cease to exist. It will take from eight to twelve hours to destroy the thrips and scales; at the expiration of that time take out the plants, place them in a warm and exposed situation, and in a few days the insects will all dry up and fall off.

Hint 835   When plants are infested in Stoves or Greenhouses with either insect, the process must be varied a little. A house twelve feet by twenty will require about two bushels of leaves; they can be bruised in the house, and placed in a tub or box, and covered with a sack or cloth, until a sufficient quantity is bruised; then they are to be strewed in the paths, and between the pots, and other vacant places, and the house must be kept as close as possible for at least twelve hours; the evening will be found the best time, so that the house can remain, closed and covered with double mats at night.

Hint 836   Aphids are easily killed by burning tobacco in a chafing-dish, provided it is done while they are in a young state; but it is expedient to have these remedies used before the plants can be injured by the attacks of insects.

Hint 837   The Scaly Insect, and Mealy Bug, when they are once perceptible to the eye, can be removed only by picking off, or washing the leaves and branches with a sponge.

Hint 838   Insects in Wood and Walls may be destroyed by washing those parts with a solution of corrosive sublimate in water. But care must be taken that none falls on the plants; and the workmen must be appraised of the strength of the poison.

Hint 839   The Black Maggot on Thorns, Pears, and Cherry trees, and the Gooseberry Caterpillars may be destroyed by slacked lime in very fine powder, dusted over the leaves while they are wet or dewy. If rain follows immediately after the dusting, the good effect will be diminished.

Like all such remedies, the earlier it is applied, after the insect is discovered, the better; and it should be done before the fruit changes colour, lest it be disfigured. Limewater, thrown by the garden engine, is also effective; but it renders the trees and borders unsightly.

Hint 840   A decoction of Elder leaves mixed with soap is also effective.

Hint 841   As a general destroyer of insects upon trees, Gas Water is exceedingly effective. Mix a pound of flour of brimstone in three gallons of gas water, with soap enough to make it adhere to the buds and branches when laid on with a painter's brush. The composition may be mixed over a fire with safety, as it is not inflammable, the gas water being merely that which is employed at gas works in the purification of gas. It does no injury to the trees, but kills the insects by its offensive odour.

Hint 842   American blight may be destroyed on trees by applying train oil, with a painter's brush, to the infected parts of the tree. No mischief will result from the application of the oil to such parts of the tree only as are affected by the insects. In America the following remedy is successfully applied:— before the sap leaves the root, take the earth from around the tree, at least for a foot and a half, and half a foot deep. Mix a quantity of coal soot with fresh rich mould, and fill up the hole again. Be careful to carry off the old earth, and to burn it, lest the insect should be generated in it by the heat of the sun. Tar, applied with a painter's brush, is also an effectual remedy, and it operates, no doubt, in the same manner as the oil, by excluding the air, and involving the insects in a mass from which they cannot escape. It is probable that the effect of the tar is more lasting than that of the oil, and that it would more completely destroy any young insects that might be produced from the latent eggs, a considerable time after their application. Tar, however, destroys the leaves and young shoots, but it does not affect the wood.

Hint 843   In applying Lime for the destruction of Snails, begin by sprinkling quicklime lightly over the beds adjoining alleys and walks about ten o'clock at night. After a wet or very dewy evening, and you will find a large number of snails, many of them exceedingly small, dead on the following morning; but some always escape, and these are probably of another species, which do not leave their hiding places so early in the evening as the others. Sprinkle the lime over the same beds and walks about three o'clock in the morning; and, by these means, in a short time you will cease to be troubled with snails of any kind. The lime used should be fresh burnt, and should be sprinkled regularly though lightly, not only over the ground, but over every plant in the vicinity.

Hint 844   Slugs may be effectually destroyed by limewater, which is superior to lime dust. Take some fresh caustic lime, and pour on it some hot water; when thoroughly dissolved, add water sufficient to make it pass through a fine rose of a water pot. Previous to the preparation, let a woman take some peas haulm, or any large leaves of the cabbage tribe, and lay them a pole distance from each other. If the weather permits, they will be found in abundance, collected under the haulm, etc., both for shelter and food; as we always find they prefer vegetables in a state of stagnation, to those luxuriant in growth; when properly collected, let a boy take up the haulm, etc., and, by a gentle shake, leave the whole of the slugs on the ground. The woman with the water pot must then pour a very small portion of the liquor on them, and the boy in the mean time must remove the haulm, etc., to a different spot in the immediate space. By pursuing this plan for one week (when the weather is favourable), they may be destroyed, as the least drop of the liquor will cause immediate death, whereas with lime they frequently leave a slimy matter behind, and escape. In the flower garden it will be found a great acquisition, by watering the edging of box, thrift, etc.; for wherever it penetrates, it is certain to kill, even in a rainy season.

To Grow Melons in the Open Air

Hint 845   The Open air Bed should be raised on the ground level, on a base twenty-four feet in length, and eight and a half feet in width. The back should be of brick work (against a south wall or paling, therefore, would do), three feet three inches high; the ends should also be of brick-work, and slope from the above height, to the level of the ground at the front. The bed should be composed of weeds, beanstalks, old tan, garden rubbish, and litter of any kind, made compact; and finally, about nine inches of only common garden soil, in which the melons are to be planted. When finished, it uniformly presents an inclined plane, facing the south or south-east.

Hint 846   The soil being raised a little higher than the back to allow for sinking, the slope should form an angle with the ground line of about twenty-three degrees. Nine plants raised singly in pots may be planted out in this slope, and, until somewhat established, they require to be protected by hand glasses; flat tiles should be then laid over the surface of the bed. The shoots or vines of the Melons need not be stopped nor thinned; in short, with the exception of merely pegging them down, no interference with their growth is required.

Hint 847   Instead of Tiles being employed, as above, Slates were formerly used; but these became at times so heated by the sun, that the plants suffered from being subjected to the vicissitudes of great heat in the day, alternately with the cold to which they were exposed at night. Tiles, on the contrary, do not absorb heat so rapidly, but retain it longer.

Hint 848 The situation of the melon bed need not be particularly sheltered. Near our own bed there is a hedge on the north side, at the distance of fifteen feet from the back of the bed, but it is not high. Two feet behind the hedge there are some tall elm trees, and at some distance there is a row of trees, which afford shelter from the west winds.

Hint 849 The mode in which the plants are reared is an important point; they are raised with as little heat as possible, and are allowed plenty of air.

Hint 850 When Melon Plants are raised for the purpose of being planted on a bed of the above description, the pots in which the seeds are sown should never be plunged in a warm dung or tan-bed; for when plants so treated are removed into the common ground, if the weather proves either cold or wet, their leaves turn yellow, and they afterwards become sickly, and continue so a long time.

Vegetable Marrow, an Excellent Substitute for or Addition to a Crop of Potatoes

Hint 851 The early potatoes having been well taken care of during the winter, the Marrows may be sown about the first week in May, in the open ground, in a warm corner. When transplanting time comes, the early potatoes will not be nearly ripe; but a root of potatoes is to be lifted every six or eight feet apart, in every sixth or eighth alternate row, and a Marrow to be inserted in its place. When thus planted, in moderately rich land, twenty tons of Marrows may be grown to the acre; and when ripe, they can be stowed away anywhere, and will keep good for a great length of time.

Hint 852 The following is a capital way of Cooking Marrows:— Cut them into short pieces, take out all the pith and seeds, and boil them in plenty of water and salt. When well boiled, scrape out all the Marrow, put it between the two dishes, and squeeze out the water, then mash it well, adding salt, pepper, and a little butter. This is a capital dish.

Hint 853 In addition to their utility as a vegetable for the dinner table. Marrows form, when boiled, a most economical food for Fattening Pigs.

Number of Seeds in a given Quantity, and the space of Ground they will Sow

Hint 854 In garden operations, it is very desirable neither to sow too thickly nor too sparely. Of the two evils the latter is the least.

The following rules as to quantity and space, in connection with some of our principal vegetables, will be of great utility to the Amateur Gardener:—

1) One ounce of Parsley Seed has in it 16,200 seeds; and a quarter of that quantity is enough for sowing a drill sixty yards long.

2) One ounce of Salmon Radish Seed contains 1,960 seeds, and will sow, broadcast, a bed containing ten square yards.

3) One ounce of Onion Seed contains 7,600 seeds, and, sown broadcast, will suffice for fourteen square yards of ground; but, if sown in drills, will be enough for twenty drills, each four yards long, or for about twenty-four square yards of ground.

4) One pint of Sun-coloured Dwarf Kidney Beans contains 750 seeds, which are enough to sow four rows each seven yards long.

5) One pint of Scarlet Runners contains 264 seeds, and is enough for four rows each nine yards long.

6) One pint of Broad Windsor Beans has 170 seeds, and is sufficient for seven rows, each four yards long.

7) One pint of Knights Dwarf Marrow Peas contains 1,720 seeds. One pint of Early Warwick Peas, 2,160. One pint of Prussian Blue Peas, 1,860. One pint of Scimetar Peas, 1,299; and any one of these pints will sow eight rows, each four yards long, as the larger peas require to be sown wider apart in the rows than the smaller seeded peas.

8) One ounce of Carrot seed or Parsnip seed, sown, broadcast, will be sufficient for a bed containing sixteen square yards, and for one containing twenty-eight square yards, if sown in drills.

9) One ounce of any kind of Cabbage or Broccoli seed will be enough for a bed containing nine square yards, if sown broadcast, or for sixteen square yards in drills.

10) To prevent Cabbages from running to long woody stalks, take a penknife and stab through the stalks of those that exhibit a tendency to shankiness; make the stab through the stalk about the middle; insert a small piece of wood to keep the incision open, and this will check the growth. By this simple plan, a good cabbage head may be secured on every stalk.

11) All flat seeds, such as Broad Beans, should be sown sideways for if laid flat on the soil they are apt to rot, and, even if this mishap does not befall them, they never germinate so readily as those placed sideways. This accounts for so many failures amongst Gourds, Melons, Cucumbers etc.

A New Method of Propagating Potatoes

Hint 855 Take off all the stems which arise from a cut of the potatoes except one, and plant them in drills, two feet apart, and one foot in the drill between the plants. The planted stems will produce an excellent yield of good sound potatoes. The potatoes from which the offsets are taken, having been left with but one stalk to each, will produce abundantly large and marketable potatoes.

A perch of twenty-one feet has been found to yield eight stone of large sound potatoes upon this system.

Hint 856 Diseased Potatoes may be preserved for many months for Pigs in the following way: — Boil the small or other diseased potatoes, and then beat them down into large casks, strewing salt over them, as they are beaten in. Keep them carefully from the air, and in a dry cool situation.

The Economy of Pig Manure and Coal Ashes

Hint 857 Have a large dry shed, in which put a layer of Coal Ashes, about a foot thick, and four feet wide. Take the excrement of the Pigs, both liquid and solid, and throw it upon the ashes. As soon as the ashes are saturated, add more, and commence a fresh layer. After it has lain for some time, let it be turned and mixed two or three times, and it will be fit for drilling.

Hint 858 The droppings of three Pigs, preserved with ashes in this way, will be ample for two acres of Turnips, and quite equal to three sacks of bone dust per acre. If we can get such valuable manure for nothing but the labour, it is better than paying money for artificial composts.

Hint 859 Pig Manure is also one of the best for Kitchen Garden crops.

Hint 860 To kill Vermin infesting Pigs, rub them with grease, or olive oil. These greasy applications are very beneficial to the Pig's health; and if, after two or three greasings they are well washed, they will improve wonderfully.

Coal Ashes Useful for Making Garden Walks

Hint 861 To three bushels of Coal Ashes, not sifted very fine, add one bushel of fine gravel. Add water to these, and mix them until they become about as soil as mortar. Spread over the walks, the surface of which should previously be slightly broken, and raked smooth. Make the mortar like mixture smooth and even by spreading it with a piece of board. It will become hard in a few days.

Value of Soot as a Manure

Hint 862 There are few manures more efficacious than Soot, and as it is in the power of every one to obtain it without expense, few gardens should be without it. Its value may soon be ascertained by the following experiment:— spread it around Cauliflower plants, about a foot in diameter, and from a quarter to half an inch in depth.

The plants treated in this manner will be ready to gather two or three weeks sooner than the others on the same piece of ground. The soot will not only act as a powerful fertilizer, but will prevent the attacks of Slugs.

Hint 863   As every chimney in which a fire is constantly kept, requires sweeping at least every four months, the sweepings for one chimney being sufficient to spread round six dozen plants, it follows that in a year's time sufficient soot may be gathered from a single chimney to treat two hundred and sixteen plants, in the manner described.

Hint 864   Soot Water is an excellent manure for Celery, and where worms and insects are troublesome, a little dry soot dashed along the rows will prevent their ravages.

To Prepare the Feathers of Geese, Fowls, etc, for
Domestic Purposes

Hint 865   Take for every gallon of clean water one pound of Quicklime, mix them well together, and when the undissolved lime is precipitated in fine powder, pour off the clean limewater for use. Put the Feathers to be cleaned in another tub, and add to them a quantity of the clean limewater, sufficient to cover them about three inches when well immersed and stirred about therein. The feathers, when thoroughly moistened, will sink down, and should remain in the limewater three or four days; after which, the foul liquor should be separated from them, by laying them in a sieve. They should be afterwards well washed in clean water, and dried upon nets, the meshes of which may be about the fineness of cabbage nets. The feathers must be, from time to time, shaken on the nets, and as they get dry, will fall through the meshes, and are to be collected for use. The admission of air will be serviceable in drying.

Hint 866   The process will be completed in three weeks; and, after being thus prepared, the feathers will only require to be beaten to get rid of the dust.

Excellent and Economical Fruit Jam, made Without
Sugar

Hint 867   It is not generally known, that boiling fruit a long time, and shimming it well, without the sugar, and without a cover to the preserving pan, is a very economical and excellent way — economical, because the bulk of the scum rises from the fruit, and not from the sugar, if the latter is good; and boiling it without a cover allows the evaporation of all the watery particles there from; the preserves keep firm, and well flavoured. The proportions are, three-quarters of a pound of sugar to a pound of fruit.

Hint 868   Jam made in this way, of Blackberries, Currants, Strawberries, Raspberries, or Gooseberries is excellent.

Usefulness of Decayed Leaves

Hint 869   Decayed Leaves make the best of soils for Potting plants; properly prepared they also make the best of manures for the Flower Bed or Border, and for the Vegetable Garden, more especially for manure for early Potatoes; they are also valuable as a fermenting leaven, of which to form Hotbeds. In this respect they are better than tanner's bark, horse dung, or any other substance whatever.

Hint 870   If wanted to make Hotbeds with, lay them on a heap in the shape of a roof of a house. This will prevent them from becoming too wet, even in the wettest weather. Turn them over with a fork every three or four weeks. If they are very dry, throw a few buckets of water upon them, as you are turning them. You may also mix any newly gathered leaves amongst those first collected. By this method duly carried on, the leaves will be well prepared to make a hotbed of lasting temperature, yet moderate heat.

Hint 871   Should the leaves not be required for the purpose of yielding heat, let them be spread as fast as they are gathered, in some convenient place, and all the slops of the house, and the refuse of the kitchen, as well as any liquid manure, be poured upon them. If a little Gypsum is procurable, it would be useful to cast it thinly over the heap from time to time. Road scrapings, also may be used to spread upon this heap of riches, for so, indeed, it truly is.

Hint 872   Plenty of the foregoing mixture laid upon, and immediately dug into, the ground, will increase the following crops tenfold,

Hint 873   Some part of the leaves may be wanted for potting purposes. Lay a heap apart, turn it more frequently, beating and chopping the leaves with a spade or fork, and lay this heap flat, in order to receive all the rains that fall, for they will materially assist decomposition.

Hint 874   Avoid all mixtures with leaves for making vegetable mould, intended ultimately, when rotted sufficiently to pass through a sieve, to mix with pure loam or peat earth, to be used for the more delicate plants, such, for instance, as Auriculas and Carnations. Lime, coarse sand, or road scrapings, would render the vegetable mould not so desirable for these finer rooted and more valuable plants.

Hint 875   When it is found necessary to reduce the number of Fowls, the proper plan is, to first kill all superfluous Cocks for the table. Some persons advise killing the Hens, but this should not be done if they are good layers, because those hens that begin by laying well, generally continue to do so, and being strong, and accustomed to the cold of winter, they are more likely to be healthy, and to lay well in the cold season, than Pullets.

Hint 876   The best plan is, to notice the Pullets when they begin to lay, and to select for killing those that do not lay well. By the month of February, the stock should be reduced to a number small in proportion to the place where they run, allowing not more than six or eight hens to each cock.

Hint 877   About this time begin to preserve Eggs for hatching. Notice those which are laid by the best hens, and let them be put aside with care; place them on end in a box of bran, with the broad end downwards. They should not have been laid more than a fortnight when they are put under the hen.

Hint 878   The Fecundity of Eggs cannot be determined otherwise than in the following manner:— at the end of about three days after setting them, they may be held to a hole in a door or shutter, against the sunshine, and those which are unproductive will look clear, while those which have been fertilised will show a darkness in one spot, and a network of veins forming over the inside of the shell.

An Excellent Yeast, easily made by Persons who Reside far from a Brewery — Parsnip Beer

Hint 879   Take a pound of flour, mix it with a pint of cold water. Boil one ounce of hops in three pints of cold water for twenty minutes; strain the hops over the flour, and let it stand until it is milk warm. Then add the "onset," and set it by the fire all night, and it will be ready for use in the morning. The "onset" is a pint of the same mixture, kept from the last baking; it will keep more than a week, or may be used sooner.

Hint 880   At the first making, Brewer's Yeast must be used for the "onset."

Hint 881   An excellent Beer maybe brewed from Parsnips by using one gallon of parsnips to every four gallons of water. The parsnips must not be scraped nor peeled.

They should be taken fresh from the ground, well washed, boiled to a pulp, the hops added and boiled, and the whole strained, cooled, and worked with yeast.

A Family Medicine Chest of Homely Drugs

Hint 882   There are few things so serviceable for a cold, as Sage, the common herb. Of this a tea should be made thus:— put a hand of sage leaves into a teapot, pour boiling water on it, and let it stand close by the fire for half an hour. Drink a teacupful. Repeat the dose for a night or two, and your cold will most likely have disappeared. In order to make the sage tea more palatable, a few leaves of lemon thyme may be added.

Hint 883   Penny Royal is also a most useful herb, and should be used in the same way.

Hint 884   Ground Ivy is most valuable for Coughs and Delicate Lungs. It is found in almost every hedge, and must be steeped in boiling water, and then allowed to get cold. It should be drunk the first thing in the mornings and if thickened with a little honey, may be sipped, with much benefit, during the day, when the cough is troublesome.

Hint 885   Half a pint of Rose Water and two teaspoonful of White Vinegar, make an excellent lotion for Pains in the Head and Face.

Hint 886   A very efficacious remedy for the Cough of a Child, is to slice a common Turnip rather thin, and to sprinkle brown sugar over it; let it stand for a few hours with a saucer pressed down on it, and the syrup which runs from it will be found very soothing to the chest, if sipped frequently.

Hint 887   To those who give medicines to the poor, the following receipt will be found useful, particularly for old people. One tablespoonful of honey, one of vinegar; let it stand by the fire until it is well mixed, then add sixty drops of ipecacuanha wine, and twenty drops of laudanum; take a teaspoonful night and morning, or more often if the cough is very troublesome.

Hint 888   How often in the case of accidents by fire is time lost, by the neighbours not knowing how to act, and waiting until the medical man arrives. If it is remembered that the very best thing to be done when any one has received a burn or a scald is, to lay on the part that is injured, a thick coating of Cotton Wool or wadding, so as to completely exclude the air, much future pain is avoided. If wool happens to be not at hand, scraped Potato, Turnip, etc., will ease the pain.

Hint 889   A capital domestic remedy for a severe cut will be found in the leaves of a common White Lily; they should be steeped in brandy for some weeks, and be kept ready for use. A leaf should be bound tightly round the wound.

Hint 890   For Ear-ache toast an Onion thoroughly, take the heart out, put it into a piece of flannel, and insert it into the ear, having previously put a few drops of hot water into the ear.
Bad Sprains or Bruises are much eased by fomentations, either of Poppy-heads or Camomile boiled in water, or plain water alone, only taking care that it is as hot as the hand can bear.

Hint 891   The White of an Egg into which a piece of Alum, about the size of a walnut has been stirred until it forms a thick jelly, is a capital remedy for sprains. It should be laid over the sprain upon a piece of lint, and be changed as often as it becomes hot or dry.

Hint 892   A lump of fresh Quicklime the size of a walnut, dropped into a pint of water, and allowed to stand all night, the water being then poured off from the sediment, and mixed with a quarter of a pint of the best vinegar, forms the best wash for scurf in the head. It is to be applied to the roots of the hair.

Various Methods of Cleaning Woollen and other Cloths

Hint 893   The art of Cleaning Cloths, without injuring the colours, supposes — First, a knowledge of the various substances that can occasion spots upon them. Secondly, that of the substances to which we must have recourse to remove those stains when deposited upon the cloth. Thirdly, that of the manner in which the colours will be affected by the re-agents meant to be employed for the removal of the spots. Fourthly, that of the manner in which the cloth itself will be affected by the re-agents. Fifthly, how to restore the colours when changed, or rendered faint. Wanting some knowledge on these points, it is evident that no person can undertake to clean cloth under all circumstances without great danger of spoiling the article.

Hint 894   Of the substances which occasion spots upon cloth some are easily known by their appearance; for instance, Grease of every kind. Others produce more complicated effects, such as Acids, Alkalies, Perspiration, Fruits, Wine, etc.

Hint 895   The effects of Acids upon blacks, purples, blues (except those produced by indigo or Prussian blue), and some other colours), and upon all those shades of colours which are produced by means of iron, archil, and astringent substances, is to turn them red. They render yellows more pale, except those produced by annatto, which they turn to an orange colour.

Hint 896   Alkalies turn scarlet's, and all reds produced by Brazil or logwood, to a violet colour; they turn green (upon woollen cloths) to yellow, and they give a reddish cast to the yellow produced by annatto. The effect of the perspiration is the same as that of the alkalies.

Hint 897   Spots made upon cloths by simple substances are easily removed by well known means. For instance, greasy substances are removed by Alkalies, by soap, by Yolk of Eggs, or by Fat Earths; Oxide of Iron, by Nitric or Oxalic Acid, Spots occasioned by Acids are removed by Alkalies, and vice versa.

Hint 898   Spots caused by Fruit upon white cloth are removed by sulphurous acid (vitriol), or what is still better, by Oxygenated Muriatic Acid.

Hint 899   But when the spots are of a complicated nature, various means must be employed successively, thus to remove a spot occasioned by the corm of carriage wheels, we must first dissolve the alkali by some of the means above mentioned, and then take away the oxide of iron by oxalic acid.

Hint 900   The colours of cloths are often injured by the re-agents made use of in order to restore them effectively; when such is the case we must thoroughly understand the art of dyeing, and know how to modify the means according to circumstances. This is sometimes difficult, because it is necessary to produce a colour similar to that of the rest of the cloth, and to apply that colour to a particular part only; sometimes also the mordant which fixed the colour, or the basis which heightened it, has also been destroyed, and must be restored. It is evident that in this case the means to be employed depend upon the nature of the colour, and that of the ingredients which produce it, for the same colour may be and often is obtainable from different substances.

Hint 901   Thus, when after using an alkali to remove an acid spot upon brown, violet, or blue cloth, etc., there remains a yellow spot, the original colour is again produced by means of a solution of Tin. A solution of the Sulphate of Iron restores the colour to those brown cloths which have been dyed with galls. Acids give to yellow cloths which have been rendered dull or brown by Alkalies, their original brightness.

Hint 902   When black cloths dyed with Logwood have any reddish spots occasioned by acids, alkalies turn such spots to a yellow colour, and a little of the astringent principle makes them black again.

Hint 903   A solution of one part of Indigo in four parts of Sulphuric Acid, properly diluted with water, may be successfully employed to restore a faded blue colour upon wool or cotton.

Hint 904   Red or scarlet colours may be restored by means of Cochineal, and a solution of Muriate of Tin, etc.

Hint 905   The choice of re-agents is not a matter of indifference; vegetable acid is generally preferable to mineral ones. The sulphurous acid, however, may be used for spots from fruit; it does not injure blue upon silk, or the colours produced by astringents; nor does it affect yellow upon cotton. The volatile alkalies succeed better than fixed alkalies in removing spots produced by acids. They are usually made use of in the form of vapour, and act quickly, seldom injuring the colour of the cloth.

Hint 906   The means of removing spots of Grease are well known, namely, Alkalies, Fuller's earth, Essential Oils dissolved in alcohol, a sufficient degree of heat to render the grease volatile, etc.

Hint 907   Spots of Inky or any other occasioned by yellow aside of iron, may be removed by Oxalic Acid. The colour may be restored by alkalies, or by a solution of the Muriate of tin. Such spots may also be taken away by oxygenated muriatic acid, when they are upon white cloth or upon paper. The effect of alkalies, and that of perspiration being the same, their spots may be removed by acids, or even by a diluted solution of Muriate of tin.

Hint 908   When the spots are owing to various unknown causes, we must have recourse to compositions possessing various powers, of which the following may be considered as one of the most efficacious:— dissolve some white soap in alcohol, mix with this solution four or five yolks of eggs; add, gradually, some spirits of turpentine, and then stir with the mixture such a quantity of Fuller's earth as will enable you to form it into balls. The manner of using these balls is to rub the spots with them, having previously wetted the place with soft water, after which the cloth is to be well rubbed and washed. By this means all kinds of spots, except those occasioned by ink or any other solution of iron, may be removed.

Hint 909   The washing of cloth takes off the gloss and leaves a dull spot disagreeable to the eye. This Gloss may be restored by passing in a proper direction over the washed part of the cloth a brush wetted with water, in which a small quantity of gum is dissolved, and then laying upon the part a sheet of paper, a piece of cloth, and a pretty considerable weight, which must remain until the cloth is quite dry. A screw press may be substituted for the weight with better effect.

Hint 910   A white Lace Veil may be cleaned by setting it in a strong lather of white soap and very clean water. Let it simmer slowly for about a quarter of an hour. Then take it out, and squeeze it well, but avoid rubbing it. Rinse it in two cold waters, adding to the last a drop of liquid blue. Have ready some very clear weak gum Arabic water, or some thin starch, or rice water. Pass the veil through it, and clear it by clapping. Then stretch it out even, and pin it to dry on a linen cloth, making the edge as straight as possible, opening out all the scallops, and fastening each with pins. When dry, lay a piece of thin muslin smoothly over it, and iron it on the wrong side.

Hint 911   A black Lace Veil may be cleaned by passing it through a warm liquor of Bullocks Gall and water; after which it must be rinsed in cold water, then cleansed for stiffening, and finished as follows:— put a piece of glue, about the size of a bean, into boiling water, and let it dissolve. Pass the veil through the solution, clap it, and then stretch on a frame, or on a linen cloth, to dry. When dry, iron on the wrong side, having laid a linen cloth under the ironing blanket.

Hint 912   Any article of Black Lace may be cleaned in the same manner.

Hint 913   Silk Lace or Blonde may be cleaned by covering a bottle with clean linen or muslin, winding the lace around it, tacking on the ends with needle and thread, not leaving the edge outward, but turning it under while winding. Set the bottle thus covered to stand in a strong lather of white soap and very clean soft water, cold, and place it in the sun, first gently rubbing the suds up and down on the lace. Keep it in the sun for several successive days, changing the latter daily, and rubbing gently each time. Take the Lace from the bottle, and pin it backward and forward on a flat board, covered with clean linen. It must be pinned carefully with small pins, so as to lie straight and even. When dry, iron or press it, without starching.

Hint 914   Thread Lace may be cleaned in the same manner. When dry, lay in long folds. Or, when the thread lace has been tacked to the bottle, take some of the best sweet oil, and saturate the lace thoroughly. Have ready in a wash-kettle, a strong cold lather of clear water, and white Castile soap. Fill the bottle with cold water, to prevent its bursting, cork it well, and stand it upright in the suds, with a string round the neck secured to the ears or handle of the kettle, to prevent its shifting about and breaking while over the fire. Let it boil in the suds for an hour or more, until the lace is clean and white all through. Drain off the suds, and dry it on the bottle in the sun.

When dry, remove the lace from the bottle and roll it round a wide ribbon-block; or lay it in long folds, place it within a sheet of smooth white paper, and press it in a large book for a few days.

Hint 915   Lace may he cleaned without washing by fixing it even in a tent, and rubbing it over with the soft part of fine bread. Afterwards dust out the crumbs.

Hint 916   Crochet collars, or other work, may be cleaned by the above methods.

Hint 917   Gold Lace may be cleaned by rubbing it with a soil brush, dipped in Roche Alum, burnt, and sifted to a very fine powder.

Hint 918   Alkaline preparations, though they clean the gold, corrode and discolour the silk of Gold Embroidery Work, and soap injures certain colours. But Spirit of Wine may be used without injury to the silk, and in many instances will restore the lustre of the gold. But if the gold is worn off, and the silver underneath tarnished to a golden colour, it will be best to let the tarnish remain.

Hint 919   Ribbons, Satins, Scarf's, etc., of one colour, should be treated as follows:— Put about a tablespoon of good spirit of wine into a gallon of very clean soft water. Wash the ribbon, or other article, in this; and next wash it through a warm lather of white soap; afterwards rinse in cold water, pull even, and dry gradually. When dry, stretch it upon an ironing table, fasten it to the cloth by pins, and sponge evenly all over with a very weak solution of isinglass, or rice water. If a ribbon, iron it upon a sheet of smooth letter paper, putting paper also over it, and move the iron quickly.

Hint 920   When the colour is Lilac, add a little dissolved Pearlash to the rinsing water; if Green, a little Vinegar; if Pink or Blue, a few drops of Vitriol; if Yellow, a little tincture of Saffron; if White, mix a salt-spoonful of Cream of Tartar with the soap suds. Other colours may be set by stirring a teaspoonful of Ox-gall into the first water.

Hint 921   Flowered Silks and White Satins may be cleaned with the following preparation:— Mix sifted bread crumbs with powder blue, and rub it thoroughly all over the article; shake well, and dust with clean soft cloths. Should there be any Gold or Silver Flowers, take a piece of crimson ingrain velvet, rub the flowers with it. And their lustre will be improved.

Hint 922   Creased Ribbons may be restored by laying them evenly on a board, and with a very clean, sponge, damping them evenly all over. Then roll them smoothly and tightly on a ribbon block, of greater breadth than the ribbon, and let them remain until dry.

Afterwards, transfer to a clean dry block. Then wrap in brown paper, and keep until wanted.

Hint 923   Ribbons and other Silks should be put away for preservation in brown paper; the chloride of lime used in manufacturing white paper frequently produces discoloration. A White Satin Dress should be pinned in blue paper, with brown paper outside, sewn together at the edges.

Hint 924   Grease Spots may be taken from silks in the following manner:— Upon a deal table lay a piece of woollen cloth or baize, upon which, lay smoothly the part stained, with the right side downwards. Having spread a piece of brown paper on the top, apply a flat iron just hot enough to scorch the paper. About five or eight seconds is usually sufficient. Then rub the stained part briskly with a piece of cap-paper.

Hint 925   Coloured or Black Silks, Stuffs, Moreens, Printed Cottons, and Chintzes, may be cleaned, without injury to their colours, by Potato Liquor. Grate raw potatoes to a fine pulp; add water in the proportion of a pint to a pound of potatoes; pass the liquid through a coarse sieve into a vessel, and allow it to remain until the fine white starch subsides to the bottom. Pour off the clear liquor, which is to be used for cleaning. Spread the article to be cleaned upon a table, which should be covered with a linen cloth; dip a sponge in the liquor, and apply it until the dirt is removed. Then rinse the article in clean cold water several times.

Hint 926   The Coarse Pulp, which does not pass through the sieve, will do to clean Worsted Curtains, Carpets, and other coarse articles; and the White Starch that subsides from the liquor may be rendered useful for ordinary starching purposes.

Hint 927   Some persons use the whole of the Pulp and water for the scouring process. Others slice the potatoes, and rub the slices on the stuff, in the same manner as soap is applied.

Hint 928   Silk Stockings may be cleaned in the following manner:— After washing them in the usual way, rinse them in clean water, and wash them well in fresh soap liquor; then make a third soap liquor, and colour it with a little stone blue; wash the stockings once more, wring them, and dry them carefully. Stove them with brimstone, drawing two stockings, one over the other, upon a wooden shape. In drawing them on, see that the two fronts, or outsides come together, to accomplish which, one stocking must be the right way, the other outside in. Polish with a glass bottle. The first two liquors should be lukewarm, but the third as hot as the hand can bear it.

Hint 929   Blondes and Gauzes may be cleaned in the same manner; but for these there should be a little gum put in the last liquor.

Hint 930   Mousselines-de-Laine may be washed in Rice water. Boil a pound of rice in five quarts of water, and, when cool, wash the material in this, using the rice for soap. Have a second quantity ready, but strain the rice from this, and use it while warm, keeping the rice strained off for a third washing. This process will stiffen the fabric, and heighten the colours.

Hint 931   The Colours of Merinos, Mousselines-de-Laine, Ginghams, Chintzes, Printed Lawns, etc., may be preserved by using a strong milk warm lather with white soap, and putting the dress into it, instead of rubbing it on the material, and stirring into a first and second tub of water a large tablespoonful of ox-gall.

Hint 932   Coloured Articles should not be allowed to remain long in water. A small piece of Alum should be boiled in the water of which the lather is to be made. They should be washed quickly, and then rinsed through two cold waters. Should alum not be added to the lather, then a teaspoonful of vinegar should be stirred into the water for each rinsing; this will help to fix and brighten the colours. After rinsing, they should be hung out immediately to dry.

Hint 933   No Coloured Articles should ever be boiled or scalded. Neither should they be allowed to freeze, or the colours will be irreparably injured. They should be ironed immediately they are dry enough, and not be allowed to lie damp over night, nor be sprinkled. They should not be smoothed with a hot iron. Pink and Green colours, though they may withstand the washing, will frequently change as soon as a hot iron is put over them.

Hint 934   Black Crape, and Mourning Dresses, may be freed from stains in the following manner:— Boil a handful of Fig leaves in two quarts of water, until reduced to a pint. Squeeze the leaves, strain the liquor, and put it into a bottle for use. Bombazines, Crape, Cloth, etc., should be rubbed with a sponge dipped in this liquor, and most stains will be instantly removed. Should there be any objection to wetting the material, French Chalk will absorb grease from the finest textiles, without injuring them. When Crape is stained with water, producing a whitish mark, spread it on a table laying on it a large book or paper weight to keep it steady and place underneath the stain a bit of waste black silk. With a camel's hair brush, dipped in good Writing Ink go over the stain, and then wipe off the ink with a little bit of black silk. The white mark will be removed.

Hint 935   Skimmed Milk and Water, with a bit of fine glue dissolved in it, made scalding hot, is an excellent restorative of rusty Black Italian Crape. It should be clapped and pulled dry, like muslin and will e greatly improved.

Hint 936   China Crape Scarf's cab be washed as frequently as may be required, in the following manner. Make a strong lather of boiling water, and allow it to cool. When cold, or nearly so, wash the scarf quickly and thoroughly, dip it immediately in cold hard water in which a little salt has been thrown, rinse, squeeze, and hang it out to dry in the open air, and the more quickly it dries, the cleaner it will be.

Hint 937   To wash; Chintzes, and preserve their colours and gloss, take two pounds of rice, and boil it in two gallons of water until soft, pour it into a tub, with the liquor; let it stand, until about the warmth generally approved for coloured linen; then put the chintz in it, and use the rice instead of soap; then boil the same quantity of rice again, but strain the rice from the water, and mix it in warm clean water. Wash in this until quite clean; afterwards rinse it in the water the rice was boiled in, and this will answer better than starch; it will be stiff as long as you wear it and will not be affected by dew. If a gown, it must be taken to pieces, and for drying be hung as smoothly as possible. When dry, rub it with a sleek stone, but do not use an iron.

Hint 938   Faded Dresses may be bleached by washing them well in hot suds and boiling them until the colour disappears; then dry in the sun.

Hint 939   Fruit Stains may generally be removed from linen by rubbing the part on each side with yellow soap, then tying up a piece of pearlash in the cloth, and soaking well in boiling water. Afterwards expose the stained part to the sun and air, until removed, and repeat if necessary.

Hint 940   Mildew may be removed from linen by soap, well rubbed in; then scrape some fine chalk, and rub it also on the linen. Lay it on the grass, in the sun. As it dries, the mildew will disappear. It may require to be repeated. If the stains are of long standing, rub them on each side with wet brown soap; mix some starch to a thick paste, with cold water, and spread it over the soaped places. Then expose as before. If the stains do not yield, try, instead of the starch, chalk, etc., boiled rice, scraped potatoes, and lastly a little chloride of lime. The stain that does not yield to one substance will probably be removed by another.

Hint 941　　　　When linen has turned Yellow, cut up a pound of fine white soap into a gallon of milk, and hang it over a fire in a wash kettle. When the soap has completely melted, put in the linen, and boil it for half an hour. Then take it out; have ready a lather of soap and water; wash the linen in it, and then rinse it through two cold waters, with a very little blue in the last.

Hint 942　　　　When Linen has been Scorched, use the following remedy:- add to a quart of vinegar the juice of half a dozen large onions, about an ounce of soap rasped down, a quarter of a pound of fuller's earth, an ounce of lime, and one ounce of pearlash. Boil all of it until it is pretty thick, and spread some of it on the scorched part. Allow it to remain until dry, then scrape it off, and wash. Two or three applications will restore the linen, unless so much scorched that the fabric is scorched.

Hint 943　　　　Iron Moulds may be removed from linen by rubbing them over with sulphuret of potash; then steep the spot in lemon juice, or citric acid, and afterwards wash well in water.

Hint 944　　　　Marking Ink may be removed from linen by a saturated solution of cyanuret of potassium, applied with a camel's hair brush. Common Ink Stains may be removed by applying, in the same manner, oxalic acid. But frequently, when the stain is caused by ink manufactured with Logwood, a red mark remains, which may be removed by the application of a little chloride of lime. All strong acids and alkalies tend to injure the fabric; therefore, immediately the stains are removed, the spots should be well rinsed in cold water.

Hint 945　　　　Grease may be taken out of Velvet by a little turpentine, poured over the spot; then rub briskly with a piece of clean dry flannel. Repeat the application, if necessary, and hang the article in the air, to remove the smell.

Hint 946　　　　When the Pile of Velvet is pressed down, hold the part over the mouth of a vessel filled with boiling water, with the inside of the velvet turned to the water. The raising of the pile may be assisted by a few strokes of a brush alternately in opposite directions, while the velvet is over the vessel.

Hint 947　　　　White Satin Shoes may be cleaned by rubbing them with stone blue and flannel, and afterwards cleaning them with bread.

Hint 948　　　　A little Pipe Clay, dissolved in the water used for washing linen will clean it thoroughly, with half the amount of soap, and a great diminution of labour; the articles will be greatly improved in colour, and the texture will be benefited.

Hint 949   Calicoes, if badly washed, are more liable than linens to assume a yellow tinge. Many persons attempt to remedy this by a strong shade of blue, which is detrimental to the appearance of the linen. Lime water, unless used too strong, will thoroughly cleanse white cotton articles without injury.

Hint 950   The method of washing with Lime is as follows:— Take half a pound of quicklime, half a pound of soap, and half a pound of soda, shred the soap and dissolve it in half a gallon of boiling water; pour half a gallon of boiling water over the soda; and enough boiling water over the quicklime to cover it. The lime must be quite fresh. Prepare each of these in separate vessels. Put the dissolved lime and soda together, and boil them for twenty minutes. Then pour them into a jar to settle. Set aside the Flannels and Coloured things, as they must not be washed in this way. The night before washing, the collars and wristbands of shirts, the feet of stockings, etc., should be rubbed well with soap and set to soak. In the morning pour ten gallons of water into the copper, and having strained the mixture of lime and soda well, taking great care not to disturb the settlings, put it, together with the soap, into the water, and make the whole boil before putting in the clothes. A plate should be placed at the bottom of the copper to prevent the clothes from burning. Boil each lot of clothes from half an hour to an hour. Wash the finer things first. Then rinse them well in cold blue water. When dry they will be beautifully white. The same water will do for three lots.

Hint 951   Rusty Black Clothes may be revived in the following manner:— Brush the garments well, then boil four ounces of logwood in a boiler or copper containing two or three gallons of water for half an hour; dip the clothes in warm water, and squeeze dry, then put them into the copper and boil for half an hour. Take them out and add three drachms of sulphate of iron; boil for half an hour then take them out, and hang them up for an hour or two; take them down, rinse them in three cold waters, dry well, and rub with a soft brush which has had a few drops of olive oil rubbed on its surface.

Hint 952   If the clothes are threadbare about the elbows, cuffs, etc., raise the nap with a teasel or half-worn hatter's card, filled with flocks, and when sufficiently raised, lay the nap the right way with a hard brush. We have seen old coats come out with a wonderful dash of respectability after this operation.

Hint 953   White or Coloured Kid Gloves may be cleaned thus:— Put the glove on your hand, then take a small piece of flannel, dip it in turpentine or camphine, and well but gently rub it over the glove, taking care not to make it too wet. When the dirt is removed, dip the flannel (or another piece, if that has become dirty) in the pipe clay and rub it over the glove.

Take it off, and hang it up in a room to dry, and in a day or two very little smell will remain and if done carefully they will be almost as good as new.

Hint 954　　　　For Coloured gloves, if yellow, use gamboge after the pipe clay, and for other colours match it in dry coloured powder.

Hint 955　　　　Or White Kid Gloves may be cleaned as follows:— Stretch them on a board, and rub the soiled spots with cream of tartar or magnesia; Let then rest for an hour. Take a mixture of alum and fuller's earth, in powder, and rub it all over the gloves with a clean brush, and let them rest for an hour or two. Then sweep it all off, and go over with a flannel dipped in a mixture of bran and finely powdered whiting. Let them rest another hour; brush off the powder, and they will be very dean.

Hint 956　　　　Coloured Gloves may also be cleaned thus:— Have ready on a table a clean towel, folded three or four times, a saucer of new milk, and another saucer with a piece of brown soap. Take one glove at a time, and spread it smoothly on the folded towel. Then dip in the milk a piece of clean flannel, rub it on the soap until you get off a tolerable quantity, and then, with the wet flannel, commence rubbing the glove. Begin at the wrist, and rub lengthways towards the end of the fingers, holding the glove firmly in your right hand. Continue this process until the glove is well cleaned all over with the milk and soap. When done, spread them out, and pin them on a line to dry gradually, and as they dry, pull them out evenly, the crossway of the leather. Stretch them on your hands.

Hint 957　　　　Furs may be cleaned as follows:— Strip the fur articles of their stuffing and binding, and lay them as much as possible in a flat position. They must then be subjected to a very brisk brushing, with a stiff clothes brush; after this, any moth-eaten parts must be cut out, and be neatly replaced by new bits of fur to match.

Hint 958　　　　Sable, Chinchilla, Squirrel, Fitch, etc., should be treated as follows:— Warm a quantity of new bran in a pan, talking care that it does not burn, to prevent which it must be actively stirred. When well warmed, rub it thoroughly into the fur with the hand. Repeat this two or three times: then shake the fur, and give it another sharp brushing until free from dust.

Hint 959　　　　White Furs, Ermine, etc., may be cleaned as follows:— Lay the fur on a table, and rub it well with bran made moist with warm water; rub until quite dry, and afterwards with dry bran. The wet bran should be put on with flannel, and the dry with a piece of book-muslin. The light furs, in addition to the above, should be well rubbed with magnesia, or a piece of book-muslin, after the bran process.

Hint 960   Or dry Flour may be used instead of wet bran. Ermine takes longer than Minevar to clean. They should be rubbed against the way of the fur.

Hint 961   Furs are usually much improved by stretching, which may be managed as follows: to a pint of soft water add three ounces of salt, dissolve; with this solution sponge the inside of the skin (taking care not to wet the fur), until it becomes thoroughly saturated; then lay it carefully on a board with the fur side downwards, in its natural disposition; then stretch as much as it will bear, and to the required shape, and fasten with small tacks. The drying may be quickened by placing the skin a little distance from the fire or stove.

Hint 962   Corrosive Sublimate dissolved in the proportion of twelve grains to one pint of warm water, will produce a wash for furs that will preserve them against Moths. The liquid is poisonous. A Tallow Candle wrapped in paper, and put away with furs in the summer, is efficacious for the prevention of moths, as also are Common Soap, Bay Leaves, Wormwood, Cedarwood, Russia Leather, Lavender, Camphor, Walnut Leaves, Rue, and Black Pepper, either in powder or whole. It is not the moth, but the maggot of the moth that destroys the fur.

Various Methods of Mending Broken Articles

Hint 963   There are a great many Cements by which broken Glass and China may be joined, and the selection of one of these, from among a number must mainly depend upon the transparency or colour of the article to be mended, the nature of the fracture, and other considerations.

Hint 964   It is an important rule in the use of all cements that only a small quantity should be employed; and that, generally speaking, thin cements, judiciously, applied, will unite articles more strongly than thick ones.

Hint 965   For uniting Glass and China, and for repairs of Cabinet Work, nothing can be better than the Liquid Glue.

Hint 966   Broken Glass may be mended as follows:— Get some cloves of Garlic, tie them in a rag, and place them in a tin pan, pounding them with a hammer, to express the juice. Wet the broken edges of the glass with this juice, and stick them firmly together; stand the article upon a plate, or other level surface, and let it remain undisturbed for a fortnight.

Hint 967   China or Glass may be mended as follows:— Slake some Quick Lime with boiled water, and collect some of the fine powder of the lime. Take the White of an Egg and well beat it with an equal bulk of water, and add the slaked lime to it, so as to form a thin paste. It must be used speedily, and will be found to be very strong, and capable of resisting the action of boiling water.

Hint 968   Cracked vessels of China, Earthenware, etc., such as chimney ornaments and vases, may be repaired by putting on the inside strips of tape, rubbed over with white Lead.

Hint 969   For uniting Cardboard, Paper, and small articles of Fancy-work, the best Glue dissolved with about one-third its weight of coarse brown sugar in the smallest quantity of boiling water is very good. When this is in a liquid state, it may be dropped in a thin cake upon a plate, and allowed to dry. When required for use, one end of the cake may be moistened by the mouth, and rubbed on the substances to be joined.

Hint 970   The uses of Flour Paste are very well known. But it will be found a great improvement to add a little Alum to it before boiling; it will then work more freely, the particles of flour will not separate from the water, and it will unite surfaces much more firmly.

Hint 971   A paste to resist the attacks of Insects may be made by omitting the alum, and putting to each half pint of paste, fifteen grains of Corrosive Sublimate in powder, and well mixing it. This paste is poisonous.

Hint 972   Rice Glue is also a very delicate and suitable article for Fancy-work. Thoroughly mix rice flour with cold water, and gently simmer over a fire. This is excellent for uniting paper, cardboard, etc., and if properly made and applied, the joining will be found, very strong. When dry it is almost transparent.

Hint 973   Plaster of Paris figures may be mended by a solution of Glue. A thin solution should be employed, and brushed over the fractured part, two or three times, and allowed to soak in; finally, a fresh thin coating of glue should be applied, and the fractured parts set together and tied in their places until the glue dries. Should a dark line be formed on the outside, it may be painted over with whiting.

Hint 974   Iron Kitchen Utensils may be cemented by six parts of potter's clay, and one part of steel filings, mixed together with a sufficient quantity of linseed oil, to make a thick paste of the consistence of putty. It should be applied to the cracked parts on both sides, and allowed to stand three or four weeks undisturbed.

Hint 975   For mending Stonework on a small scale, such as Marble Mantelpieces, the corners of Hearth Stones, or the edges of Steps, Mastic Cement, made by mixing twenty parts of well washed and sifted, sand, with two parts of litharge, and one of freshly burned and slaked quicklime, in fine dry powder, is very good. It may be used for filling up the missing parts; it sets in a few hours and has the appearance of light stone. In stones of dark colour, it may be painted over to match.

Hint 976   Another form of Mastic Cement, or Mastic Glue, suitable for China, Glass, Earthenware, the finer Stones and Marbles, and even for Metals, is prepared as follows:— To an ounce of mastic add as much highly rectified spirits of wine as will dissolve it. Soak an ounce of isinglass in water until quite soft, then dissolve it in pure rum or brandy, until it forms a strong glue to which add about a quarter of an ounce of gum-ammoniac, well rubbed and mixed. Put the two mixtures together in an earthen vessel over a gentle heat; when well united put into a phial and keep it well stopped. When wanted for use, the bottle must be set in warm water, when the china or glass articles must be also warmed and the cement applied. The broken surfaces, when carefully fitted, should be kept in close contact for twelve hours at least, until the cement is fully set; after which the fracture will be found as secure as any part of the vessel, and scarcely perceptible.

Hint 977   In melting ordinary Glue in the double vessel containing water, it is an excellent method to add Salt to the water. It will not boil then, until heated considerably above the ordinary boiling point; the consequence is, the heat is retained, instead of passing off by evaporation, and when the water boils, the glue will be found to be thoroughly and evenly melted.

Hint 978   An adhesive material for joining Leather, Cloth, etc., which may be useful in certain cases, is made as fellows:- Take one pound of Gutta Percha, four ounces of India rubber, two ounces of pitch, one ounce of shellac, and two ounces of oil. Melt these ingredients together, and use them while hot.

Hint 979   The Red Cement used for uniting glass to metals, may be purchased at the tool shops. It is made by melting five parts of black resin, one part of yellow wax, and then stirring in gradually one part of red ochre or Venetian red, in fine powder, and previously well dried. This cement requires to be melted before use, and it adheres better if the objects to which it is applied are warmed.

Hint 980   A soft cement, of a somewhat similar character, may be found useful for covering the Corks of Preserved Fruits, and other bottles.

It is made by melting yellow wax with an equal quantity of resin, or of common turpentine (not oil of turpentine, but the resin), using the latter for a very soft cement, and stirring in, as before, some dried Venetian red.

To obtain a Constant Supply of Mushrooms

Hint 981   Mushrooms are second only to beef and mutton, and, either by their substance or their juice, they may be made to enrich every kind of savoury dish. They may be grown in or out of doors, in brick pits, under sheds, walls, railway or other arches, in stables, lofts, coach-houses, yards, cellars, large boxes, etc.

Hint 982   To obtain the Spawn, see 775; or buy the Bricks of Spawn, which are sold at sixpence each.

Hint 983   A Bed of Dung should be made, about one foot deep. The heat should be about 60 to 70 degrees on the surface, and when the temperature gets too high, it may be kept down by uncovering, or by making rows of holes about six inches deep, and a foot apart. When the heat is properly regulated, the holes should be filled to within three inches of the surface, and the spawn then put into the holes, and cover with a little droppings. The bed should then be covered with any kind of soil which is not chalky or limey. About four inches in depth of this should be laid on and well beaten down, and matting or hay may be thrown over open beds. The bed should be watered occasionally with soft water, which in the winter should be chilled. Water should not be given too often — excess of heat and moisture are to be carefully guarded against, and water must be sparingly applied after the mushrooms have shown above the surface.

Hint 984   The Covering of the Bed, whether matting or hay, must be occasionally removed to allow moisture and heat to escape, and prevent mouldiness. The mushrooms ought not to appear sooner than two months after spawning; but then a constant supply may be kept up.

Hint 985   In gathering Mushrooms, never cut them, but twist them gently off, and others will spring up from underneath.

Hint 986   Mushrooms are very liable to attacks from the Woodlouse, or Cheesebug. The best method of destroying them is to frequently pour boiling water into the cracks between the stones and boards where they hide.
They may be destroyed in Melon, Strawberry, and Cucumber beds, in the same manner.

Flowers that should be Cultivated Early in the Season for Bees

Hint 987   The first offering of Flora to the honey-gatherers, appears as the Christmas rose, *Helleborus Niger*, raising its white blossoms above the snow, and is greatly prized by the Bees. Then follows the Crocus, rich in pollen; and the delicate odours of the *Hepatica* are rivalled by their tempting sweets, but they must be the single kinds. Another very valuable flower is the White Arabis; it blooms for many weeks during spring, and its evergreen leaves, and close habit of growth, not rising above three inches from the ground, render it peculiarly well adapted for rock work; it has likewise the advantage of being exceedingly hardy, and is easily propagated by cuttings. A few of these plants in the neighbourhood of the apiary would be a great assistance to the bees, and are also easy of cultivation; and as they are propagated by division of roots, they may be transplanted early in the season, if care is taken to have a good ball of earth about the roots.

Hint 988   Borage is an excellent plant to cultivate for Bees, Two great recommendations in its favour are the easiness of its culture, and the length of time it remains in flower. The first sowing should be made in August or September, which will survive the winter, and begin to flower in May or June; a second sowing may be made in March, and a third in the end of April or beginning of May; these latter will continue in flower until cut down by the frosts of winter. The seed may be sown in patches about the size of the top of a hat between the gooseberry and currant bushes in cottage gardens; or, if a whole bed can be spared, it may be sown in rows about a foot apart. In either case, the plants should be thinned in coming up, as two or three in full flower will cover a square yard.

The Best Methods of Producing Summer and Winter Salads

Hint 989   The principal ingredients used in Salads in England, are Lettuce, Endive, Chicory, Radishes, Beet, Celery, Tarragon, Chervil, Nasturtium, Burnet, Small Salad, and Cucumbers,

Hint 990   Lettuces are of two kinds, Cos and Cabbage, and their duration may be extended over the greater part of the year by a little management. The first crop may be got in about the middle of April, and will be most valuable for salad at that period. The kind called the Dutch forcing lettuce, if sown about the 25th of August, and preserved in a cold frame during the winter, may be planted on a slight hot-bed about the end of February; or potted and plunged to the rims of the pots. The greatest difficulty is to preserve the plants from damping.

It will bear almost as much heat as a cucumber, but requires shading in bright sunshine, and is at the season in which it comes in a luxury but little known in English gardens, although common in Holland.

Hint 991   Those Cos and Cabbage Lettuces which were sown in August to stand the winter in the open ground, will succeed in May, and the succession will be continued by sowing a few in a little heat early in Spring to succeed these. A crop sown broadcast in the open ground, and hoed out (previously giving a slight dressing of guano) will give fine summer lettuces. Similar successional sowings up to July will continue the supply; but those sown the end of that month will make fine lettuces if transplanted in the cooler nights and under the refreshing dews of autumn. If some of this sowing is taken up with balls, and put in a dryhouse or frame, they will continue the supply until Christmas, or even later.

Hint 992   The culture of Radishes needs little comment; the early frame is best for winter and spring use, and the turnip-rooted kinds for summer. For winter, a frame may be sown the end of September, and a fortnight later; and the next sowing may be upon a south border.

Hint 993   Of Beets, a sowing made in the beginning of May, in drills, will give a supply.

Hint 994   Celery is one of the most important crops; its use for culinary purposes, as well as salads, renders its being of good quality a great desideratum. It is much in request in large families, both for stewing and salads, and forms a most important item of the kitchen garden. The first sowing must be made about the middle of February, in pits in heat, or on a slight hotbed. As soon as the plants are large enough, they should be pricked down upon four inches of rotten dung, laid upon an impervious bottom, which causes them to produce a dense mass of fibrous roots when taken up for replanting in trenches. The distance at which Celery is planted is generally regulated by the ground and convenience; but, like all other vegetables, if it is to be fine it must not be crowded; it requires plenty of water during its growth, and should have a spit of good rotten dung or leaf mould to grow in. The latest crop may be sown about the middle of April; intermediate sowings being also made between it and the first.

Hint 995   Chervil is an annual which only requires successional sowings for winter; some may be sown in pots about the end of July.

Hint 996   Tarragon is much in request by French cooks, for flavouring soups, and mixing in salads. It increases readily by slips or cuttings.

It should never have its tops cut off in the winter, but when it has shot a little in spring, remove them. A store of pots must be provided for winter supply, and gently forced.

Hint 997   Every tyro is familiar with the culture of Small Salad, and that of Cucumbers is fully before the Gardening World.

Hint 998   Endive, when well blanched, is a most useful winter salad. Successional sowings should be made of it from the middle of June to the middle of August, and in the early part of November a quantity should be taken up and protected in cold frames or pits. It blanches in a very superior manner if potted and introduced into a mushroom house.

Hint 999   Chicory should be sown in April or May in drills, and should be six or eight inches apart. The roots may be taken up in autumn, cutting off the tops, and placing them in layers of rather dry soil in a mushroom shed. It soon produces new leaves, which, when well blanched, are of a moist, mild, and agreeable flavour.

Hint 1000   The flowers of the Nasturtium, and the leaves of the Burnet are sometimes used in salads; and the common Corn Salad is an agreeable addition, which is much valued in France, where greater attention is paid to salads generally than we give them in this country.

Hint 1001   In growing produce of this kind, the cultivator will have occasion to exercise his judgment in the various processes of accelerating, retarding, increasing, or diminishing, the supply required. The great point to attend to, in keeping up a supply, is to make frequent sowings, and to be as frequently planting out small proportions.

Selection of the Best Fruits and Vegetables

Hint 1002   As, generally speaking, the poor varieties of Fruits and Vegetables occupy as much ground, and demand as great attention as the better sorts, it is obviously an important element of economy to know the best kinds to cultivate. Select, therefore, as nearly as possible in the order in which they are placed, the following varieties, modifying the selection by such attendant circumstances as cannot be laid down in general rules:—

Apples for the kitchen — Alfriston, large and heavy, November to April; Lord Suffield, large, August; Bedfordshire Foundling, November to March; Codlin, Manks, September to November; Codlin, Keswick, August and September; French Crab may be kept two years.

Dumelow's Seedling, November to April; Hawthornden, September to January; Nonsuch, September to October; Northern Greening, November to April; Pippin, Gooseberry, will keep until the next crop ripens; Brownlee's Seedling, January to April; Royal Russet, November to May; Winter Colmar, November to May; Yorkshire Greening, October to January.

<u>Apples for the Kitchen and for Dessert</u> — Golden Harvey; Pearmain; Herefordshire; Pippin Blenheim; King of the Pippins, October to January; Pippin, Ribston; Pippin Sturmer, very late; Reinette du Canada.

<u>Apples for Dessert</u> — Barcelona Pearmain, November to March; Beachamwell Seedling, December to March; Court of Wick, October to March; Court Pendu Piatt, November to April; Early Harvest, July and August; Lord Suffield; Margaret, Joaneting, August; Nonpareil, January to May; Pitmaston Nonpareil, November; Pearmain, Adams's, December to February ; Golden Pippin, November to March; Pippin, Kerry, September to October; Stanford Pippin, December to April; Reinette, Golden; Reinette, Van Mons, Aromatic, December to May; Russet, Boston, January to April; Russet, Syke House, November to February.

<u>Cherries for the Kitchen</u>— Morello, Kentish; Elton; Belle Magnifique.

<u>Cherries for the Dessert</u> — Belle d'Orleans; Bigarreau, Black Eagle; Black Heart; Werdy's Early Black Heart; Downton Elton; May Duke; Late Duke; Coe's Late Carnation.

<u>Apricots</u> — Early: Royal, Shipley, Kaisha. Late: Breda for preserving), Alsace, Peach, Moorpark.

<u>Currants</u> — Black Naples, Common Red; Red Dutch, Myatt's Red Grape; White Dutch; Holland's White.

<u>Grapes</u> — Open air: Black July; Chasselas Musque; white; Esperione, purple; Hamburg, Black, Royal Muscadine, white; Pitmaston Cluster, white; Dutch Sweetwater, white; Early Black Muscat. Cool Vinery: Duc de Malakoff, white; Early Black Muscat Hamburg; Barbarossa, black; Black Prince; Madeira Muscat; Chasselas Vibert; Golden Hamburg; West's St. Peter's, black; White Romain. For Forcing:- Bowood Muscat ; Golden Hamburg; Mill Hill Hamburg; West's St. Peter's; Muscat of Alexandria, white; Cannon Hall Muscat, late white; Black Hamburg; White Sweetwater.

<u>Gooseberries for the Kitchen and Dessert</u> — Early White; White Eagle; Whitesmith; Bright Venus; White Champagne. Yellow: Early Sulphur; Rockwood; Rumbullion; Yellow Champagne. Green: Greengage; Green Orleans; Greenwood; Large Late Green.

Green Gascoigne; Hepburn Prolific. Red: Wilmot's Early; Red Champagne, Jackson's Red (for preserving); Lancaster Hero; Rough Red, late (best for preserving); Wonderful; Red Warrington ; Keen's Seedling; Ironmonger.

Melons — Red: Turner's Scarlet Gem, early, handsome and excellent flavour; Atkinson's Cranmore Hall; Frogmore Scarlet; McEwen's Hybrid Scarlet; Victoria Windsor Prize; Green Carter's Excelsior; Beechwood; Bromham Hall; Golden Ball; Boosie's Incomparable; Victory of Bath.

Nectarines - Early: Stanwick requires warmth, end of August; Elruge, forces well, end of August; Imperatrioe, excellent for forcing; Murray, good flavour, end of August; Newington Early, excellent flavoured, beginning of September; Pitmaston Orange, best yellow-fleshed, end of August; River's Orange, August and September; Violet Hative, best for forcing, end of August. Late: Old Newington, prized when shrivelling, middle of September; Peterborough, October.

Peaches — Early: Red Nutmeg, small, handsome, musky, July and August; Grosse Mignonne, first rate for forcing, end of August and beginning of September; Noblesse, best for general purposes, end of August; Early York, medium size, richly flavoured, beginning of August; Royal George, first-rate for forcing, end of August; Crawford's Early, one of the best, end of August. Late: Admirable, late for forcing, September; Admirable (Walburton), forces well, middle of September; Bellegarde, succeeds Royal George, beginning and middle of September; Shanghai, the largest grown, middle of September; Pucelle de Malines, very hardy, end of September; Salway, aromatic and juicy, beginning of November.

Pears for the Kitchen — Bellissime d'Hiver, good stewer; Catillac, first-rate for baking; Uvedale St. Germain, largest stewing; Black Worcester, for preserving. Dessert: Aston Town, bears well as a standard; Bergamotte (Gansell's), rich flavour; Bergamotte (Esperen's), hardy; Beurre d'Amanlis, large and melting; Beurre d'Aremberg, hardy as a standard; Beurre Bose, half melting, requires a wall; Brown Beurre, bears abundantly; Beurre de Capiaumont, fine melting; Beurre de Mons, crisp flavour; Beurre Diel, large melting; Easter Beurre, a valuable spring pear; Beurre Rance, melting and beautiful; Beurre Van Mons, melting, very rich. Bon Chretien d'Auch, rich, but rather gritty, without heat; Bon Chretien Fondante, cool, refreshing juice; Bon Chretien Musque, slightly perfumed; Bon Chretien (William's), requires a warm situation; Chaumontel, buttery, splendid as pyramid; Colmar, requires a wall; Crassane, requires a warm wall; Crassane Althorp, good as a standard; Doyenne Gray, hardy autumnal; Duchesse d' Angouleme, large and melting; Dunmore, good as a standard; Mathews' Eliza, large melting, valuable in the smallest collection.

Foulle, melting, speckled like a trout; Glout Morceau, very late, requires a wall; Incomparable (Hacon's), melting; Inconnue, Van Mons, melting; Jargonelle, very juicy, early; Josephine de Malines, aromatic flavour; Louise Bonne of Jersey, handsome; Marie Louise, best on a wall, very buttery; Ne Plus Meuris, best late; Passe Colmar, melting, great bearer; Saint Denis, melting; Seckel, good bearer; Swan's Egg, good bearer; Thompson's, very rich; Van Mons, melting; Vicar of Winkfield, very large; Winter Nells, very melting, deserving a wall.

<u>Twelve Best Pears for a Small Collection</u> – Knight's Monarch, Thompson's Marie Louise, Louise Bonne of Jersey, Beurre Bosc, Beurre Hardy, Winter Nells, Beurre Diel. Glout Morceau, Passe Colman, Eastern Beurre, Beurre Rance.

<u>Six of the Best Early Pears</u> - Doyenne d'Ete, Jargonelle, Beurre Goubalt, Bon Chretien, Summer Beurre, Gifford Rose.

<u>Plums for the Kitchen</u> — Victoria, red, large; a great bearer and very hardy, ripe in July; Goliah, very large purple, excellent for Preserving; Winesour, for Preserving; Mitchelson's, most prolific.

<u>Plums for Dessert</u> — Peach, July Green Gage, equal to Green Gage, and earlier; Early Favourite, best early; Jefferson, better as a standard than Green Gage; Reine Claude Violet, bears freely as standard; Denyer's Victoria, bears well as standard; Kirke's; Purple Gage; Topaz.

<u>Plums for Kitchen and Dessert</u> — Coe's Golden Drop, excellent as standard; Green Gage, well known; Imperatrice, blue, requires a wall; Orleans, Prince of Wales, finer than old Orleans; Prince Eaglebert.

<u>Raspberries, Early</u> — Black Cap; Carter's Prolific; Red Antwerp, unequalled; Beehive, large; Fastolff, first-rate; Prince of Wales. Late. — Double-bearing; Victoria, October Red, October Yellow. These must be cut down to the ground in February.

<u>Strawberries</u> — Early: Black Prince, forces well; May Queen; Keen's Seedlings; Prolific Hautbois; Grove End Scarlet; Carolina Superba. Medium: British Queen, uncertain; Alice Maud; Comte de Paris; Kitley's Goliath; Sir Charles Napier; Sir Harry; Oscar; Myatt's Eliza. Late: Elton Pine, fertilized; Hautbois; Eleanor; Red and White Alpines.

<u>Beans</u> — Earliest: Marshall's Early Dwarf; Early Long-pod. Main Crop: Conqueror; Green Long-pod; Hangdown (good for market); Johnson's Wonderful. Late; Taylor's Windsor; Green Windsor; Thick-seeded Windsor.

French Beans — Early and for Forcing: Newington Wonder; Fulmer's Forcing; Robin's Egg; Six Weeks. Main Crop: Dark Dun; Negro. Late: Dwarf Dutch; Red-speckled.

Beet — Whyte's Black Red; Cattell's Dwarf; Henderson's Dwarf-top White Silesian; White Spinach Beet.

Borecole — Cottager's Kale (Turner); Dwarf Green; Hardy Purple; Ragged Jack; Tall Curled; Variegated, for garnishing.

Broccoli — Cumming's (new); Meville's White May; Snow's Winter; Grange's Walcheren; Chappel's Cream; Early Sprouting; Mitchell's Ne Plus Ultra; Dwarf Siberian.

Brussels Sprouts — Rosebury, and the old sort imported.

Cabbage — Early Fulham; Early York; Early Admirable; West Ham; Nonpareil; Shilling's Queen; Sprotsborough; Vanack; Green Colewort; East Neuk ap Fife.

Carrots — Early: Horn; Long Orange; Surrey Altringham; Improved, has green top, but Is the most productive of any, and excellent flavour.

Cauliflower — Mitchell's Hardy; Early London; Haage's Forcing; Stadtholder.

Celery - Cole's Red; Cole's White; Giant White; Laing's Mammon; Red; Manchester Red.

Cucumbers — Exhibition; Improved Manchester; Norfolk Hero; Hunter's Prolific; Essex Rival; Cunning's Prolific (excellent for winter and spring); Carter's Champion Ipswich Standard; Latter's Victory.

Gourds — Custard Long Green; Dancer's Ribbed; American Marrow; Citronelli, and common Pumpkin. There are almost as many varieties of Marrow as there are days in the year, and there is but little difference as to their several merits, but the Custard is the best flavoured.

Lettuce — Brighton Cos; Brown; White and Black Bath Cos; Fulham Cos; Malta (fine); Hammersmith; Sicilian Cabbage; (fine), Neapolitan, Snow's Compact.

Onions — White Spanish (hardy), Deptford; James Kuping Tripoli; Welsh (for salading); Silver Skin, for pickling; for which purpose also use White Globe, sown thick on poor ground, and the Tree Onion.

<u>Peas</u> — Earliest: Sangster's No.1; Eastring's Early Dwarf; Emperor; Early Charlton: Second Early and Succession: Alliance; Harrison's; Glory; Blue Perfection; Wrench's Perfection; Veitch's Perfection; Hair Dwarf Mammoth; Harrison's Napoleon; Warwick; Charlton; Taylor's Prolific; Shilling's Grotts Ringwood Marrow; Cotterell's Wonder; Dickson's Favourite; Dwarf Green Mammoth; Prize-taker; Bedman's Imperial; Carter's Champion, King of Marrows, (very large); Prussian Blue (if true, first-rate); Waterloo Marrow, Burbidge's Eclipse (very prolific).

<u>Potatoes</u> — Regent; Forty-fold; Onwards; Flower-ball; Early Fulham; Ash-leaf; Lapstone; Flukes; Myatt's Brockley; Red Ash-leaf.

<u>Savoy</u> — Barnes' Feather-stemmed; Early Ulm; Cattel's Green Curled Dwarf Drumhead.

The names of the months indicate the times when the fruit or vegetable is best for the table. All the best known varieties are included in the above judicious selection, which has been extracted and revised from The Garden Oracle.

PART 3

MISCELLANEOUS HINTS

1003   Port Wine Sediment is excellent as a flavouring to coffee.

1004   Biscuits, broken, and biscuit dust are good for puddings.

1005   Chestnuts may be made into soups or puddings.

1006   Milk, morning is richer than that of the evening.

1007   Leeks, green tops of, sliced thin, capital flavouring for soups.

1008   Wood ashes form a good lye for softening water.

1009   Bricks covered with baize, serve to keep open doors.

1010   Rye, roasted, is the best substitute for coffee, with chicory.

1011   Turnip peel, washed clean, and tied in a net, imparts good flavour to soups

1012   Cold green tea, well sweetened, put into saucers, will destroy flies.

1013   Celery leaves and ends, are useful for flavouring soups, gravies, sauces, etc.

1014   Beans, roasted, form an agreeable substitute for coffee, with chicory.

1015   Walnuts, the outer green husks supply, with vinegar, a very good ketchup.

1016   Cherry kernels, broken, steeped in brandy, make a nice flavouring for tarts.

1017   Mulberry juice in small quantity greatly improves the colour and flavour of cider.

1018   Wheat, roasted, forms an agreeable substitute for coffee, with chicory.

1019   Cloth of old clothes, may be made into door mats, pen-wipers, etc.

1020   Bay leaves, in their green state, allay the inflammation of bee stings.

1021   Linen rags should be washed and preserved for various domestic uses.

1022   Apple pips impart a fine flavour to tarts and dumplings.

1023   Old shoes make excellent slippers, and being occasionally polished look very well.

1024   The Soot should be brushed from the backs of kettles daily, and the front parts be polished.

1025   Sage leaves in small quantity, make an excellent addition to tea.

1026   Lemon juice will allay the irritation caused by the bites of gnats and flies.

1027   Clothes lines should be well wiped before they are put away. Gutta Percha lines are best.

1028   Ashes and soap suds are a good manure for shrubs and young plants.

1029   An Oyster shell, put into a teakettle, will prevent its becoming furred.

1030   The white of egg, beaten to a froth with a little butter, is a good substitute for cream in tea or coffee.

1031   Honey and castor oil mixed are excellent for the asthmatic, a teaspoonful night and morning.

1032   Soap suds, and soapy watery supply a good manure for garden soils.

1033   Cold potatoes, mashed with peas, make an excellent and light peas pudding.

1034   Wooden spoons are generally best for articles that require beating or stirring in cookery.

1035   Milk when slightly acid, mixed with a little lukewarm water, is a cooling drink for invalids.

1036   Bran, dusted over joints of meat when hung, will keep them good for an extra time.

1037   As much carbonate of soda as will lie on a four penny piece, added to tea, will increase its strength.

1038   Parsley eaten with vinegar will remove the unpleasant effects of eating onions.

1039   Fine coals are excellent for cleaning bottles. Put them in with a little hot or cold water, and shake well.

1040   Lemon Peel is useful for flavouring gravies, sauces, puddings, punch, grog, etc.

1041   Plum stones, broken, and steeped in brandy, afford an excellent flavouring for tarts.

1042   The juice of Bean Pods is an effective cure for warts.

1043   Eggs white are useful for clearing coffee; and as a cement for broken china, with lime.

1044   A little cider added to apple tarts, greatly improves them.

1045   Fried cucumber, added to Soups, greatly improves them. They should be fried in slices.

1046   Gas meters may be prevented from freezing by keeping one burner lighted during the whole day.

1047   Scotch oatmeal, carefully dried, will keep cream cheese good and dry, if laid over it.

1048   The leaves and roots of the blackberry shrub make an excellent and refreshing tea. The berries are a corrective of dysentery.

1049   Stale bread, after being steeped in water, and re-baked for about an hour, will be nearly equal to new.

1050   Pea-shell and haulm are excellent food for horses, mixed with bruised oats, or bran. Good also for pigs.

1051   Butter which has been used for covering potted meats, may be used for basting, or in paste for meat pies.

1052   Bleeding from the nose may be stopped by putting bits of lint into the nostrils; and by raising the arms over the head.

1053   Egg shells are useful for the stockpot, to clarify the stock.

1054   In winter, get the work forward by daylight, which will prevent many accidents and inconveniences with candles, etc.

1055   In ironing, be careful first to rub the iron over something of little value; this will prevent the scorching and smearing of many articles.

1056   When chamber towels wear thin in the middle, cut them in two, sew the selvages together, and hem the sides.

1057   One flannel petticoat will wear nearly as long as two, if turned hind part before, when the front begins to wear thin.

1058   For turning meats while broiling or frying, small tongs are better than a fork. The latter lets out the juice of the meat.

1059   Persons of weak sight, when threading a needle, should hold it over something white, by which the sight will be assisted.

1060   Lemon and orange seeds either steeped in spirits, or stewed in syrups, supply an excellent bitter tonic.

1061   Gutta Percha is useful for filling decayed teeth, stopping crevices in windows and floors, preventing windows from rattling, etc.

1062   Potatoes may be prevented from sprouting in the spring season, by momentarily dipping them into hot water.

1063   To loosen a glass stopper pour round it a little sweet oil, close to the stopper, and let it stand in a warm place.

1064   Raspberries, green, impart an acidity to spirit more grateful than that of the lemon. A decoction in spirit may be kept for flavouring.

1065   Acorns if roasted, form a substitute for coffee, and produce a beverage scarcely less agreeable especially if with an addition of chicory.

1066 The presence of copper in liquids may be detected by a few drops of hartshorn, which produces, when copper is present, a blue colour.

1067 Cold melted butter may be warmed by putting the vessel containing it into boiling water, and allowing it to stand until warm.

1068 Cabbages, (red), for pickling, should be cut with a silver knife. This keeps them turning black, as they do when touched with iron.

1069 Common radishes, when young, tied in bunches, boiled for twenty minutes, and served on buttered toast, are excellent.

1070 Eel skins, well cleansed, to clarify coffee, etc. Sole skins, well cleansed, to clarify coffee, etc., and making fish soups and gravies.

1071 Charcoal powder is good for polishing knives, without destroying the blades. It is also a good toothpowder, when finely pulverised.

1072 The earthy mould should never be washed from potatoes, carrots, or other roots, until immediately before they are to be cooked.

1073 Apple pips, and also the pips of pears, should be saved, and put into tarts, bruised. They impart a delicious flavour.

1074 Potato water, in which potatoes have been scraped, the water being allowed to settle, and afterwards strained, is good for sponging dirt out of silk.

1075 Sitting to sew by candlelight, before a table with a black cloth on it, is injurious to the eyes. When such work must be done, lay a black cloth before you.

1076 Straw matting may be cleaned with a large coarse cloth, dipped in salt and water, and then wiped dry. The salt prevents the straw from turning yellow.

1077 Cold boiled potatoes used as soap, will cleanse the hands, and keep the skin soft and healthy. Those not over-boiled are best.

1078 In mending sheets, shirts, or other articles, let the pieces put on be fully large, or when washed the thin parts will give way, and the work be all undone.

1079 Leaves, green, of any kind, worn inside the hat in the heat of summer, are said to be an effectual preventive of sunstroke.

1080   Cakes, Puddings, etc., are always improved by making the currants, sugar, and flour hot, before using them.

1081   It is an error to give fowls egg shells, with the object of supplying them with lime. It frequently induces in fowls a habit of eating eggs.

1082   Buttermilk is excellent for cleaning sponges. Steep the sponge in the milk for some hours, then squeeze it out, and wash in cold water.

1083   Lamp shades of ground glass should be cleaned with soap or pearlash; these will not injure or discolour them.

1084   When reading by candlelight, place the candle behind you, that the light may pass over your shoulder and fall upon the book from behind.

1085   Walnut pickle, after the walnuts are consumed, is useful for adding to gravies and sauces, especially for minced cold meats, and hashes.

1086   Coffee grounds are a disinfectant and deodorizer, being burnt upon a hot fire shovel, and borne through any apartment.

1087   Cold boiled eggs may be warmed by putting them into cold water and warming them gradually, taking them out before the water boils.

1088   The best plan to collect dripping is, to put it while warm into water nearly cold. Any impurities it may contain will sink to the bottom.

1089   Hay, sprinkled with a little chloride of lime, and left for one hour in a closed room, will remove the smell of new paint.

1090   Tea leaves, used for keeping down the dust when sweeping carpets, are apt to stain light colours; in which case, use newly mown damp grass instead.

1091   Moths deposit their eggs in May and June. This, therefore, is the time to dust furs, etc., and to place bits of camphor in drawers and boxes.

1092   Bran may be used for cleaning damask or chintz. It should be rubbed over them with a piece of flannel.

1093   A cut lemon kept on the washing stand, and rubbed over the hands daily after washing, and not wiped off for some minutes, is the best remedy for chapped hands. Lemon juice, or Salts of Lemon, will clean Sponges perfectly.

1094   Elderflowers, prepared in precisely the same manner as 1153, furnish a very cooling ointment, for all kinds of local irritation, and especially for the skin when sunburnt.

1095   Common washing soda dissolved in water, until the liquid will take up no more, is an effective remedy for warts. Moisten the warts with it, and let them dry, without wiping.

1096   Bran water, or water in which bran has been steeped, greatly improves bread, instead of plain water. The bran may afterwards be given to fowls, or pigs.

1097   After washings, look over linen, and stitch on buttons, hooks and eyes. For this purpose keep a box or bag well supplied with sundry threads, cottons, buttons, hooks and eyes, etc.

1098   It has been suggested that the sex of eggs may be determined by the situation of the air cell; but careful experiments have shown that no dependence can be put upon this criterion.

1099   The leaf of the common dock, bruised and rubbed over the part affected, will cure the stings caused by nettles. Leaves of sage, mint, or rosemary are also good for the same purpose.

1100   Pudding cloths should never be washed with soap. They should be rinsed in clean water, dried, and be put away in a drawer, where they will be free from dust.

1101   Add a teaspoon of Alum, and a teaspoonful of salt, to each three gallons of Vinegar for Pickling, and immerse in it whole pepper, ginger root, and mixed spices, and it will be greatly improved.

1102   It is a great economy in serving Dinners to provide a plentiful supply of good vegetables, thoroughly hot. For which purpose they should not be served up all at once, but a reserve "to follow" should be the plan.

1103   It is an error to wash weak children, in cold water, with the view of strengthening them. The temperature should be modified to their condition, and be lowered as they are found to improve.

1104   Onions, shallots, scallions, chives, garlic, and rocambole are pretty much the same, and may be substituted one for the other in many instances, as a matter of convenience or economy.

1105   For Soft Corns, dip a piece of linen rag in Turpentine, and wrap it round the toe on which the corn is situated, night and morning. The relief will be immediate, and after a few days the corn will disappear.

1106   The Juice of an Onion will relieve the pain from a beesting; dusting the blue from a washerwoman's "blue bag" will have a similar effect. The venom must first be pressed out.

THE END

INDEX

The Numbers Refer to the Hints, or Paragraphs.

** We recommend this work for keeping the promise of its Title-page. The demon of Cold Mutton is effectually exorcised from the domestic table; and if the Wife has only the genius for following good advice, no Husband can henceforth have an excuse for dining at his Club — nor will the wife, even on a washing day, have any plea for not producing a good dinner. The Family Receipts are garnished with sippets of wise apothegms, or seasoned with the salt of lively anecdote; and there is an Appendix of instructions how to repair or obviate every damage that may attaint the perfectness of the household goods, from chipped mantel-pieces to broken china or faded curtains; whilst there is abundant comfort prepared for other small evils. 'The Family Save-all' will be an invaluable work, if it meets with an intelligent Reader.'

Lightning Source UK Ltd.
Milton Keynes UK
30 December 2009

147973UK00001B/29/P